BIRTHRIGHT

VOLUME TWO
CALL TO ADVENTURE

www.skybound.com

IMAGE COMICS, INC.
Robert Kirkman *Chief Operating Officer*
Erik Larsen *Chief Financial Officer*
Todd McFarlane *President*
Marc Silvestri *Chief Executive Officer*
Jim Valentino *Vice-President*

Eric Stephenson *Publisher*
Corey Murphy *Director of Sales*
Jeremy Sullivan *Director of Digital Sales*
Kat Salazar *Director of PR & Marketing*
Emily Miller *Director of Operations*
Branwyn Bigglestone *Senior Accounts Manager*

www.imagecomics.com

Sarah Mello *Accounts Manager*
Drew Gill *Art Director*
Jonathan Chan *Production Manager*
Meredith Wallace *Print Manager*
Randy Okamura *Marketing Production Designer*
David Brothers *Branding Manager*
Ally Power *Content Manager*
Addison Duke *Production Artist*
Vincent Kukua *Production Artist*
Sasha Head *Production Artist*
Tricia Ramos *Production Artist*
Emilio Bautista *Sales Assistant*
Chloe Ramos-Peterson *Administrative Assistant*

Robert Kirkman *CEO*
David Alpert *President*
Sean Mackiewicz *Editorial Director*
Shawn Kirkham *Director of Business Development*
Brian Huntington *Online Editorial Director*
June Alian *Publicity Director*
Rachel Skidmore *Director of Media Development*
Michael Williamson *Assistant Editor*
Dan Petersen *Operations Manager*
Sarah Effinger *Office Manager*
Nick Palmer *Operations Coordinator*
Genevieve Jones *Production Coordinator*
Andres Juarez *Graphic Designer*
Stephan Murillo *Administrative Assistant*

International inquiries: *foreign@skybound.com*
Licensing inquiries: *contact@skybound.com*

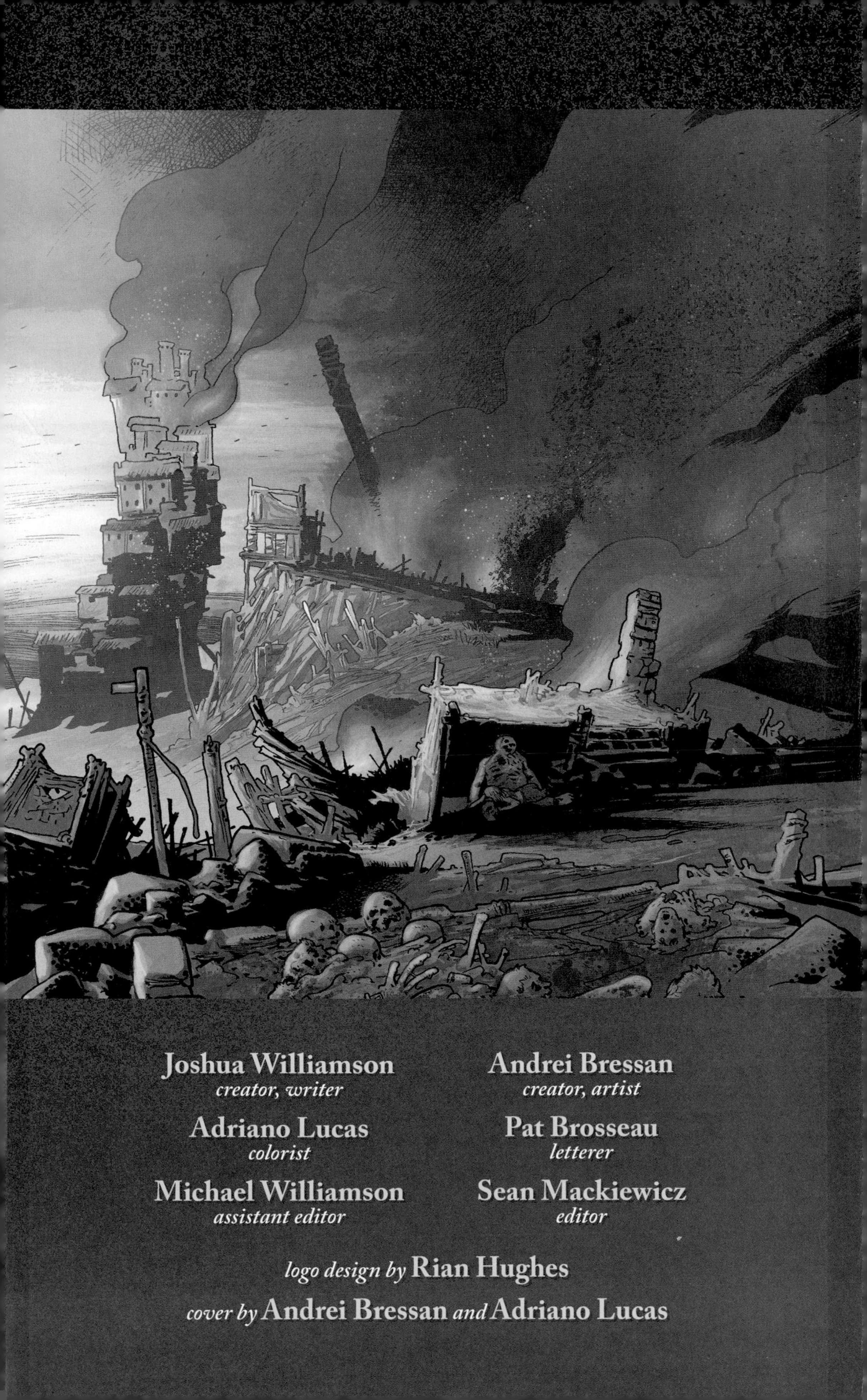

Joshua Williamson
creator, writer

Andrei Bressan
creator, artist

Adriano Lucas
colorist

Pat Brosseau
letterer

Michael Williamson
assistant editor

Sean Mackiewicz
editor

logo design by **Rian Hughes**

cover by **Andrei Bressan** *and* **Adriano Lucas**

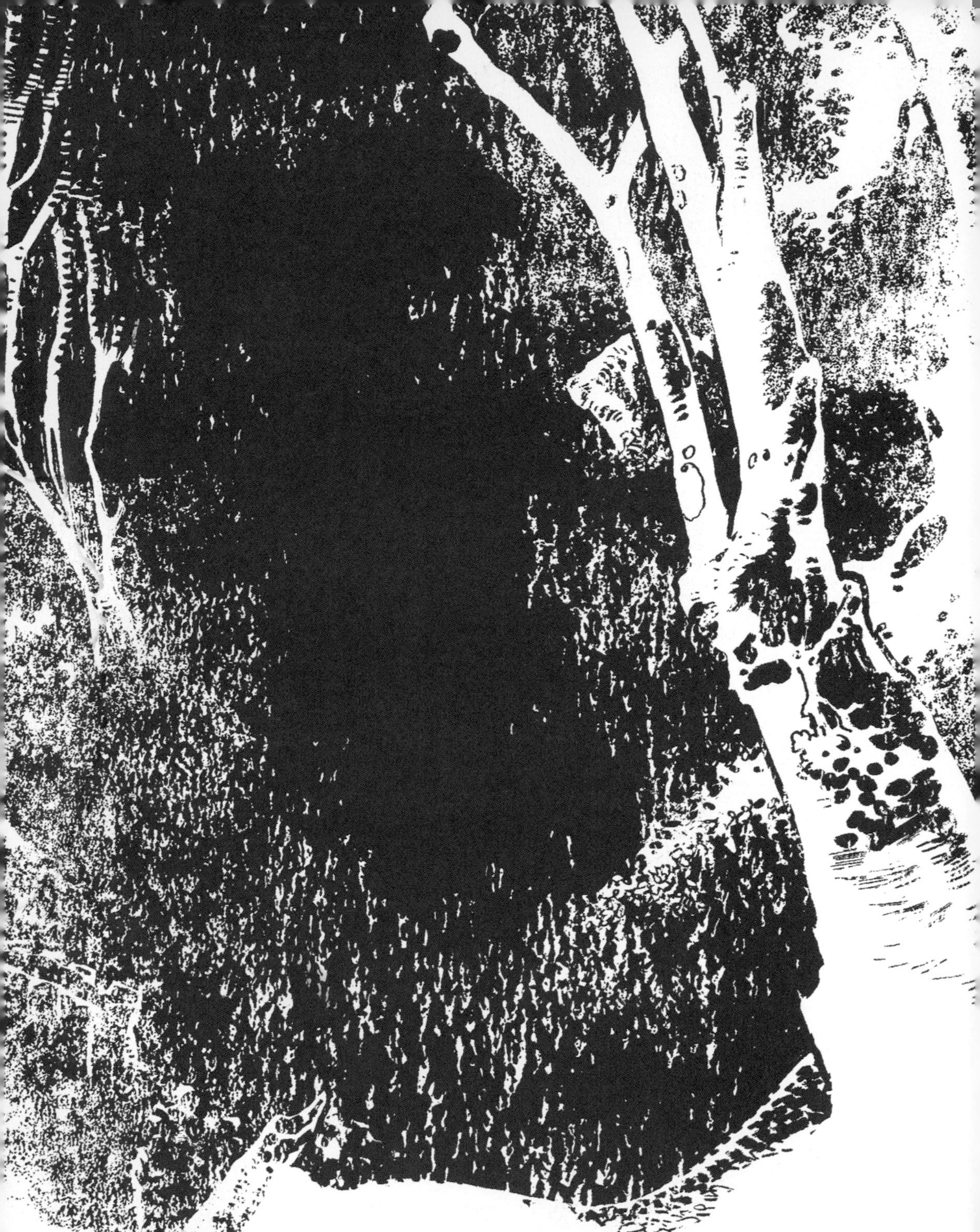

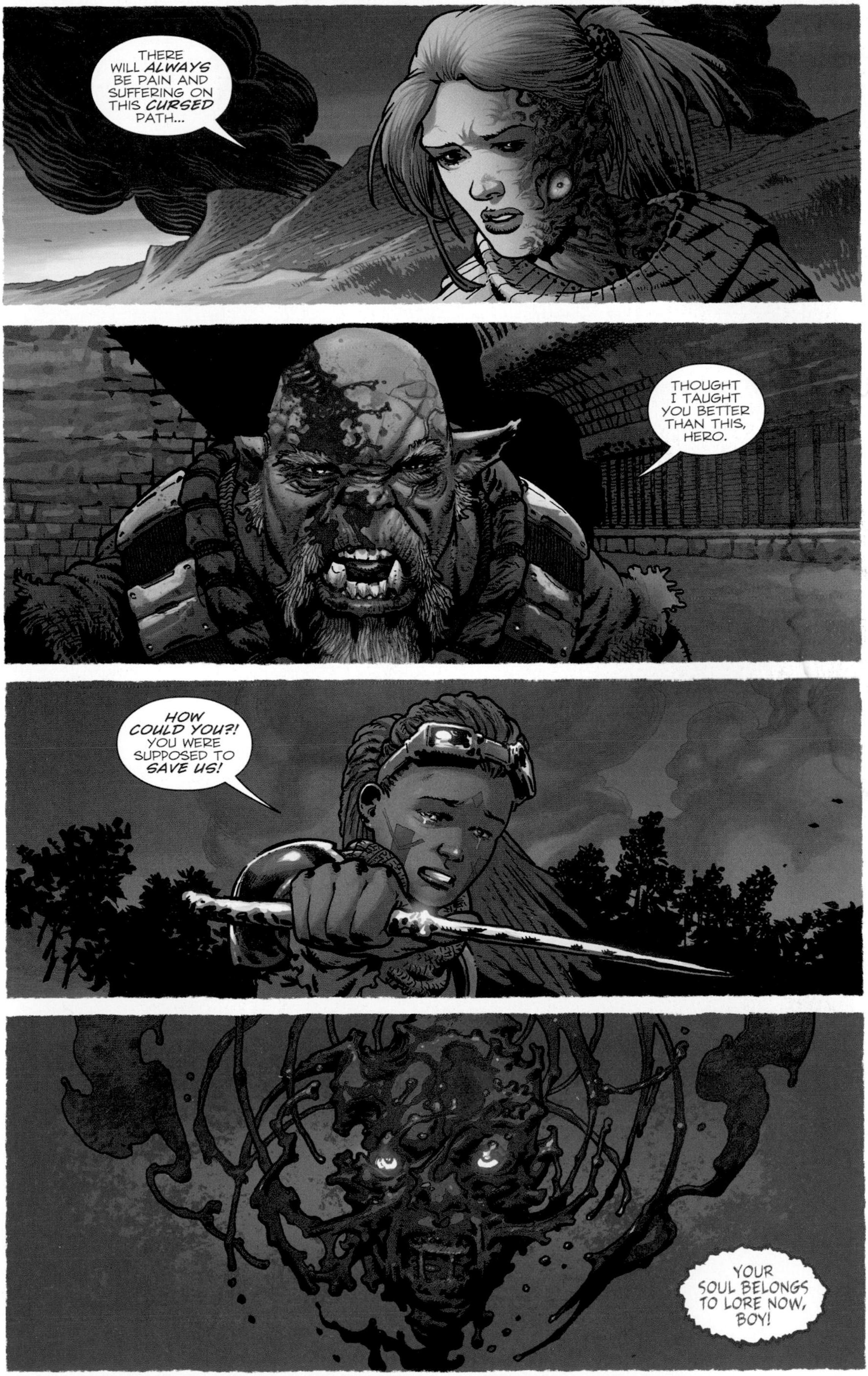
THERE WILL ALWAYS BE PAIN AND SUFFERING ON THIS CURSED PATH...
THOUGHT I TAUGHT YOU BETTER THAN THIS, HERO.
HOW COULD YOU?! YOU WERE SUPPOSED TO SAVE US!
YOUR SOUL BELONGS TO LORE NOW, BOY!

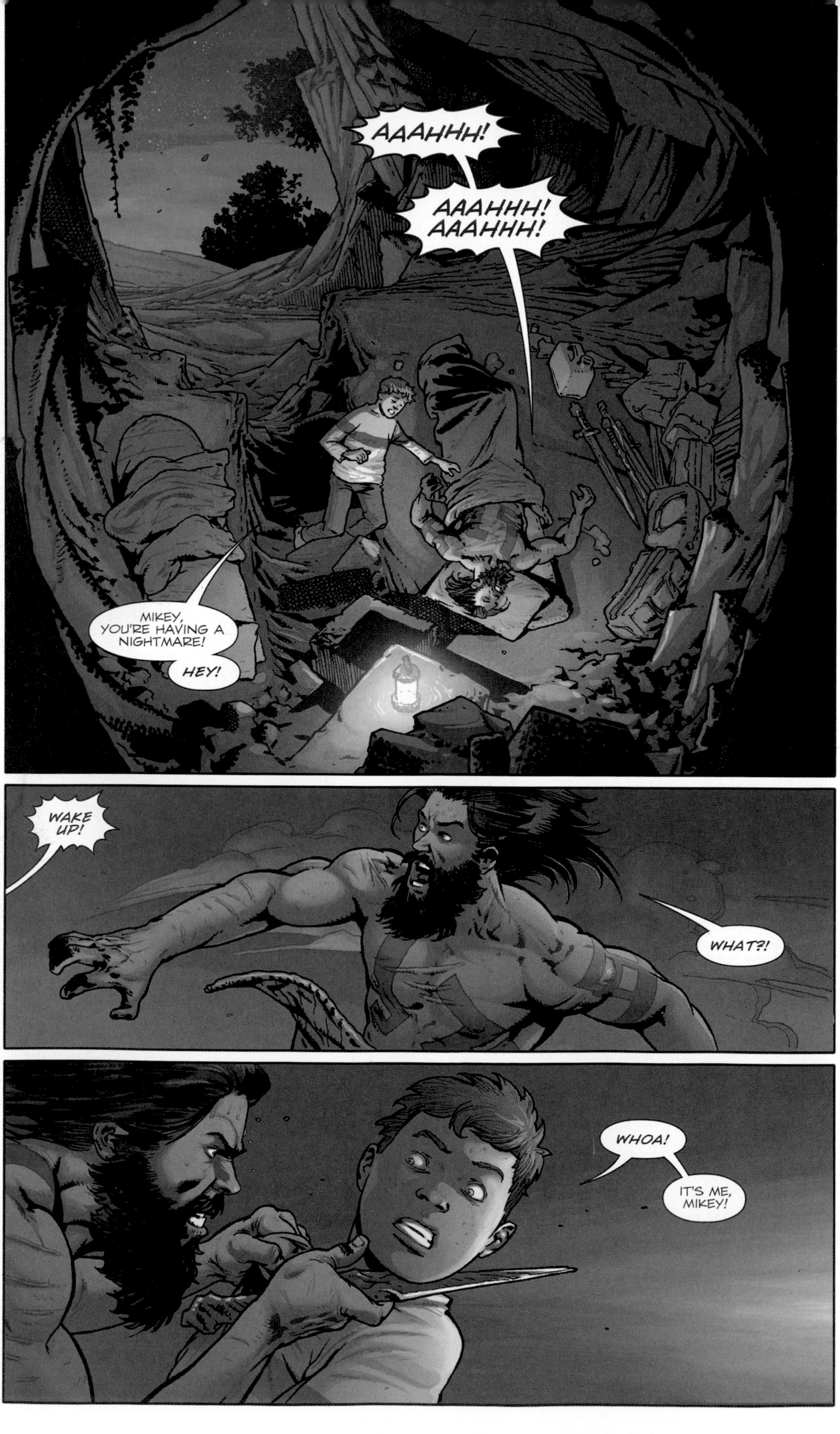
AAAHHH!
AAAHHH! AAAHHH!
MIKEY, YOU'RE HAVING A NIGHTMARE!
HEY!
WAKE UP!
WHAT?!
WHOA!
IT'S ME, MIKEY!

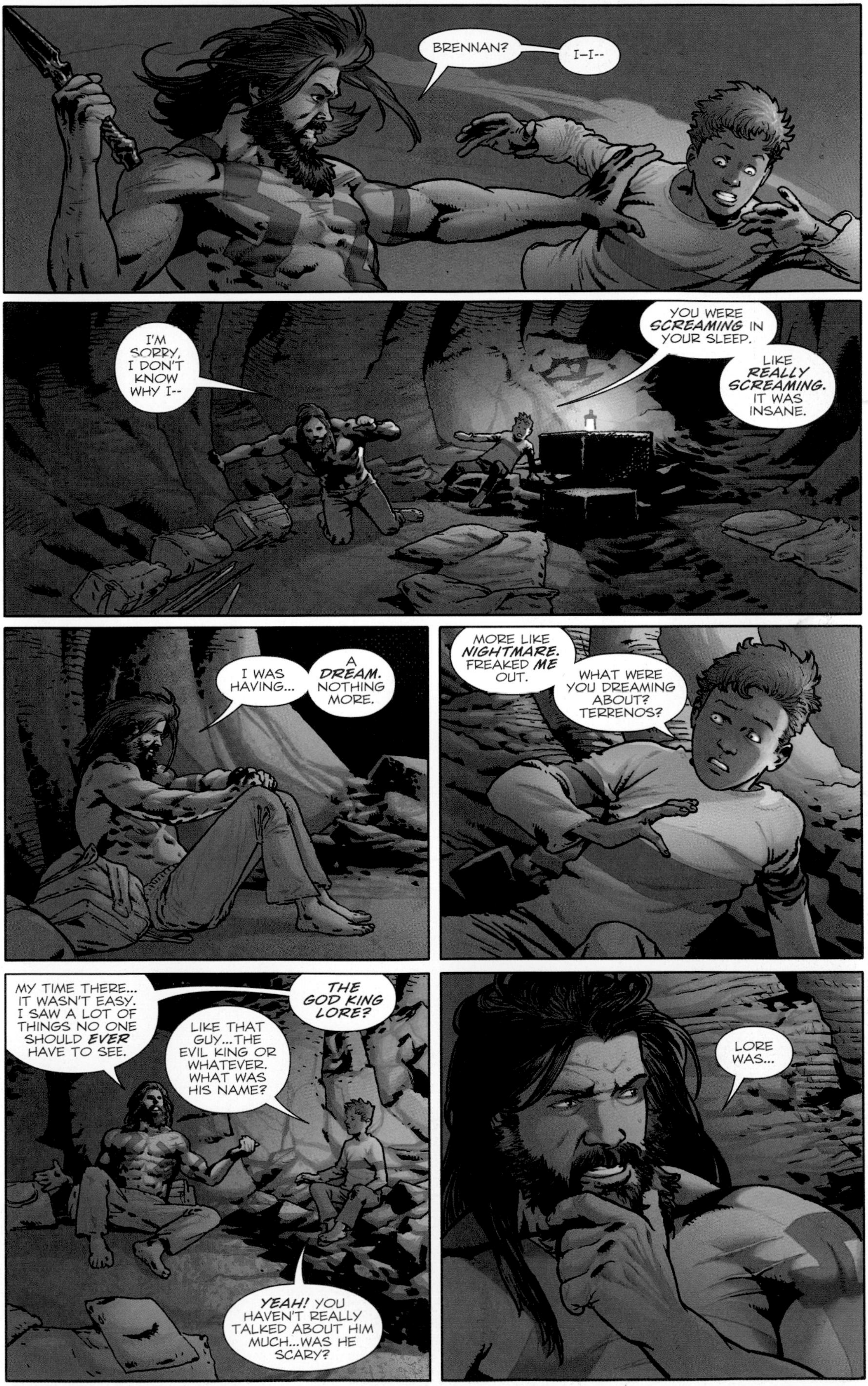
BRENNAN?
I--I--
I'M SORRY, I DON'T KNOW WHY I--
YOU WERE SCREAMING IN YOUR SLEEP.
LIKE REALLY SCREAMING. IT WAS INSANE.
I WAS HAVING...
A DREAM. NOTHING MORE.
MORE LIKE NIGHTMARE. FREAKED ME OUT.
WHAT WERE YOU DREAMING ABOUT? TERRENOS?
MY TIME THERE... IT WASN'T EASY. I SAW A LOT OF THINGS NO ONE SHOULD EVER HAVE TO SEE.
LIKE THAT GUY...THE EVIL KING OR WHATEVER. WHAT WAS HIS NAME?
THE GOD KING LORE?
YEAH! YOU HAVEN'T REALLY TALKED ABOUT HIM MUCH...WAS HE SCARY?
LORE WAS...

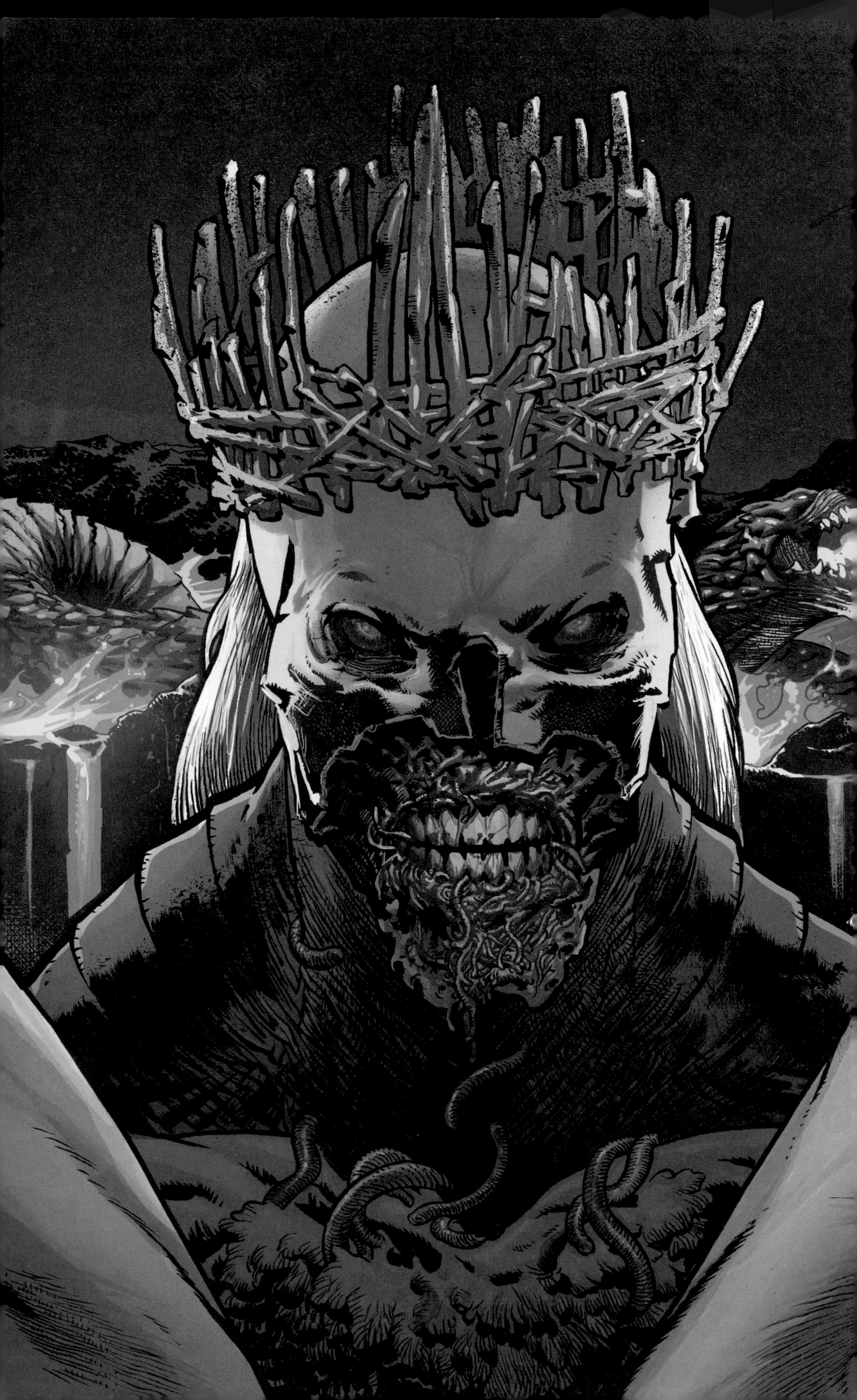

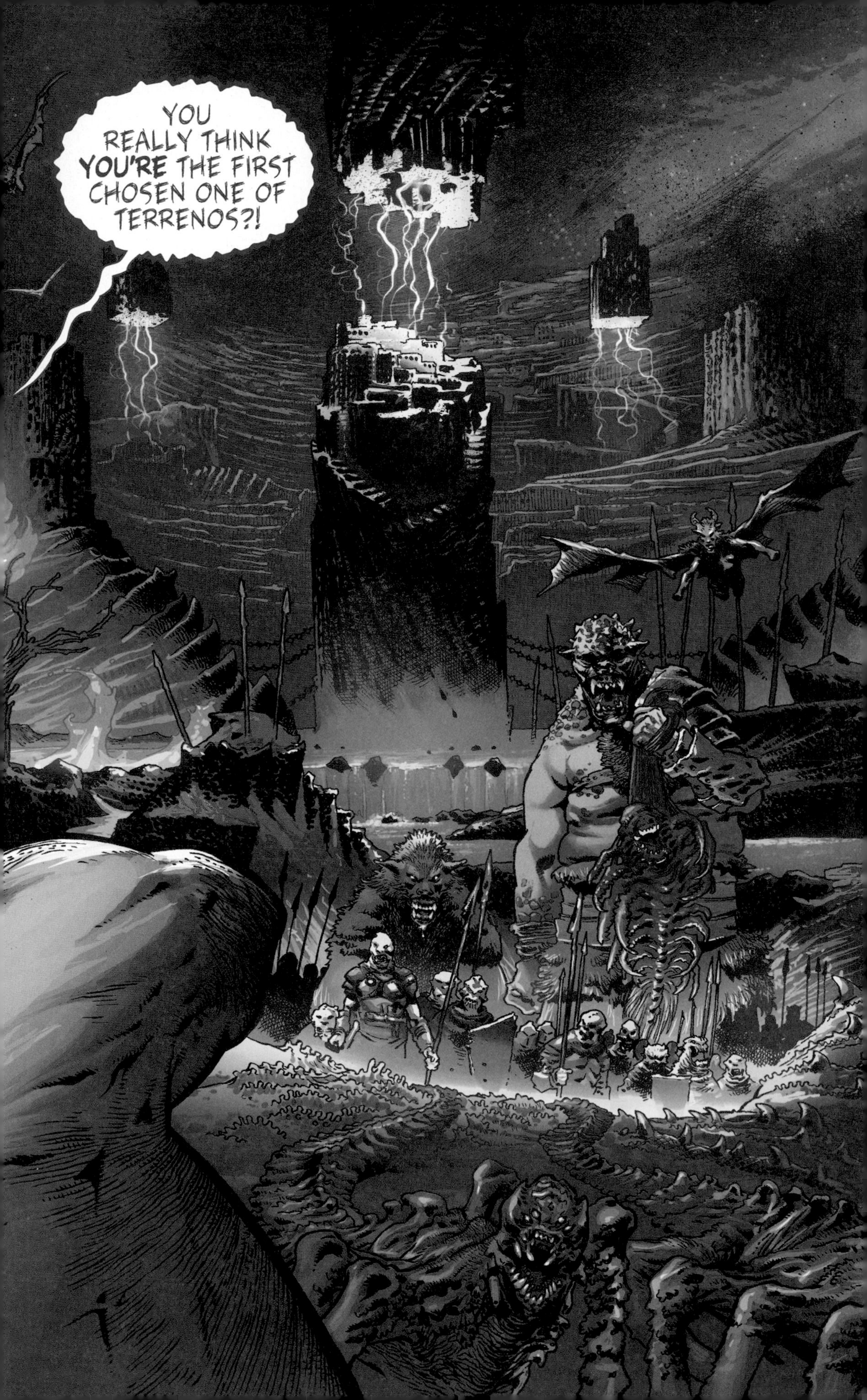
YOU REALLY THINK **YOU'RE** THE FIRST CHOSEN ONE OF TERRENOS?!

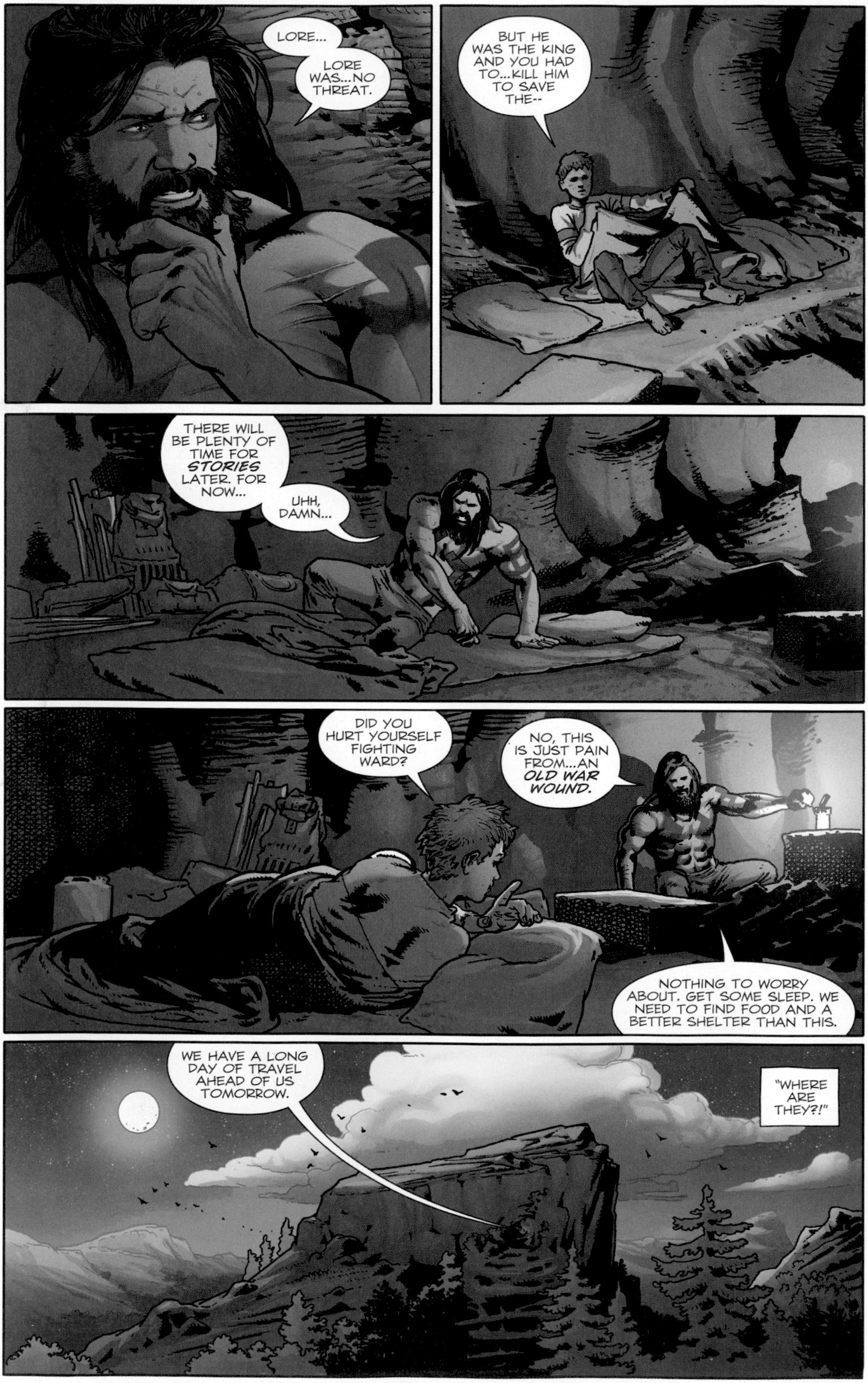

LORE...
LORE WAS...NO THREAT.
BUT HE WAS THE KING AND YOU HAD TO...KILL HIM TO SAVE THE--
THERE WILL BE PLENTY OF TIME FOR STORIES LATER. FOR NOW...
UHH, DAMN...
DID YOU HURT YOURSELF FIGHTING WARD?
NO, THIS IS JUST PAIN FROM...AN OLD WAR WOUND.
NOTHING TO WORRY ABOUT. GET SOME SLEEP. WE NEED TO FIND FOOD AND A BETTER SHELTER THAN THIS.
WE HAVE A LONG DAY OF TRAVEL AHEAD OF US TOMORROW.
"WHERE ARE THEY?!"

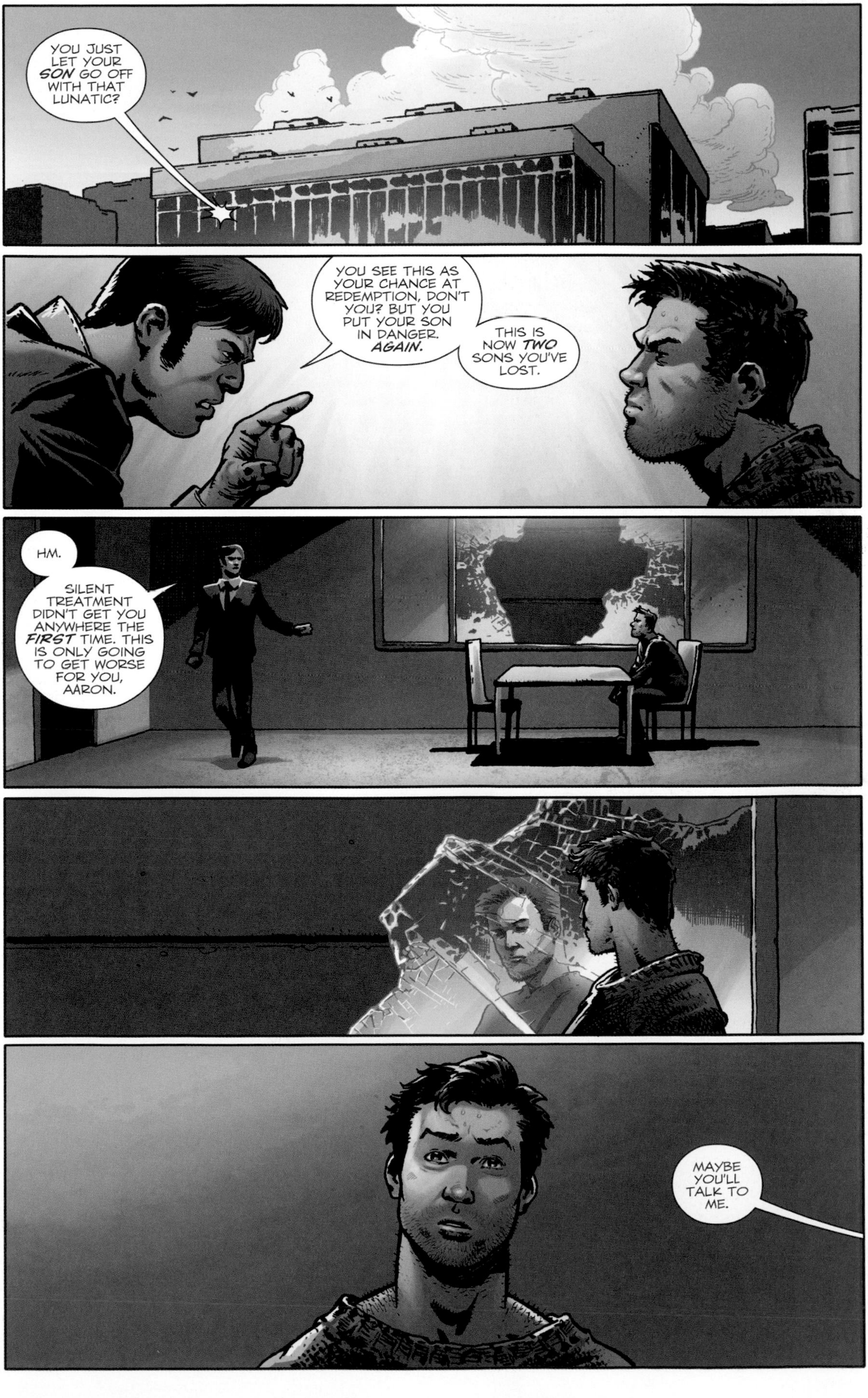
YOU JUST LET YOUR SON GO OFF WITH THAT LUNATIC?
YOU SEE THIS AS YOUR CHANCE AT REDEMPTION, DON'T YOU? BUT YOU PUT YOUR SON IN DANGER. AGAIN.
THIS IS NOW TWO SONS YOU'VE LOST.
HM.
SILENT TREATMENT DIDN'T GET YOU ANYWHERE THE FIRST TIME. THIS IS ONLY GOING TO GET WORSE FOR YOU, AARON.
MAYBE YOU'LL TALK TO ME.

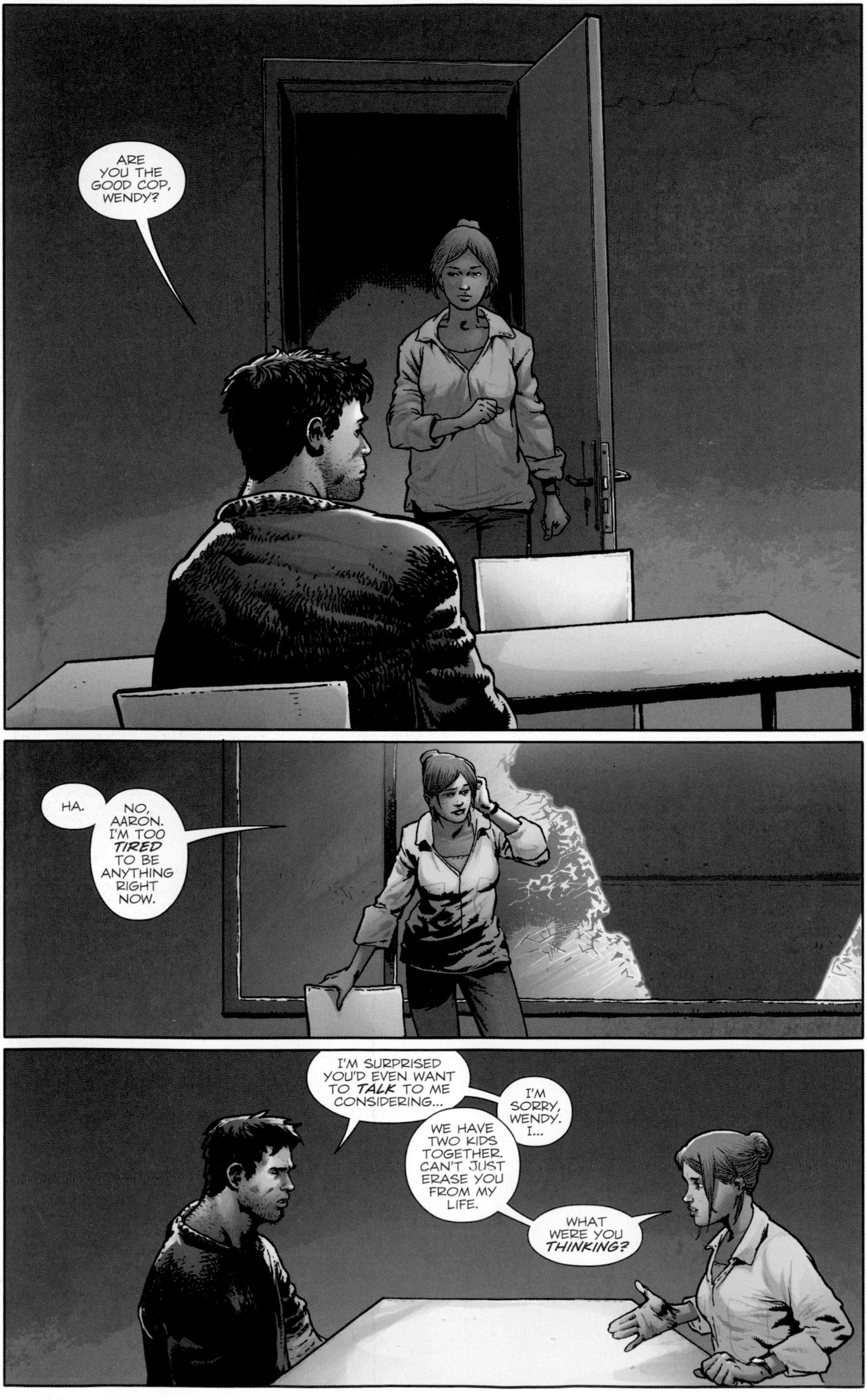
ARE YOU THE GOOD COP, WENDY?
HA.
NO, AARON. I'M TOO TIRED TO BE ANYTHING RIGHT NOW.
I'M SURPRISED YOU'D EVEN WANT TO TALK TO ME CONSIDERING...
I'M SORRY, WENDY. I...
WE HAVE TWO KIDS TOGETHER. CAN'T JUST ERASE YOU FROM MY LIFE.
WHAT WERE YOU THINKING?

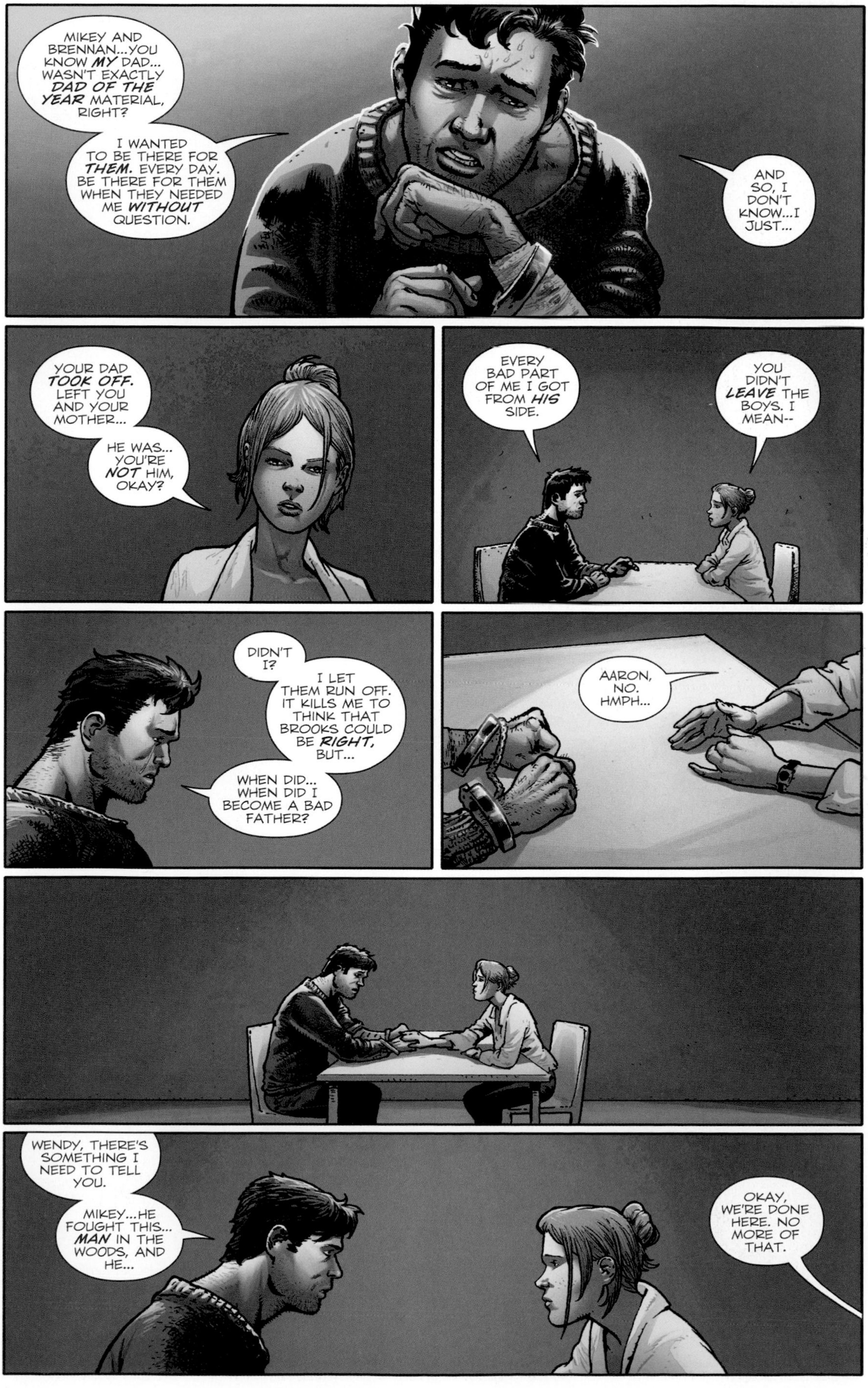
MIKEY AND BRENNAN...YOU KNOW MY DAD... WASN'T EXACTLY DAD OF THE YEAR MATERIAL, RIGHT?
I WANTED TO BE THERE FOR THEM. EVERY DAY. BE THERE FOR THEM WHEN THEY NEEDED ME WITHOUT QUESTION.
AND SO, I DON'T KNOW...I JUST...
YOUR DAD TOOK OFF. LEFT YOU AND YOUR MOTHER...
HE WAS... YOU'RE NOT HIM, OKAY?
EVERY BAD PART OF ME I GOT FROM HIS SIDE.
YOU DIDN'T LEAVE THE BOYS. I MEAN--
DIDN'T I?
I LET THEM RUN OFF. IT KILLS ME TO THINK THAT BROOKS COULD BE RIGHT, BUT...
WHEN DID... WHEN DID I BECOME A BAD FATHER?
AARON, NO. HMPH...
WENDY, THERE'S SOMETHING I NEED TO TELL YOU.
MIKEY...HE FOUGHT THIS... MAN IN THE WOODS, AND HE...
OKAY, WE'RE DONE HERE. NO MORE OF THAT.

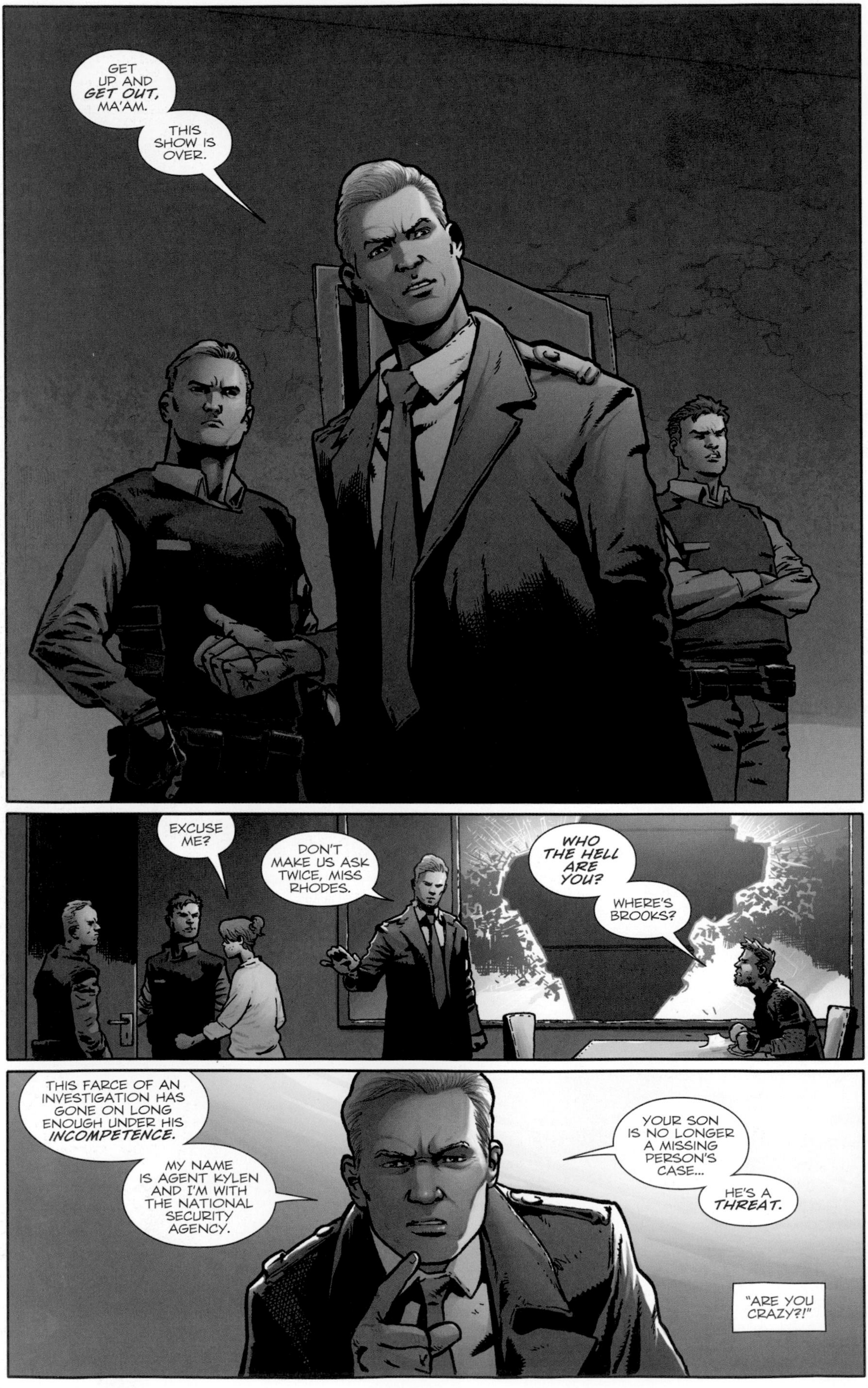
GET UP AND *GET OUT,* MA'AM.
THIS SHOW IS OVER.
EXCUSE ME?
DON'T MAKE US ASK TWICE, MISS RHODES.
WHO THE HELL ARE YOU?
WHERE'S BROOKS?
THIS FARCE OF AN INVESTIGATION HAS GONE ON LONG ENOUGH UNDER HIS *INCOMPETENCE.*
MY NAME IS AGENT KYLEN AND I'M WITH THE NATIONAL SECURITY AGENCY.
YOUR SON IS NO LONGER A MISSING PERSON'S CASE...
HE'S A *THREAT.*
"ARE YOU CRAZY?!"

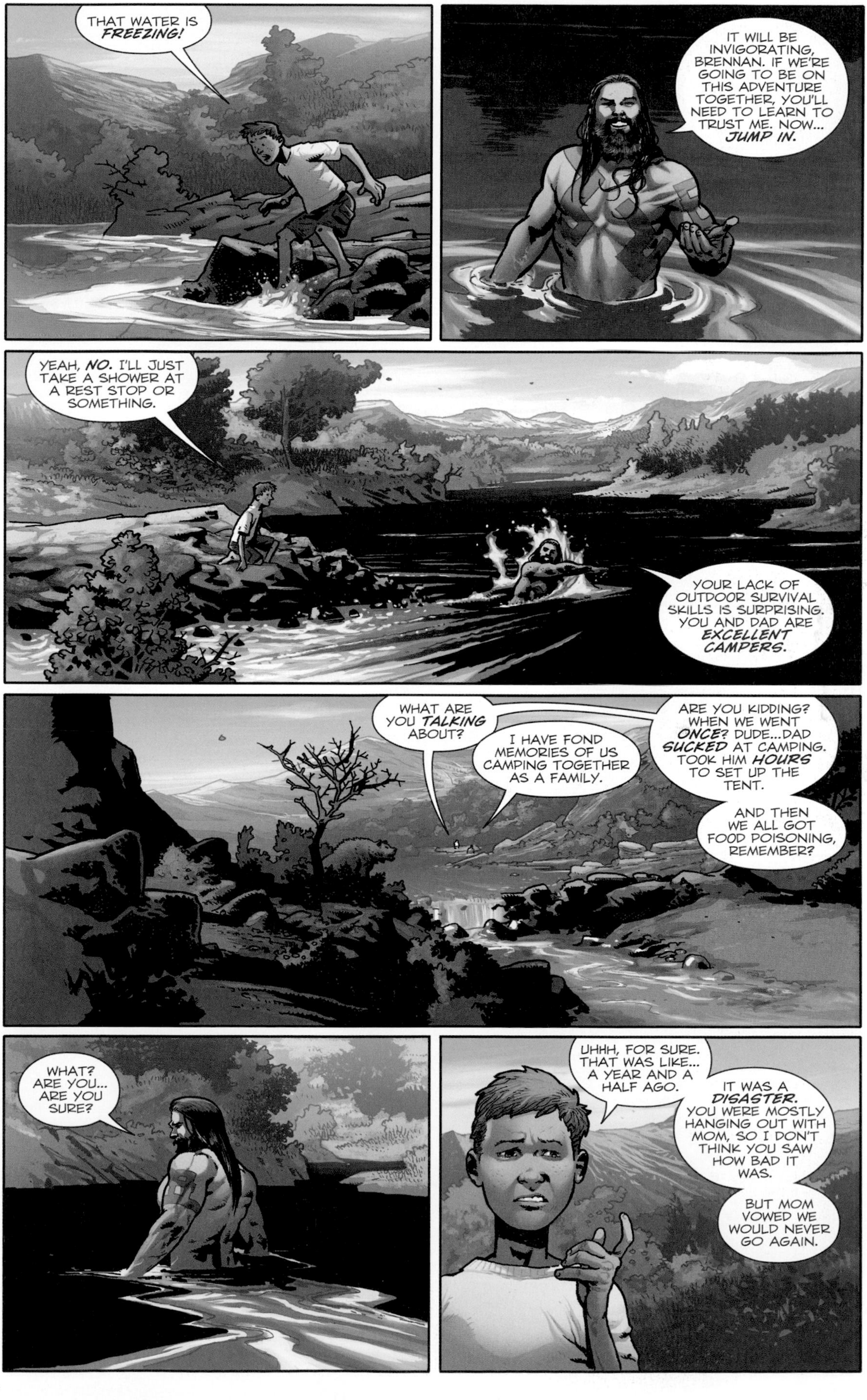
THAT WATER IS *FREEZING!*
IT WILL BE INVIGORATING, BRENNAN. IF WE'RE GOING TO BE ON THIS ADVENTURE TOGETHER, YOU'LL NEED TO LEARN TO TRUST ME. NOW... *JUMP IN.*
YEAH, *NO.* I'LL JUST TAKE A SHOWER AT A REST STOP OR SOMETHING.
YOUR LACK OF OUTDOOR SURVIVAL SKILLS IS SURPRISING. YOU AND DAD ARE *EXCELLENT CAMPERS.*
I HAVE FOND MEMORIES OF US CAMPING TOGETHER AS A FAMILY.
WHAT ARE YOU *TALKING* ABOUT?
ARE YOU KIDDING? WHEN WE WENT *ONCE*? DUDE...DAD *SUCKED* AT CAMPING. TOOK HIM *HOURS* TO SET UP THE TENT.
AND THEN WE ALL GOT FOOD POISONING, REMEMBER?
WHAT? ARE YOU... ARE YOU SURE?
UHHH, FOR SURE. THAT WAS LIKE... A YEAR AND A HALF AGO.
IT WAS A *DISASTER.* YOU WERE MOSTLY HANGING OUT WITH MOM, SO I DON'T THINK YOU SAW HOW BAD IT WAS.
BUT MOM VOWED WE WOULD NEVER GO AGAIN.

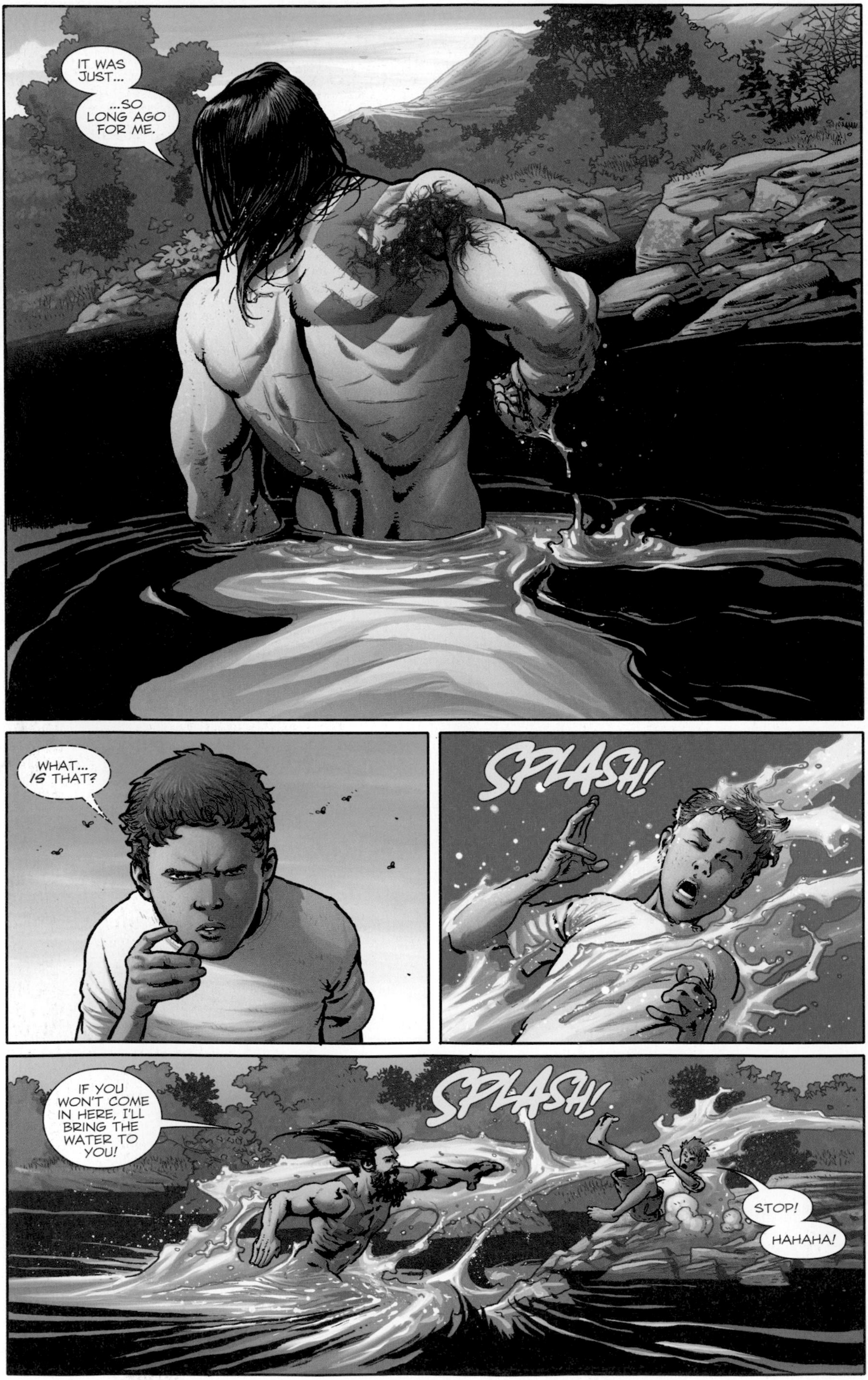
IT WAS JUST...
...SO LONG AGO FOR ME.
WHAT... IS THAT?
SPLASH!
IF YOU WON'T COME IN HERE, I'LL BRING THE WATER TO YOU!
SPLASH!
STOP!
HAHAHA!

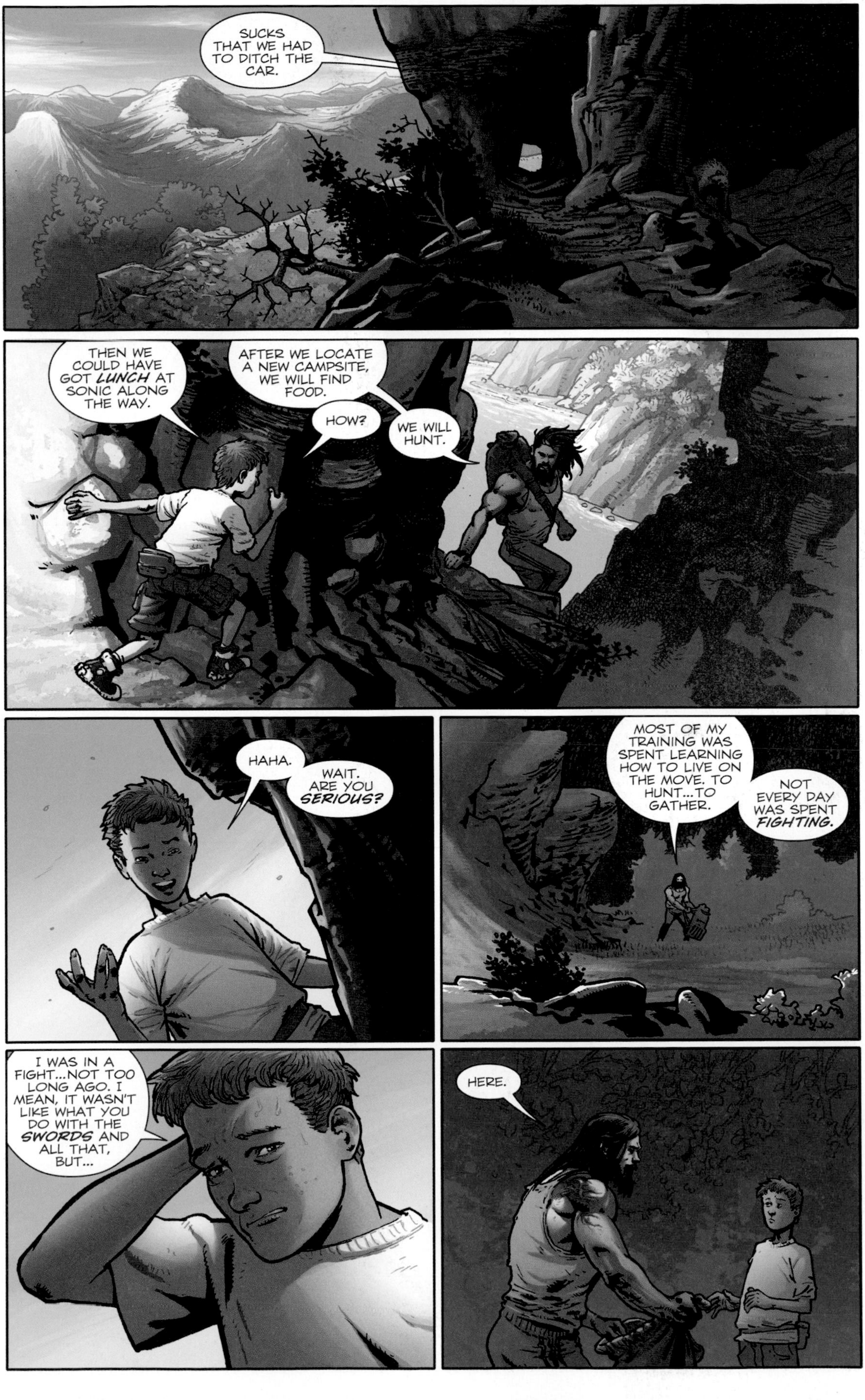
SUCKS THAT WE HAD TO DITCH THE CAR.
THEN WE COULD HAVE GOT *LUNCH* AT SONIC ALONG THE WAY.
AFTER WE LOCATE A NEW CAMPSITE, WE WILL FIND FOOD.
HOW?
WE WILL HUNT.
HAHA.
WAIT. ARE YOU *SERIOUS?*
MOST OF MY TRAINING WAS SPENT LEARNING HOW TO LIVE ON THE MOVE. TO HUNT...TO GATHER.
NOT EVERY DAY WAS SPENT *FIGHTING*.
I WAS IN A FIGHT...NOT TOO LONG AGO. I MEAN, IT WASN'T LIKE WHAT YOU DO WITH THE *SWORDS* AND ALL THAT, BUT...
HERE.

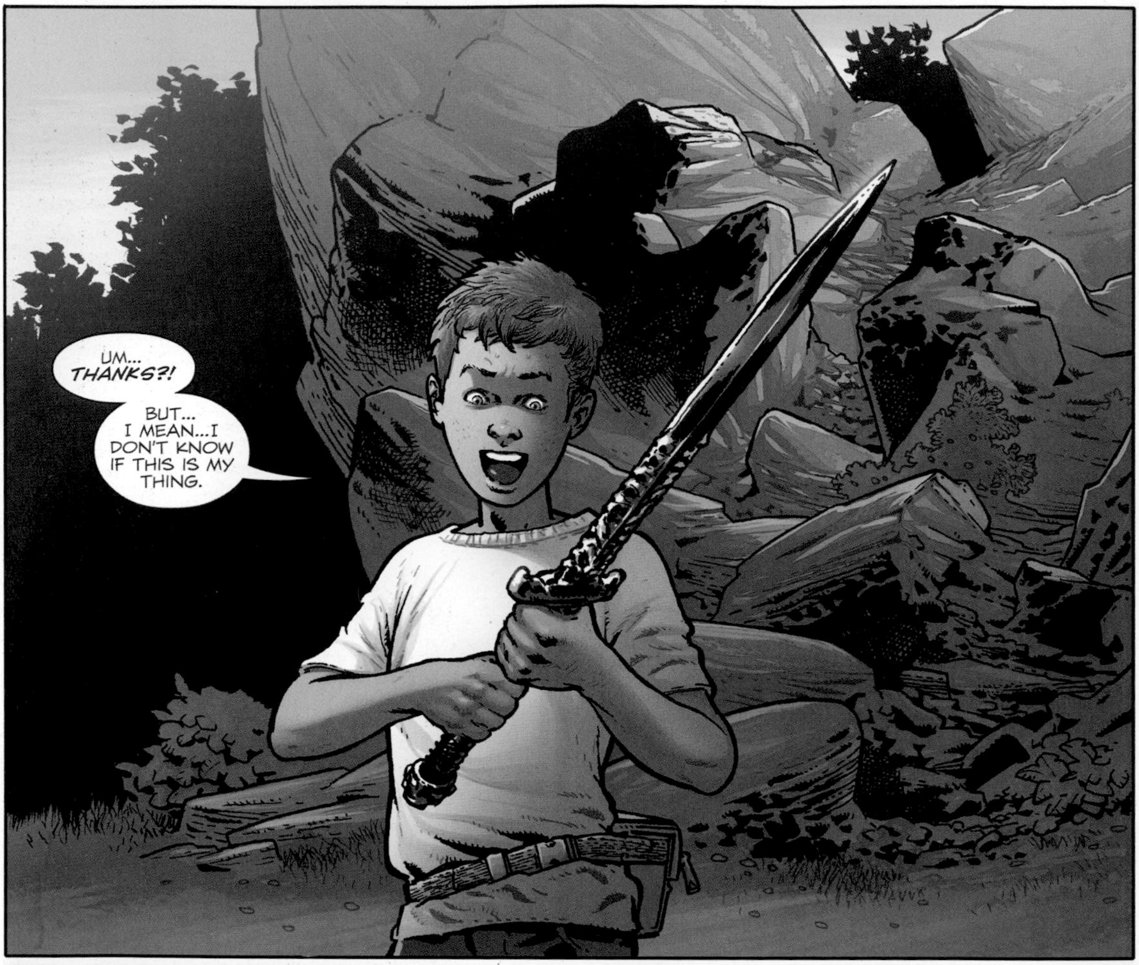
UM... THANKS?!
BUT... I MEAN...I DON'T KNOW IF THIS IS MY THING.

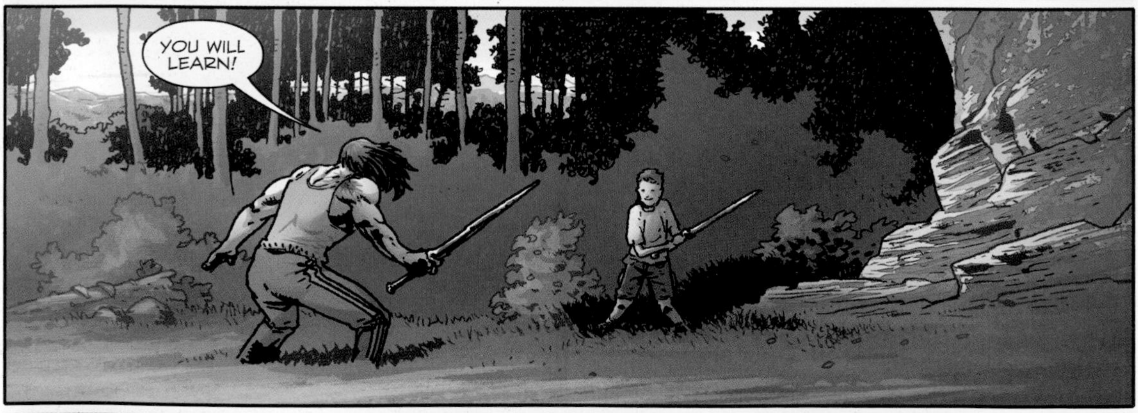
YOU WILL LEARN!

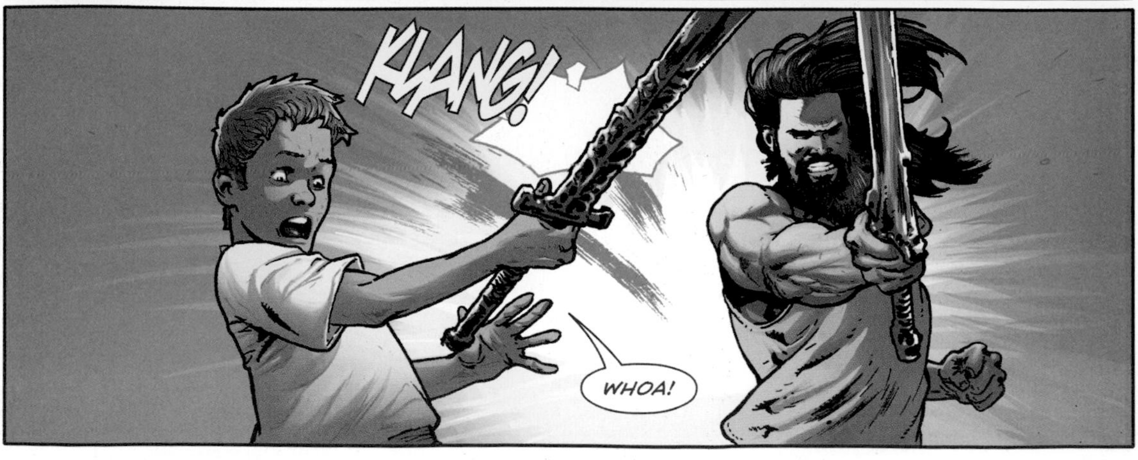
KLANG!
WHOA!

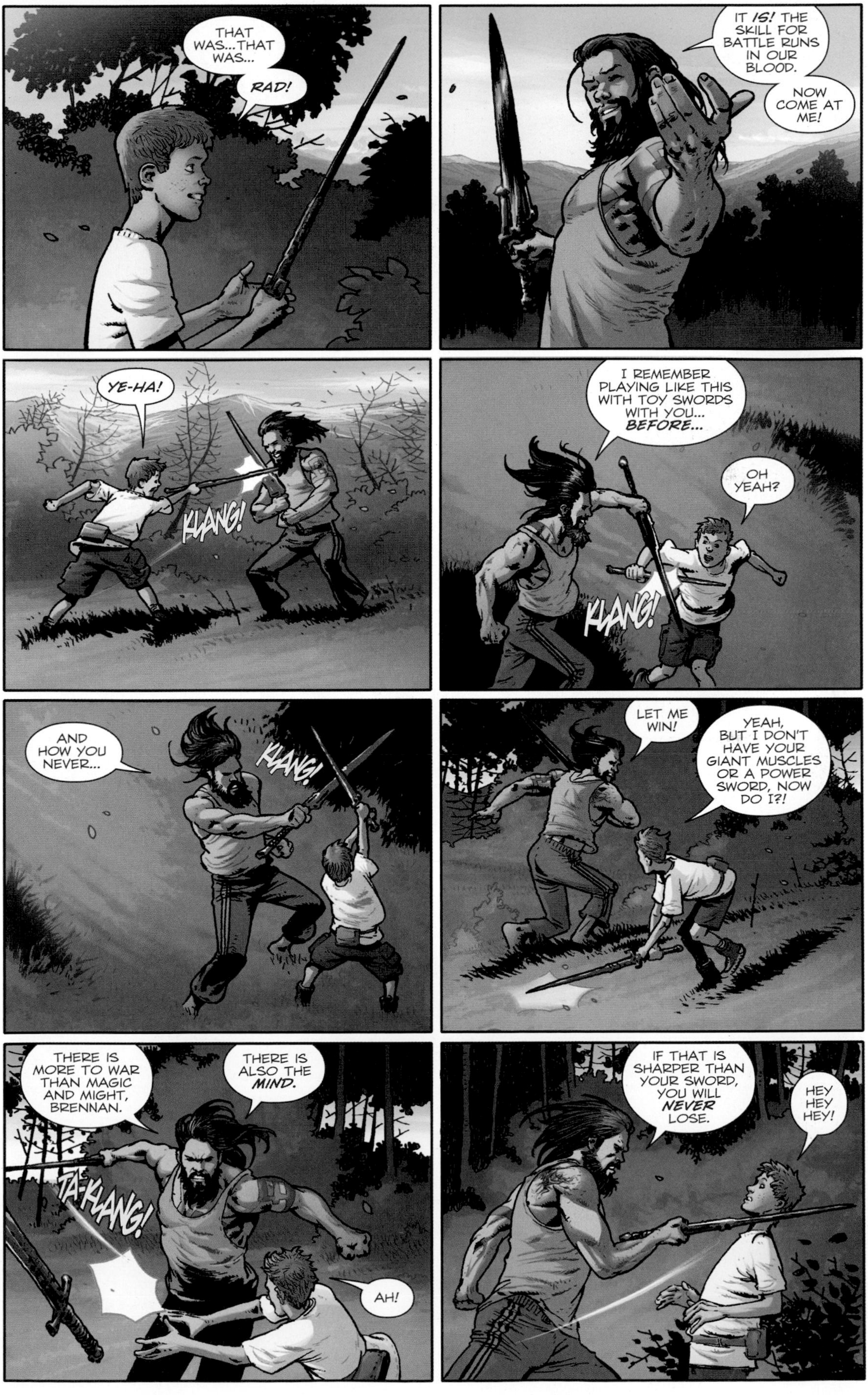
THAT WAS...THAT WAS...
RAD!
IT IS! THE SKILL FOR BATTLE RUNS IN OUR BLOOD.
NOW COME AT ME!
YE-HA!
KLANG!
I REMEMBER PLAYING LIKE THIS WITH TOY SWORDS WITH YOU... BEFORE...
OH YEAH?
KLANG!
AND HOW YOU NEVER...
KLANG!
LET ME WIN!
YEAH, BUT I DON'T HAVE YOUR GIANT MUSCLES OR A POWER SWORD, NOW DO I?!
THERE IS MORE TO WAR THAN MAGIC AND MIGHT, BRENNAN.
THERE IS ALSO THE MIND.
TA-KLANG!
AH!
IF THAT IS SHARPER THAN YOUR SWORD, YOU WILL NEVER LOSE.
HEY HEY HEY!

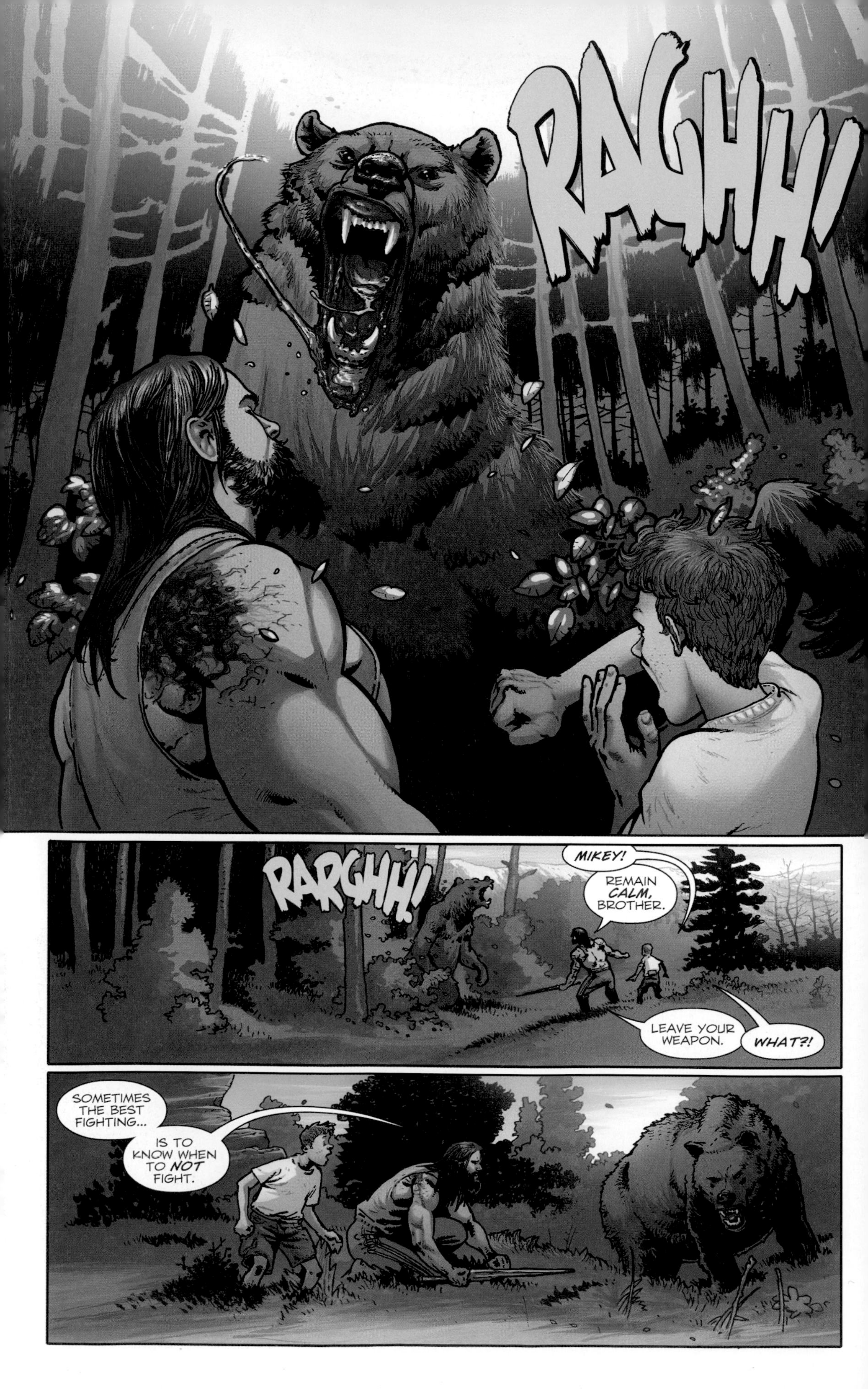
RAGHH!
RARGHH!
MIKEY!
REMAIN CALM, BROTHER.
LEAVE YOUR WEAPON.
WHAT?!
SOMETIMES THE BEST FIGHTING...
IS TO KNOW WHEN TO NOT FIGHT.

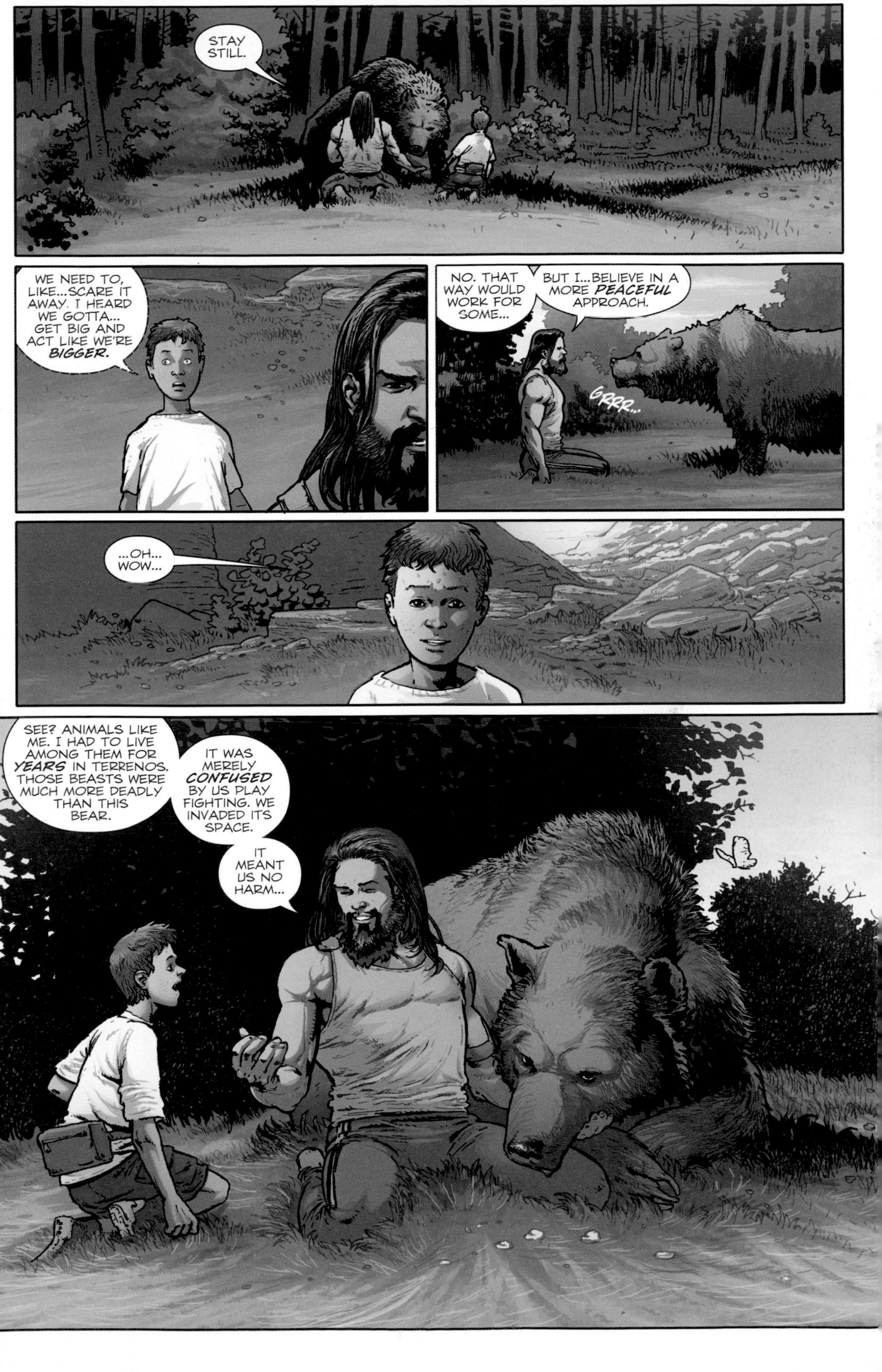
STAY STILL.
WE NEED TO, LIKE...SCARE IT AWAY. I HEARD WE GOTTA... GET BIG AND ACT LIKE WE'RE BIGGER.
NO. THAT WAY WOULD WORK FOR SOME...
BUT I...BELIEVE IN A MORE PEACEFUL APPROACH.
GRRR...
...OH... WOW...
SEE? ANIMALS LIKE ME. I HAD TO LIVE AMONG THEM FOR YEARS IN TERRENOS. THOSE BEASTS WERE MUCH MORE DEADLY THAN THIS BEAR.
IT WAS MERELY CONFUSED BY US PLAY FIGHTING. WE INVADED ITS SPACE.
IT MEANT US NO HARM...

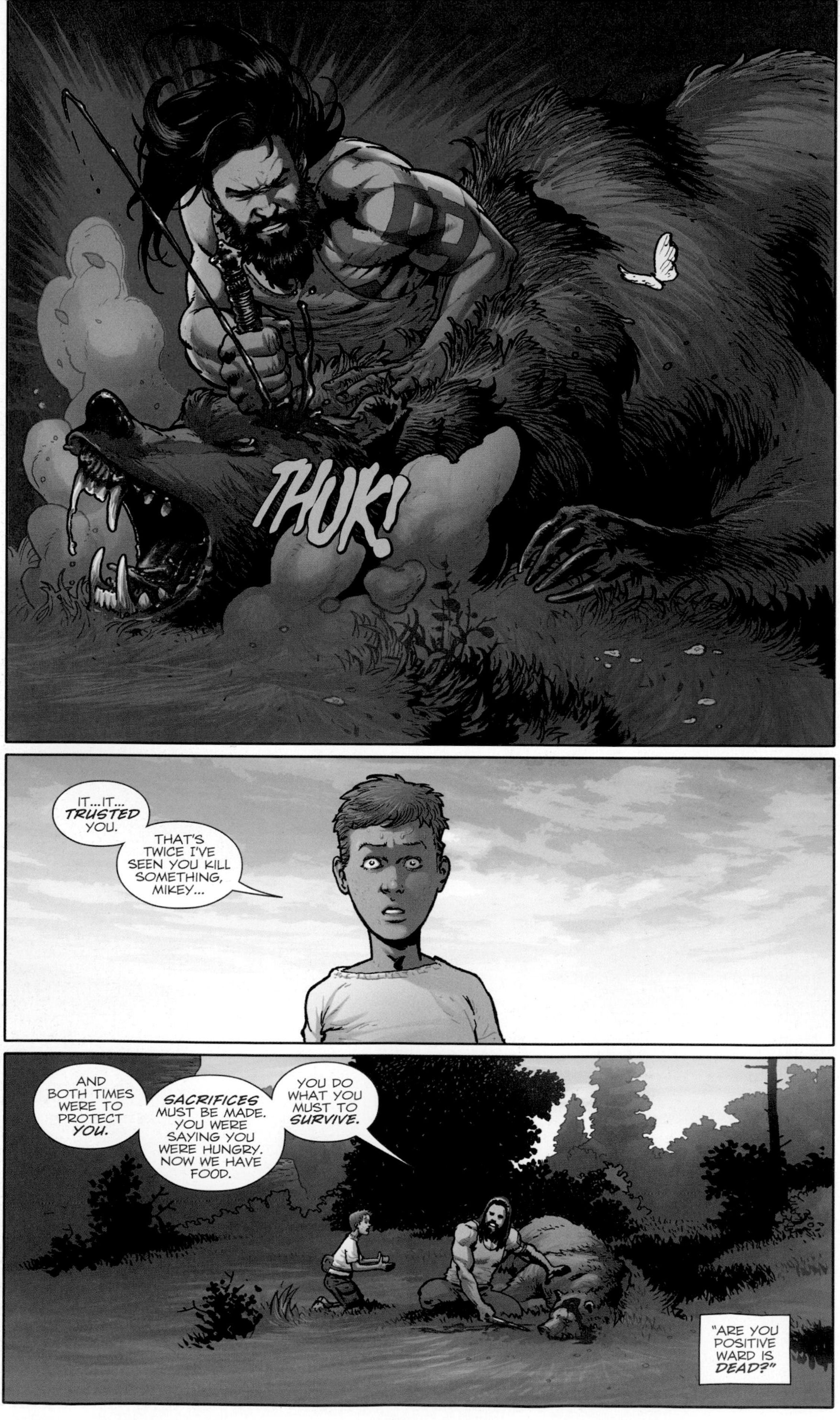
THUK!
IT...IT... TRUSTED YOU.
THAT'S TWICE I'VE SEEN YOU KILL SOMETHING, MIKEY...
AND BOTH TIMES WERE TO PROTECT YOU.
SACRIFICES MUST BE MADE. YOU WERE SAYING YOU WERE HUNGRY. NOW WE HAVE FOOD.
YOU DO WHAT YOU MUST TO SURVIVE.
"ARE YOU POSITIVE WARD IS DEAD?"

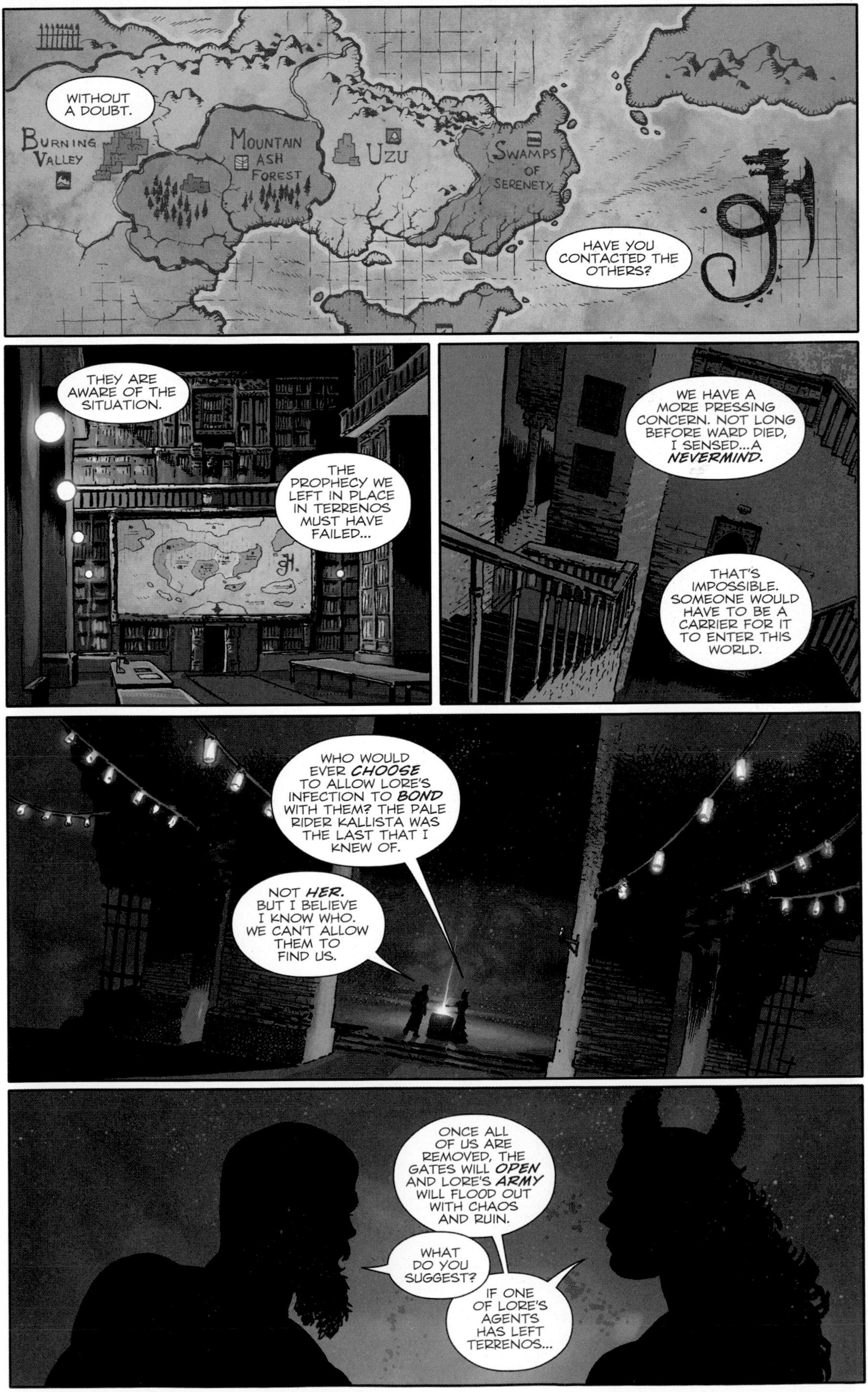
WITHOUT A DOUBT.
BURNING VALLEY
MOUNTAIN ASH FOREST
UZU
SWAMPS OF SERENETY
HAVE YOU CONTACTED THE OTHERS?
THEY ARE AWARE OF THE SITUATION.
THE PROPHECY WE LEFT IN PLACE IN TERRENOS MUST HAVE FAILED...
WE HAVE A MORE PRESSING CONCERN. NOT LONG BEFORE WARD DIED, I SENSED...A NEVERMIND.
THAT'S IMPOSSIBLE. SOMEONE WOULD HAVE TO BE A CARRIER FOR IT TO ENTER THIS WORLD.
WHO WOULD EVER CHOOSE TO ALLOW LORE'S INFECTION TO BOND WITH THEM? THE PALE RIDER KALLISTA WAS THE LAST THAT I KNEW OF.
NOT HER. BUT I BELIEVE I KNOW WHO. WE CAN'T ALLOW THEM TO FIND US.
ONCE ALL OF US ARE REMOVED, THE GATES WILL OPEN AND LORE'S ARMY WILL FLOOD OUT WITH CHAOS AND RUIN.
WHAT DO YOU SUGGEST?
IF ONE OF LORE'S AGENTS HAS LEFT TERRENOS...

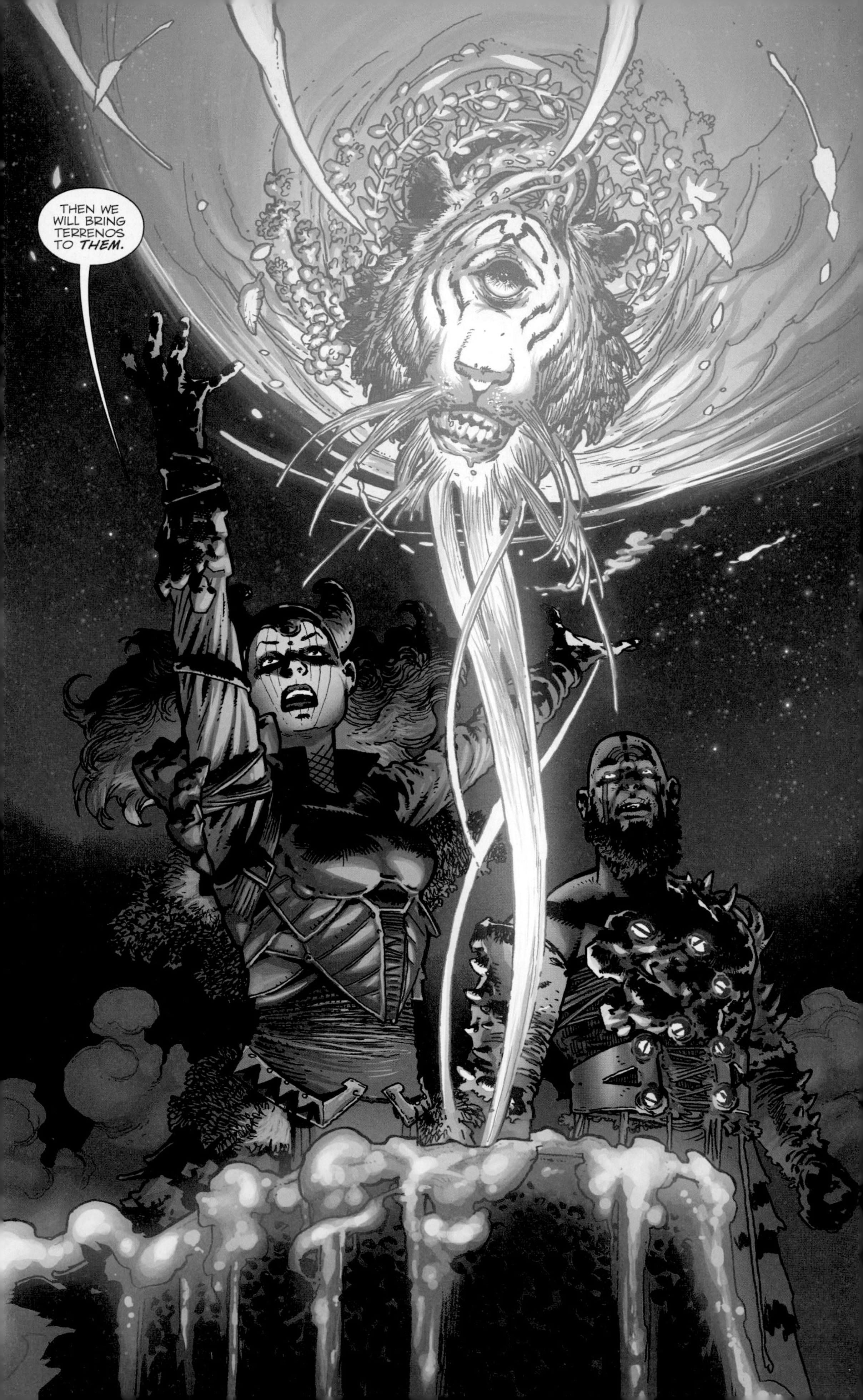
THEN WE WILL BRING TERRENOS TO *THEM*.

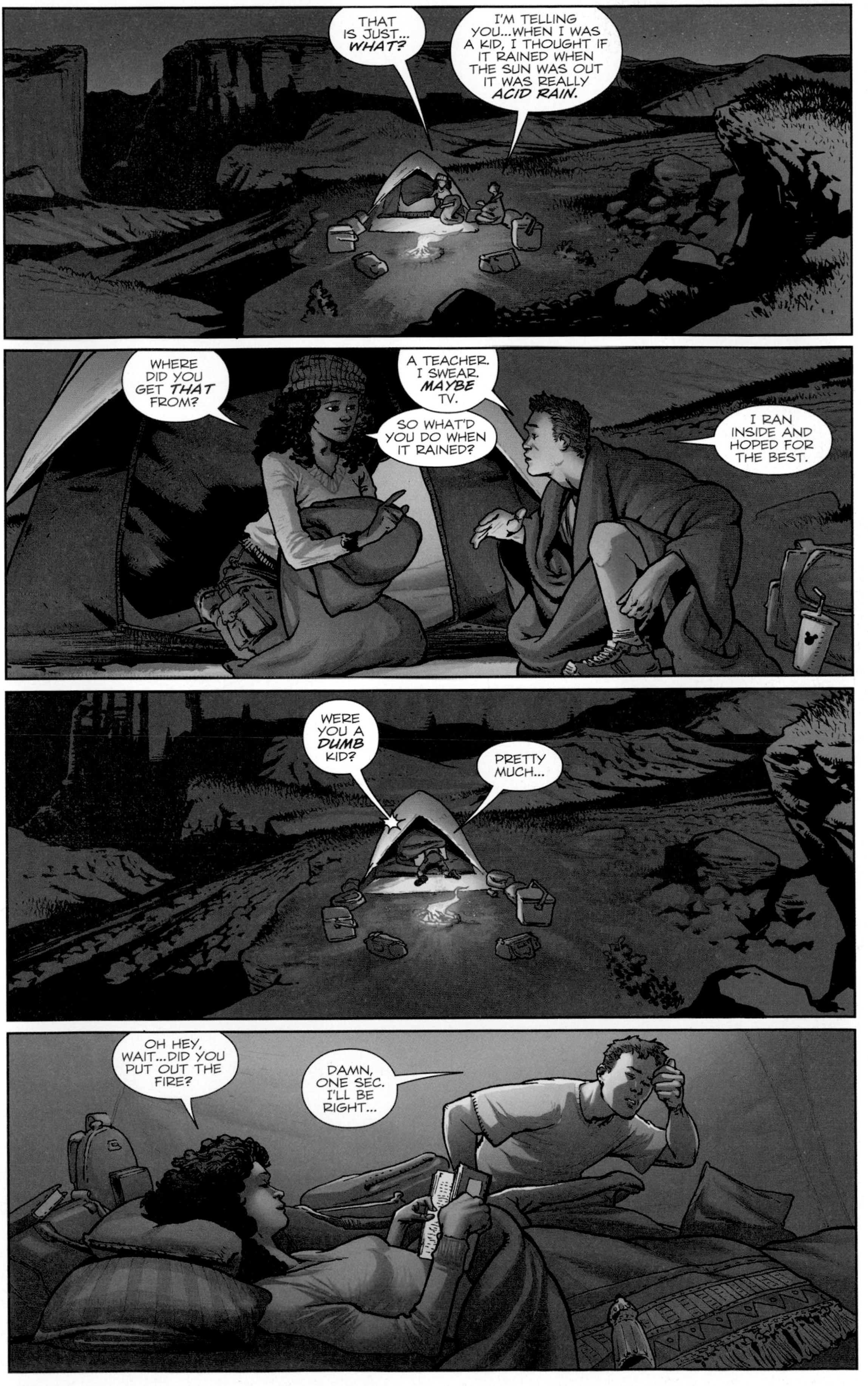
THAT IS JUST... WHAT?
I'M TELLING YOU...WHEN I WAS A KID, I THOUGHT IF IT RAINED WHEN THE SUN WAS OUT IT WAS REALLY ACID RAIN.
WHERE DID YOU GET THAT FROM?
A TEACHER. I SWEAR. MAYBE TV.
SO WHAT'D YOU DO WHEN IT RAINED?
I RAN INSIDE AND HOPED FOR THE BEST.
WERE YOU A DUMB KID?
PRETTY MUCH...
OH HEY, WAIT...DID YOU PUT OUT THE FIRE?
DAMN, ONE SEC. I'LL BE RIGHT...

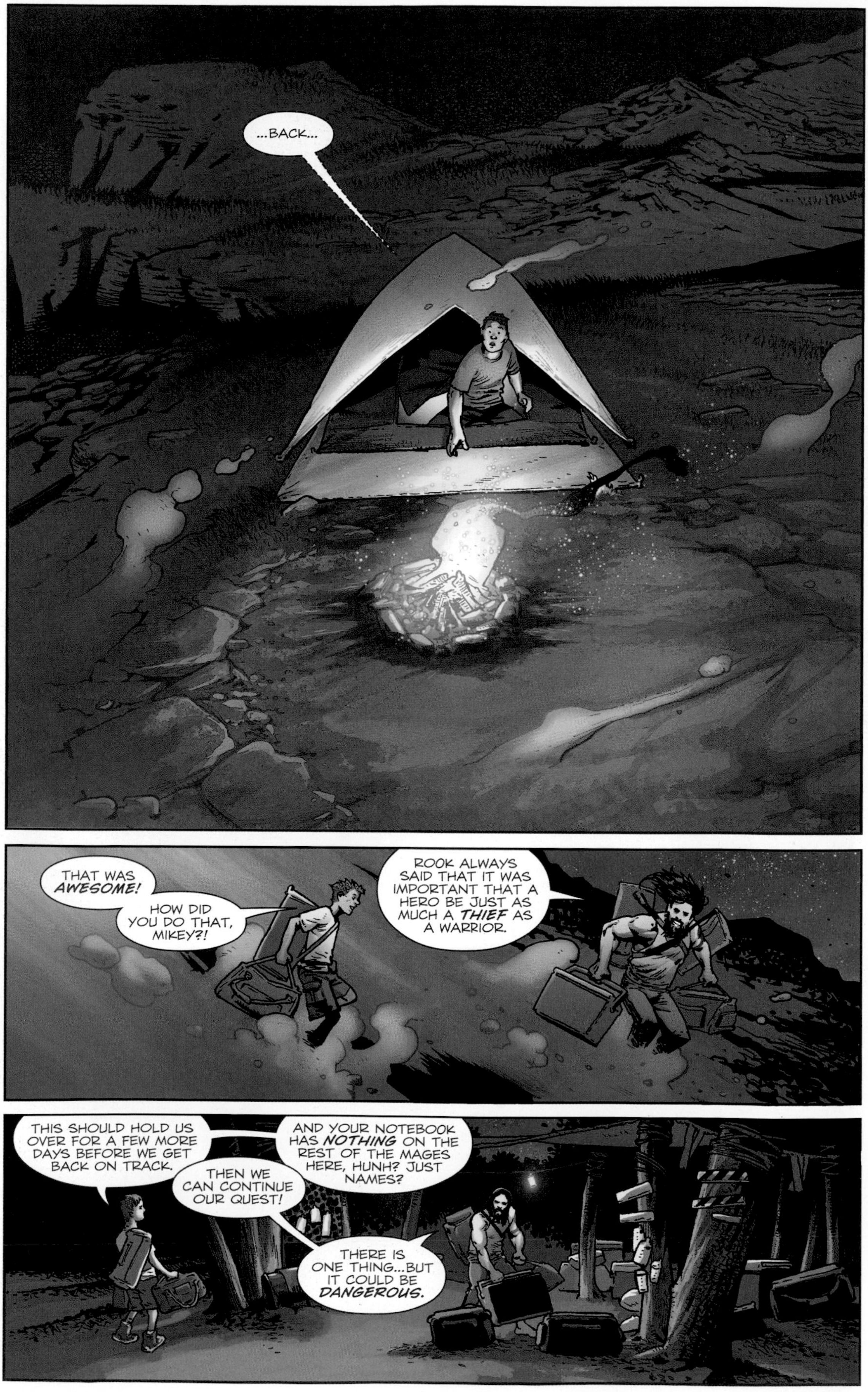
...BACK...
THAT WAS AWESOME!
HOW DID YOU DO THAT, MIKEY?!
ROOK ALWAYS SAID THAT IT WAS IMPORTANT THAT A HERO BE JUST AS MUCH A THIEF AS A WARRIOR.
THIS SHOULD HOLD US OVER FOR A FEW MORE DAYS BEFORE WE GET BACK ON TRACK.
THEN WE CAN CONTINUE OUR QUEST!
AND YOUR NOTEBOOK HAS NOTHING ON THE REST OF THE MAGES HERE, HUNH? JUST NAMES?
THERE IS ONE THING...BUT IT COULD BE DANGEROUS.

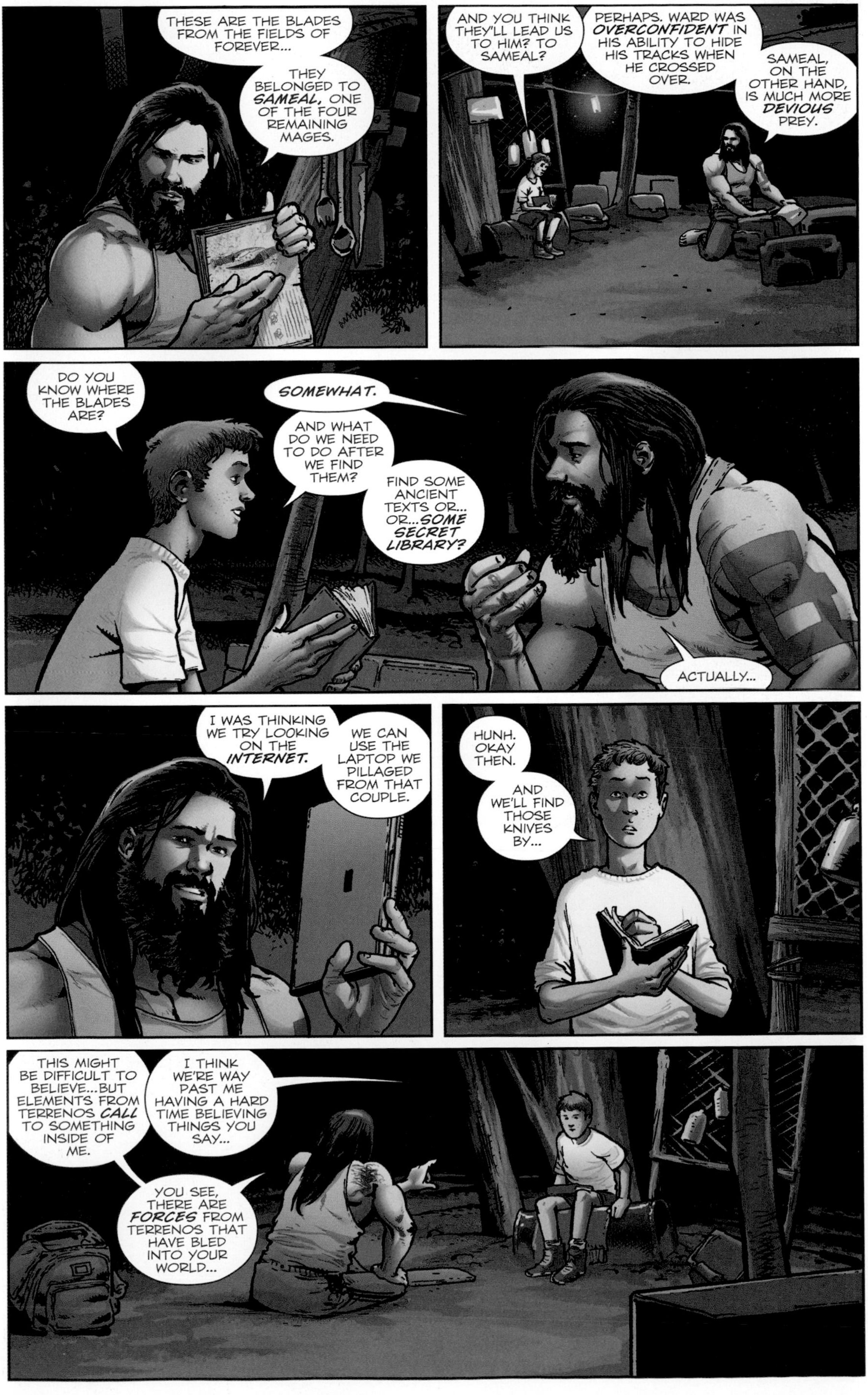
THESE ARE THE BLADES FROM THE FIELDS OF FOREVER...
THEY BELONGED TO SAMEAL, ONE OF THE FOUR REMAINING MAGES.
AND YOU THINK THEY'LL LEAD US TO HIM? TO SAMEAL?
PERHAPS. WARD WAS OVERCONFIDENT IN HIS ABILITY TO HIDE HIS TRACKS WHEN HE CROSSED OVER.
SAMEAL, ON THE OTHER HAND, IS MUCH MORE DEVIOUS PREY.
DO YOU KNOW WHERE THE BLADES ARE?
SOMEWHAT.
AND WHAT DO WE NEED TO DO AFTER WE FIND THEM?
FIND SOME ANCIENT TEXTS OR... OR...SOME SECRET LIBRARY?
ACTUALLY...
I WAS THINKING WE TRY LOOKING ON THE INTERNET.
WE CAN USE THE LAPTOP WE PILLAGED FROM THAT COUPLE.
HUNH. OKAY THEN.
AND WE'LL FIND THOSE KNIVES BY...
THIS MIGHT BE DIFFICULT TO BELIEVE...BUT ELEMENTS FROM TERRENOS CALL TO SOMETHING INSIDE OF ME.
I THINK WE'RE WAY PAST ME HAVING A HARD TIME BELIEVING THINGS YOU SAY...
YOU SEE, THERE ARE FORCES FROM TERRENOS THAT HAVE BLED INTO YOUR WORLD...

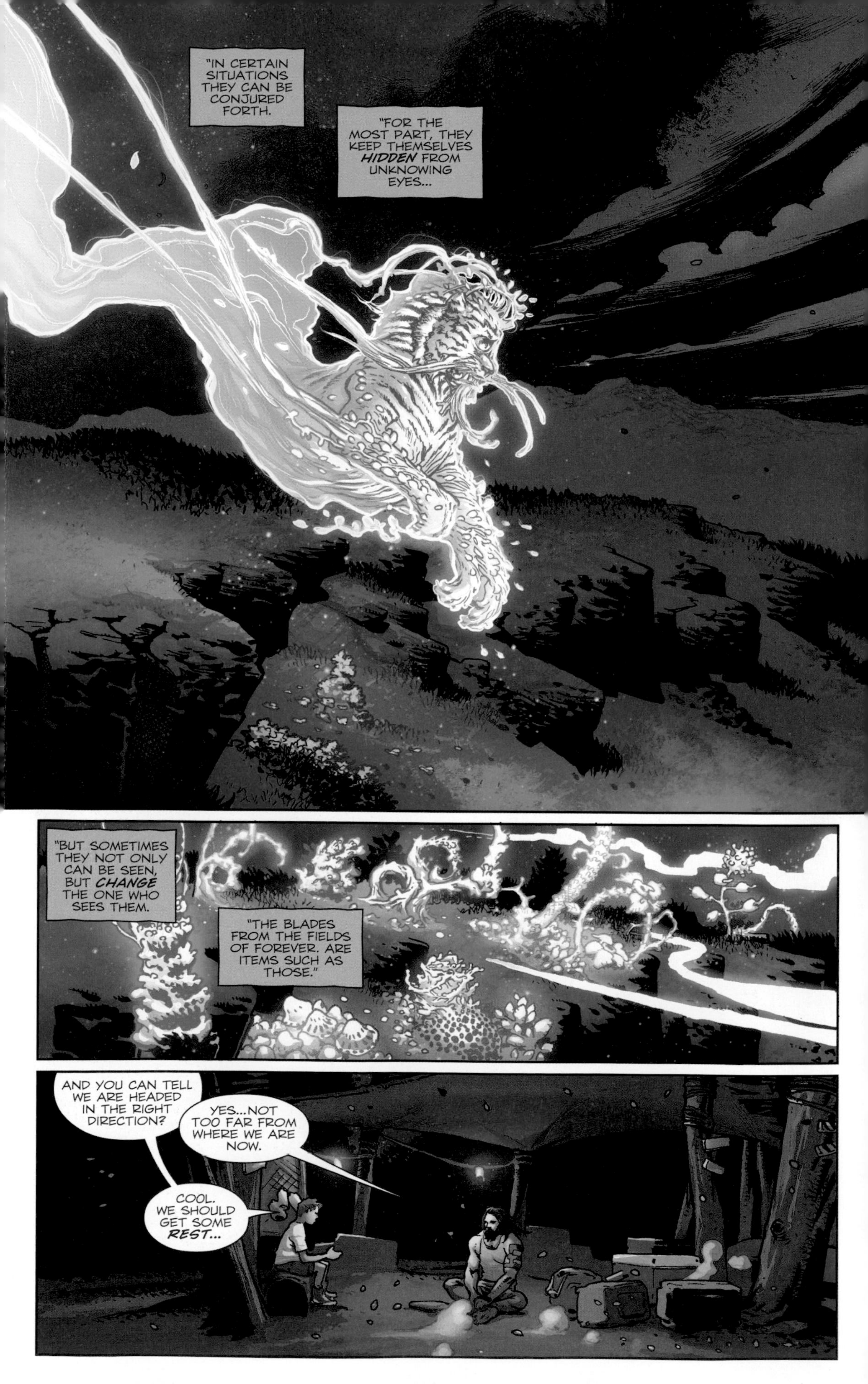
"IN CERTAIN SITUATIONS THEY CAN BE CONJURED FORTH.
"FOR THE MOST PART, THEY KEEP THEMSELVES HIDDEN FROM UNKNOWING EYES...
"BUT SOMETIMES THEY NOT ONLY CAN BE SEEN, BUT CHANGE THE ONE WHO SEES THEM.
"THE BLADES FROM THE FIELDS OF FOREVER. ARE ITEMS SUCH AS THOSE."
AND YOU CAN TELL WE ARE HEADED IN THE RIGHT DIRECTION?
YES...NOT TOO FAR FROM WHERE WE ARE NOW.
COOL. WE SHOULD GET SOME REST...

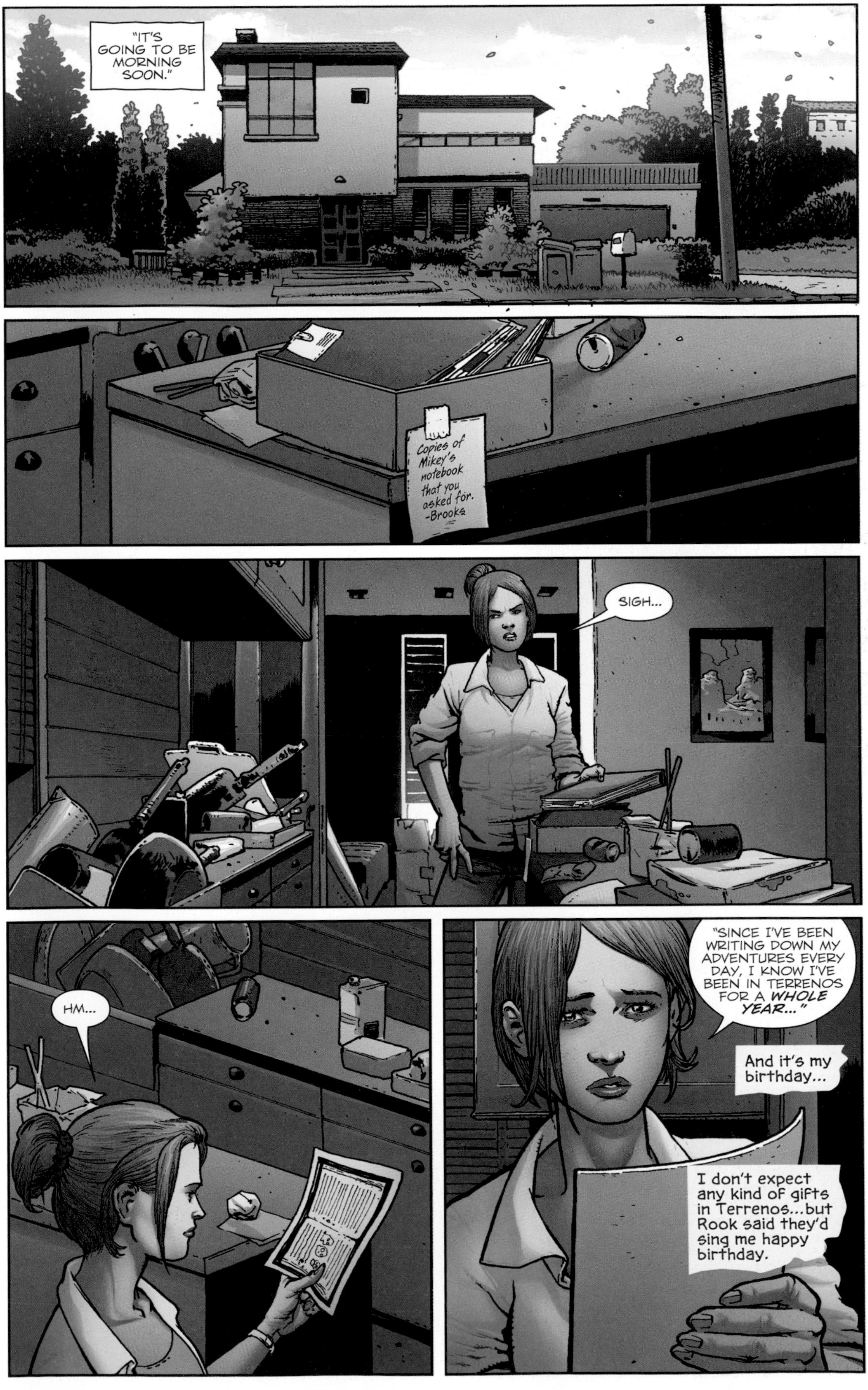

"IT'S GOING TO BE MORNING SOON."
Copies of Mikey's notebook that you asked for. -Brooks
SIGH...
HM...
"SINCE I'VE BEEN WRITING DOWN MY ADVENTURES EVERY DAY, I KNOW I'VE BEEN IN TERRENOS FOR A *WHOLE YEAR...*"
And it's my birthday...
I don't expect any kind of gifts in Terrenos...but Rook said they'd sing me happy birthday.

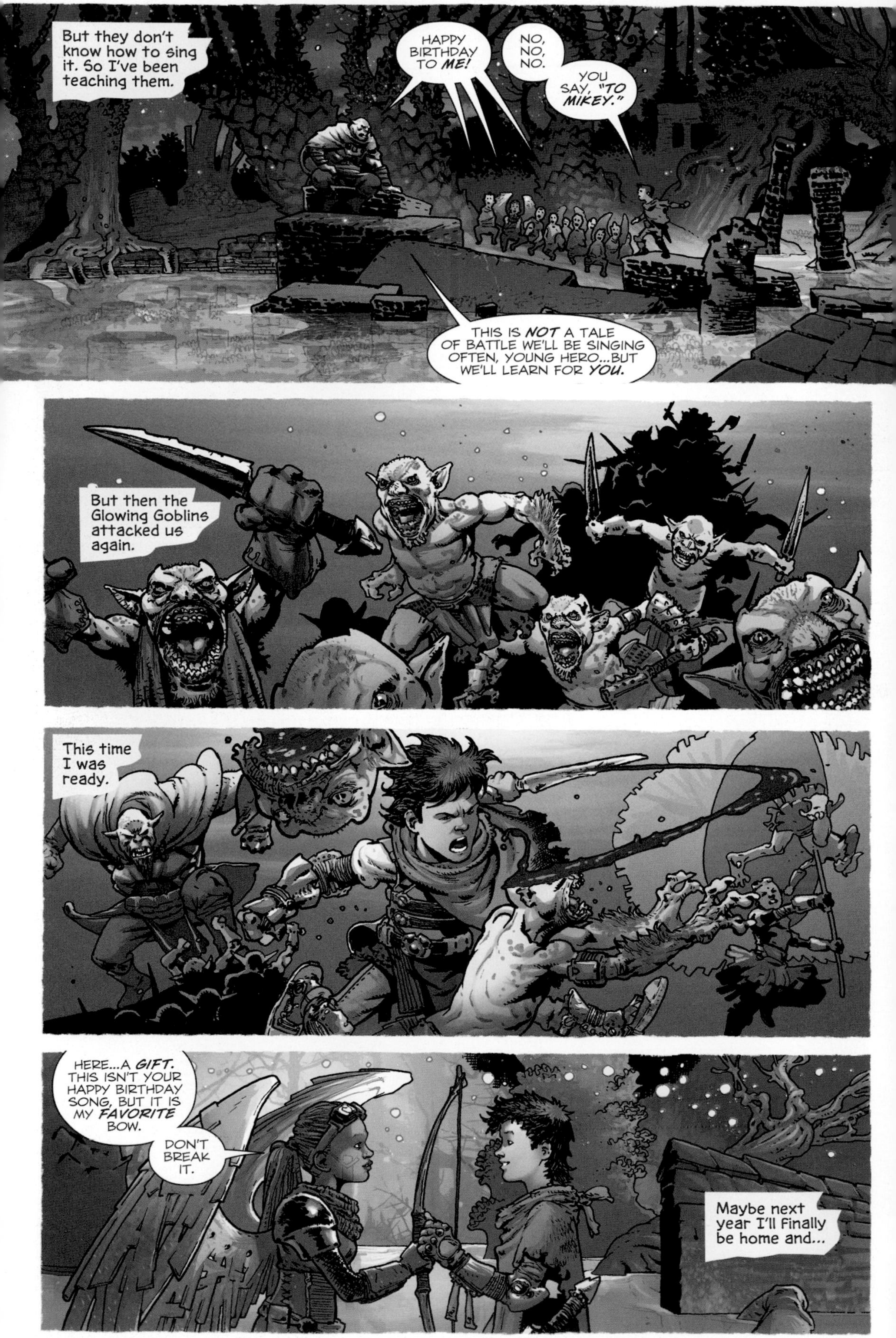
But they don't know how to sing it. So I've been teaching them.
HAPPY BIRTHDAY TO ME!
NO, NO, NO.
YOU SAY, "TO MIKEY."
THIS IS NOT A TALE OF BATTLE WE'LL BE SINGING OFTEN, YOUNG HERO...BUT WE'LL LEARN FOR YOU.
But then the Glowing Goblins attacked us again.
This time I was ready.
HERE...A GIFT. THIS ISN'T YOUR HAPPY BIRTHDAY SONG, BUT IT IS MY FAVORITE BOW.
DON'T BREAK IT.
Maybe next year I'll Finally be home and...

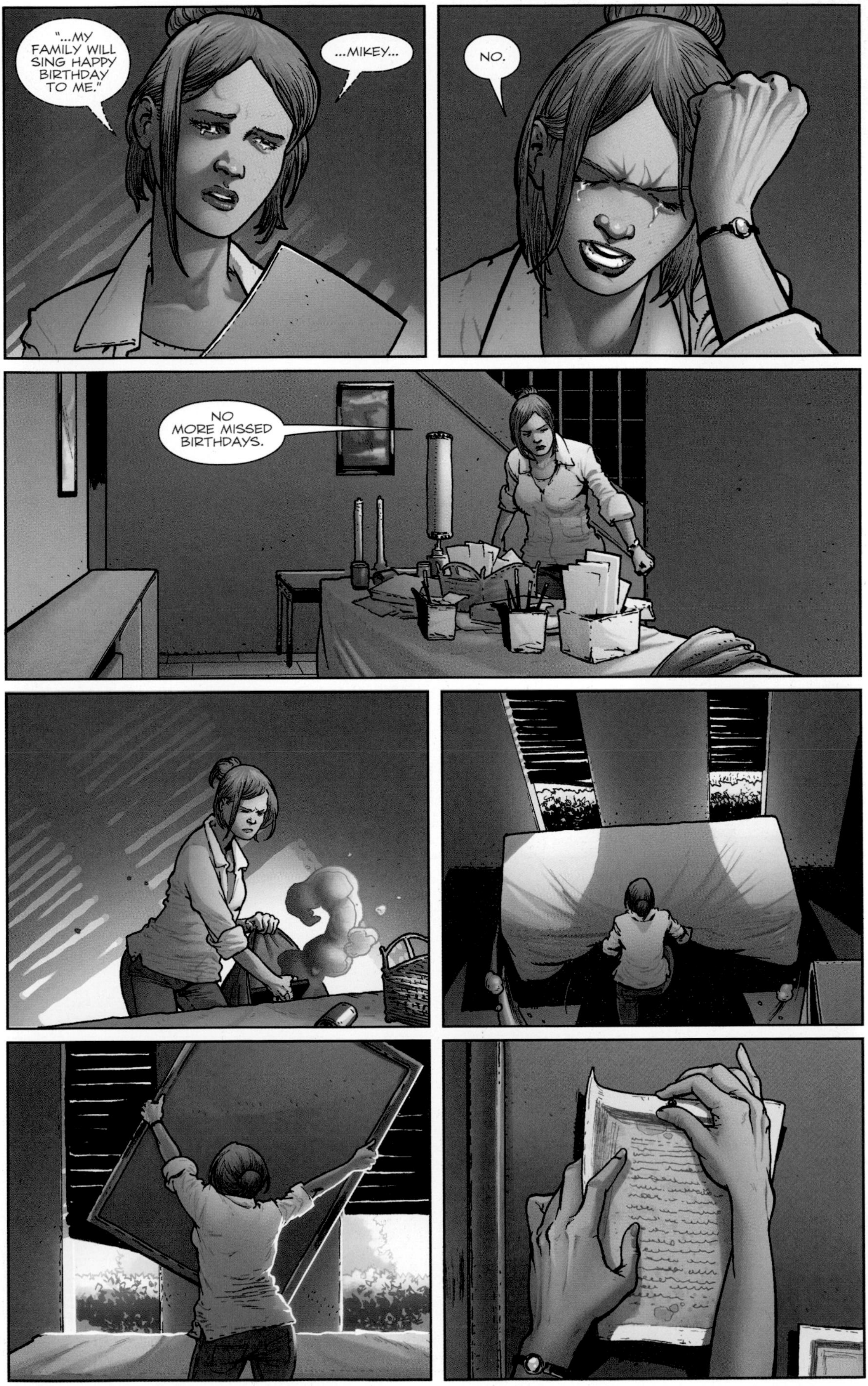
"...MY FAMILY WILL SING HAPPY BIRTHDAY TO ME."
...MIKEY...
NO.
NO MORE MISSED BIRTHDAYS.

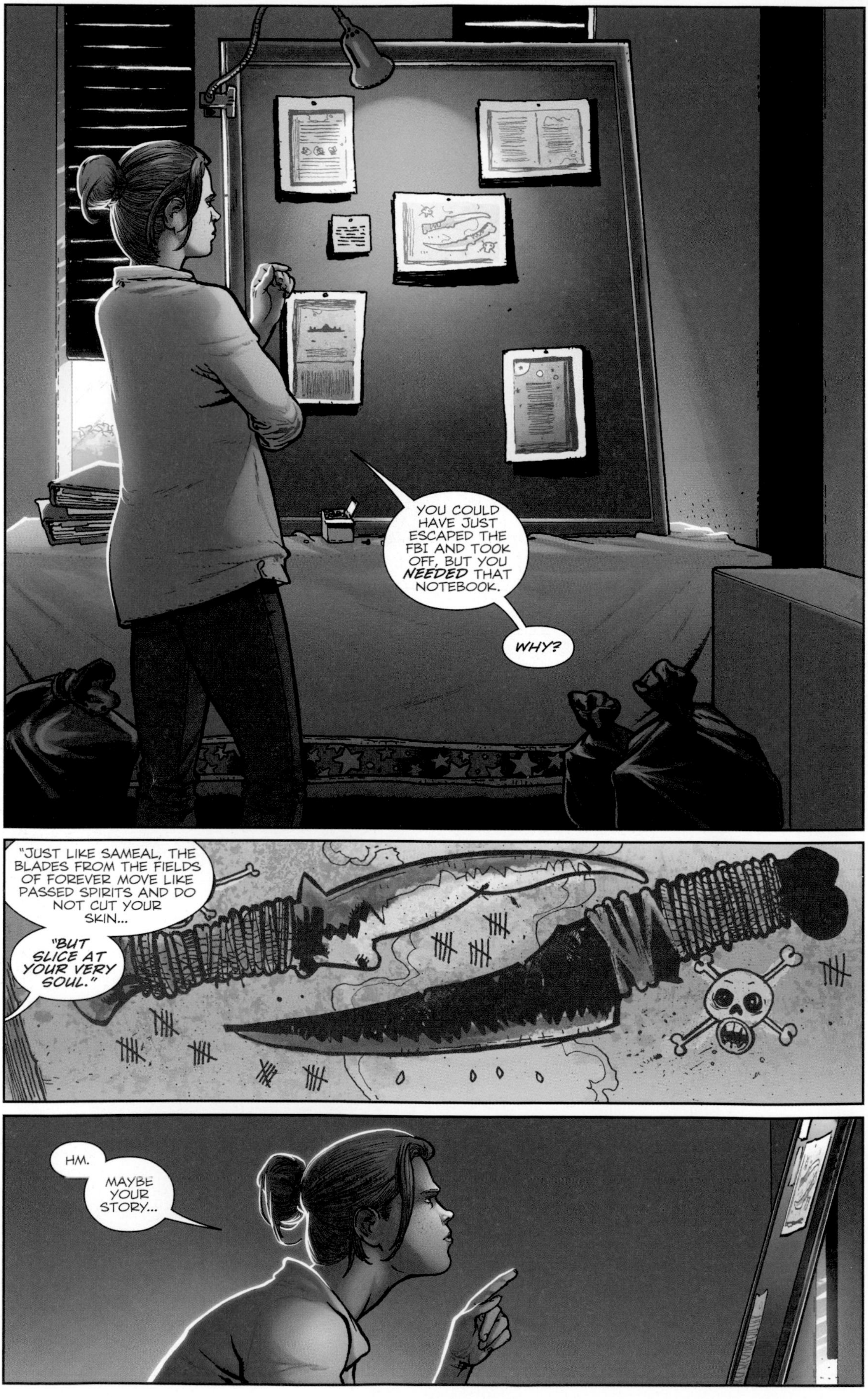
YOU COULD HAVE JUST ESCAPED THE FBI AND TOOK OFF, BUT YOU NEEDED THAT NOTEBOOK.
WHY?
"JUST LIKE SAMEAL, THE BLADES FROM THE FIELDS OF FOREVER MOVE LIKE PASSED SPIRITS AND DO NOT CUT YOUR SKIN...
"BUT SLICE AT YOUR VERY SOUL."
HM.
MAYBE YOUR STORY...

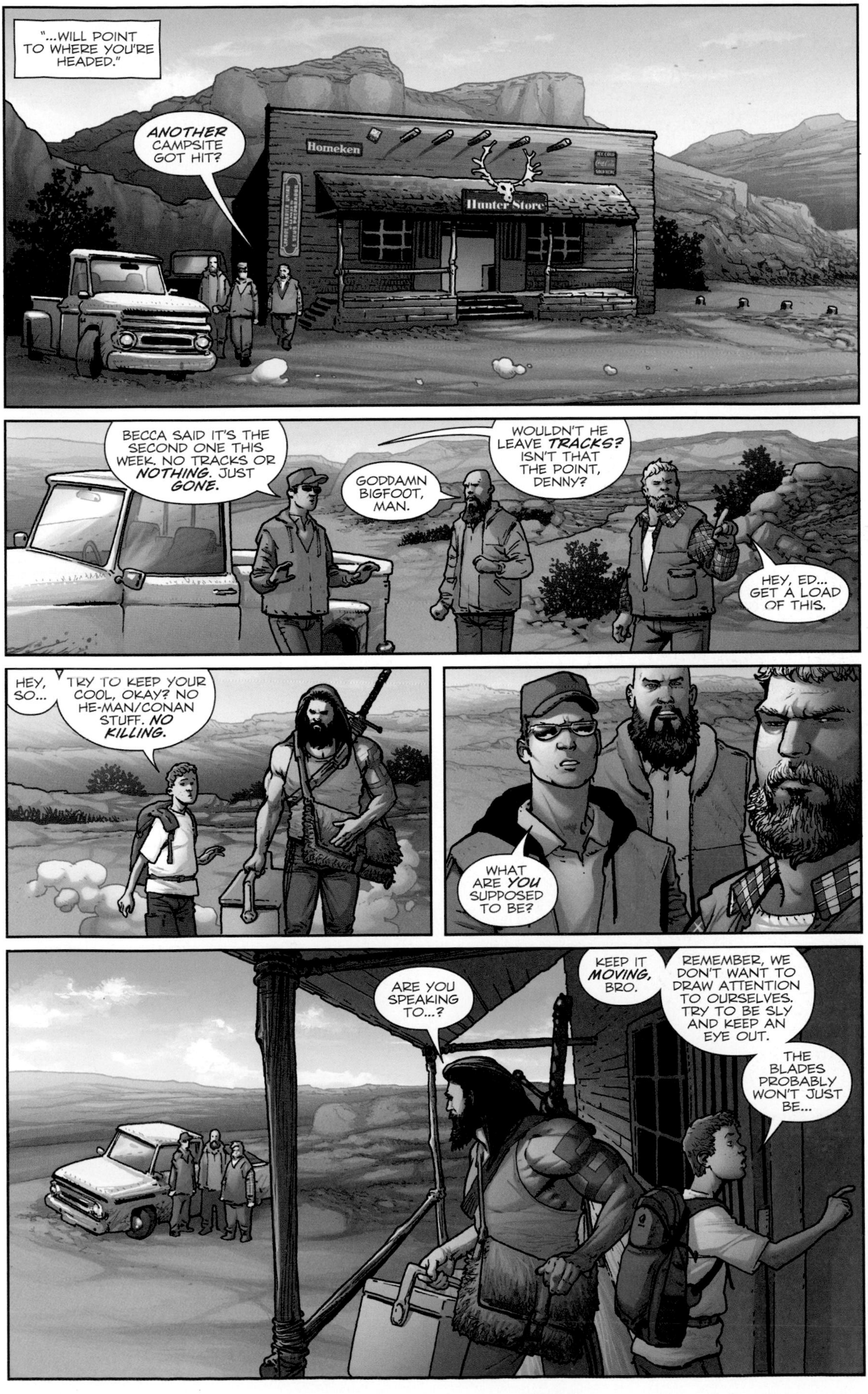
"...WILL POINT TO WHERE YOU'RE HEADED."
Homeken
Hunter Store
ANOTHER CAMPSITE GOT HIT?
BECCA SAID IT'S THE SECOND ONE THIS WEEK. NO TRACKS OR *NOTHING*. JUST *GONE*.
GODDAMN BIGFOOT, MAN.
WOULDN'T HE LEAVE *TRACKS?* ISN'T THAT THE POINT, DENNY?
HEY, ED... GET A LOAD OF THIS.
HEY, SO...
TRY TO KEEP YOUR COOL, OKAY? NO HE-MAN/CONAN STUFF. *NO KILLING*.
WHAT ARE *YOU* SUPPOSED TO BE?
ARE YOU SPEAKING TO...?
KEEP IT *MOVING*, BRO.
REMEMBER, WE DON'T WANT TO DRAW ATTENTION TO OURSELVES. TRY TO BE SLY AND KEEP AN EYE OUT.
THE BLADES PROBABLY WON'T JUST BE...

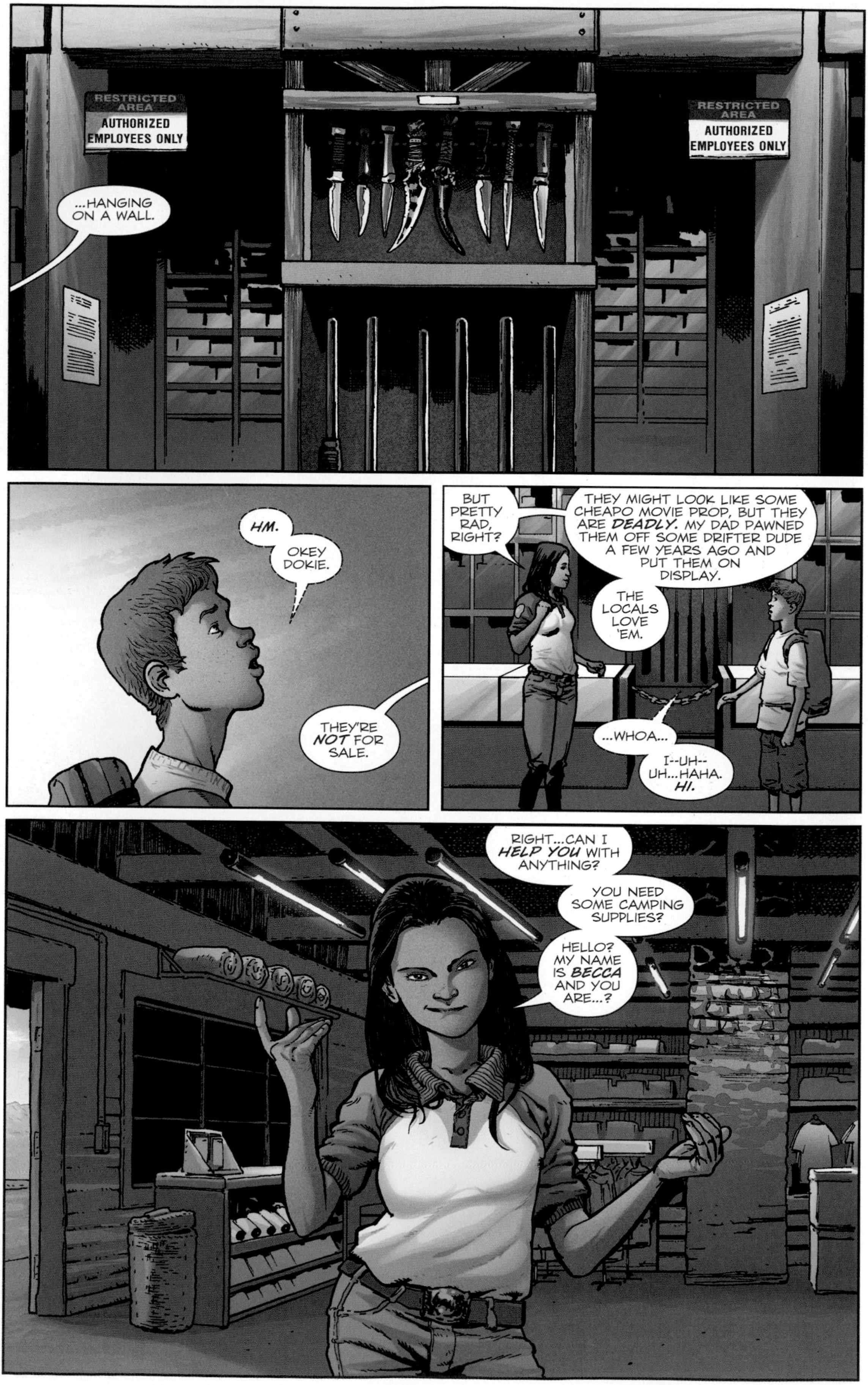
RESTRICTED AREA
AUTHORIZED EMPLOYEES ONLY
RESTRICTED AREA
AUTHORIZED EMPLOYEES ONLY
...HANGING ON A WALL.
HM.
OKEY DOKIE.
THEY'RE NOT FOR SALE.
BUT PRETTY RAD, RIGHT?
THEY MIGHT LOOK LIKE SOME CHEAPO MOVIE PROP, BUT THEY ARE DEADLY. MY DAD PAWNED THEM OFF SOME DRIFTER DUDE A FEW YEARS AGO AND PUT THEM ON DISPLAY.
THE LOCALS LOVE 'EM.
...WHOA...
I--UH-- UH...HAHA. HI.
RIGHT...CAN I HELP YOU WITH ANYTHING?
YOU NEED SOME CAMPING SUPPLIES?
HELLO? MY NAME IS BECCA AND YOU ARE...?

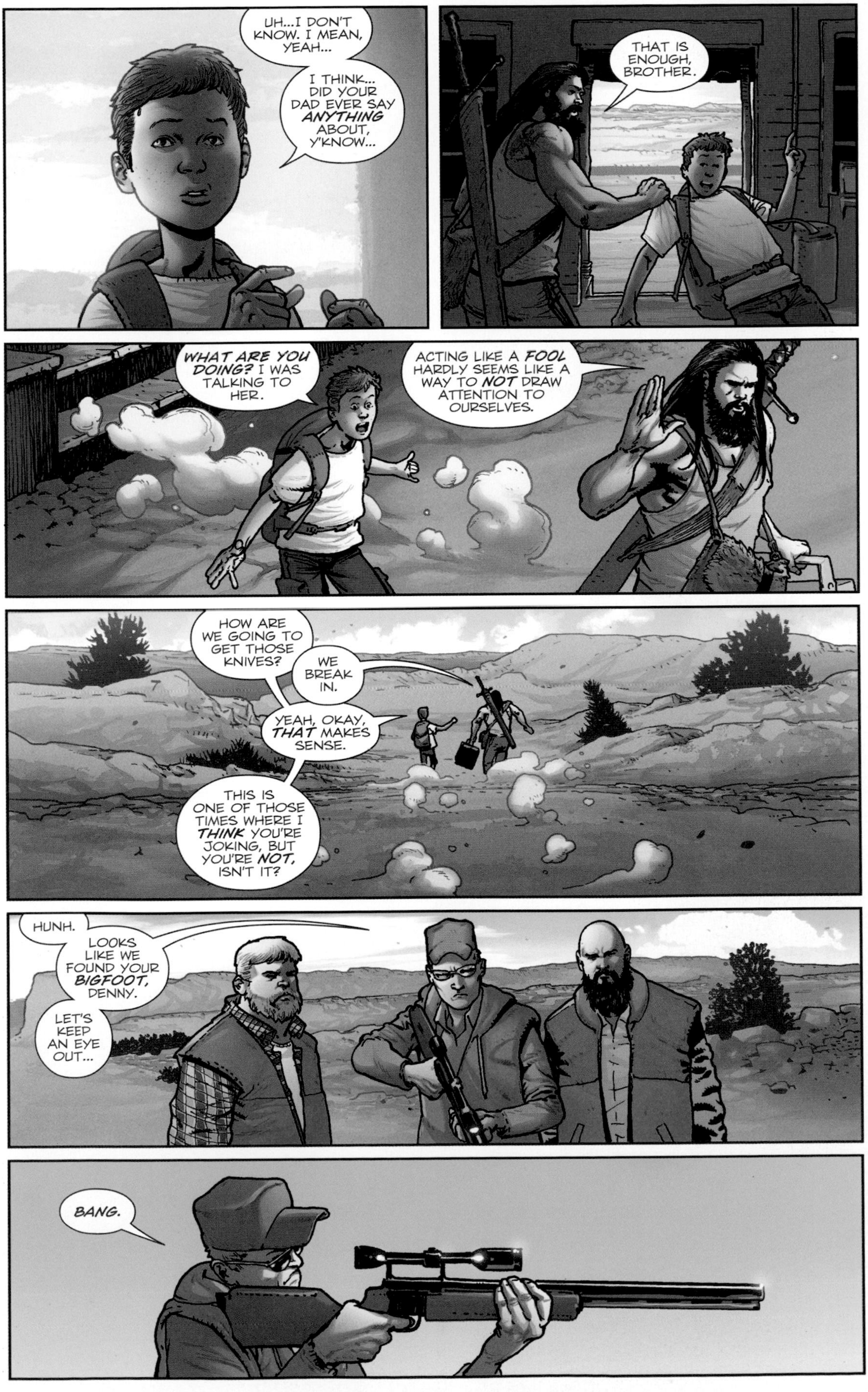
UH...I DON'T KNOW. I MEAN, YEAH...
I THINK... DID YOUR DAD EVER SAY ANYTHING ABOUT, Y'KNOW...
THAT IS ENOUGH, BROTHER.
WHAT ARE YOU DOING? I WAS TALKING TO HER.
ACTING LIKE A FOOL HARDLY SEEMS LIKE A WAY TO NOT DRAW ATTENTION TO OURSELVES.
HOW ARE WE GOING TO GET THOSE KNIVES?
WE BREAK IN.
YEAH, OKAY, THAT MAKES SENSE.
THIS IS ONE OF THOSE TIMES WHERE I THINK YOU'RE JOKING, BUT YOU'RE NOT, ISN'T IT?
HUNH.
LOOKS LIKE WE FOUND YOUR BIGFOOT, DENNY.
LET'S KEEP AN EYE OUT...
BANG.

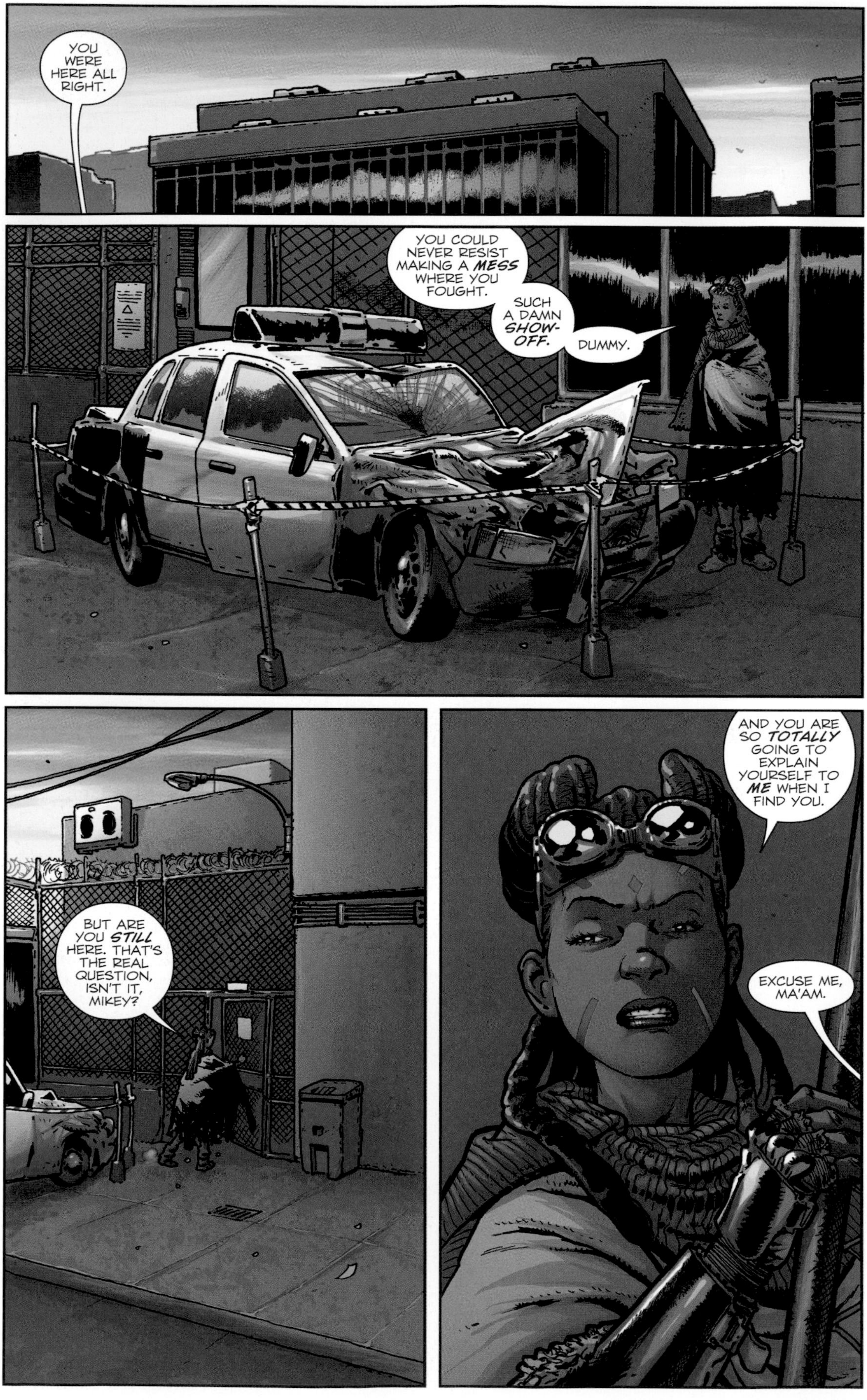
YOU WERE HERE ALL RIGHT.
YOU COULD NEVER RESIST MAKING A MESS WHERE YOU FOUGHT.
SUCH A DAMN SHOW-OFF.
DUMMY.
BUT ARE YOU STILL HERE. THAT'S THE REAL QUESTION, ISN'T IT, MIKEY?
AND YOU ARE SO TOTALLY GOING TO EXPLAIN YOURSELF TO ME WHEN I FIND YOU.
EXCUSE ME, MA'AM.

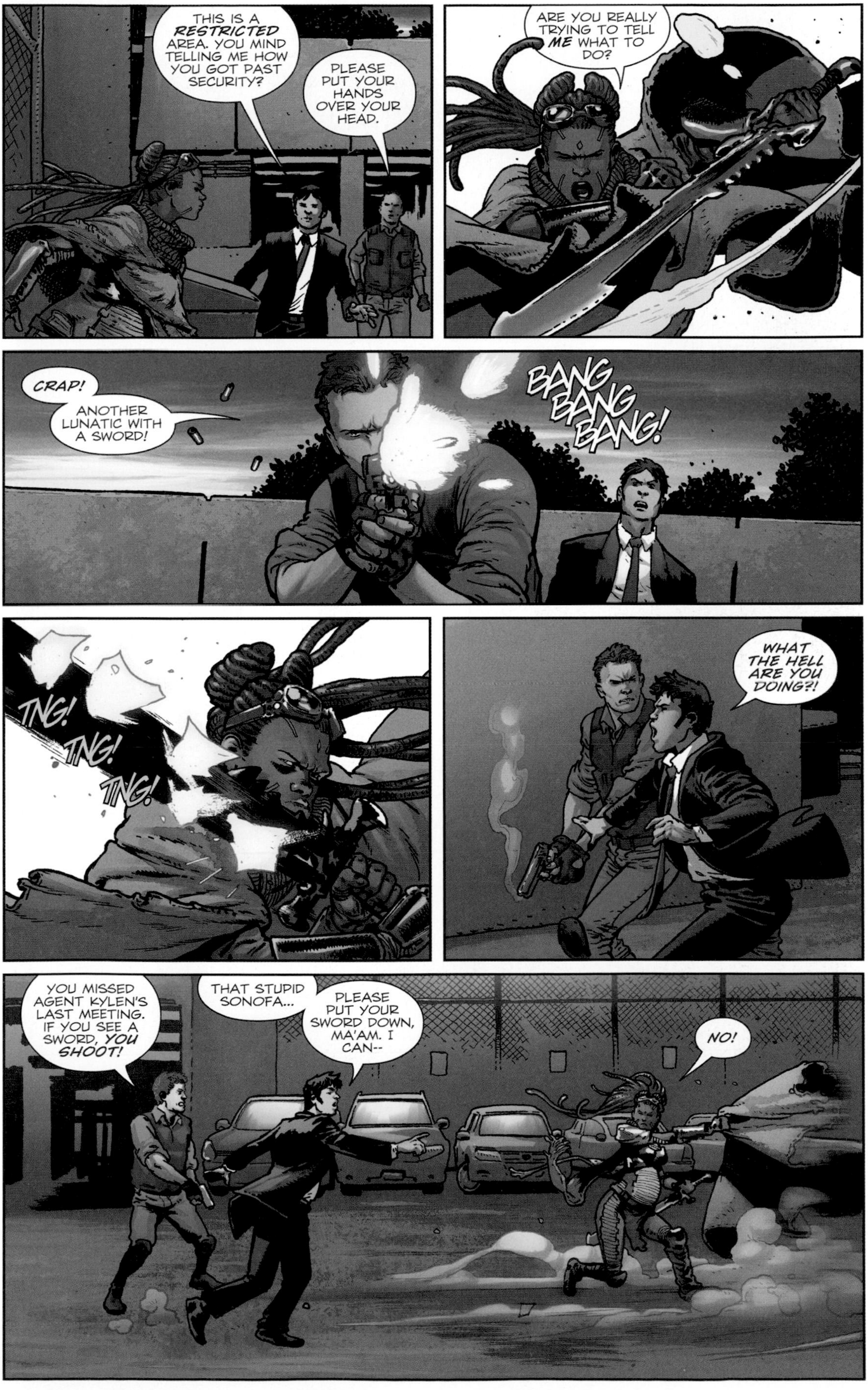
THIS IS A *RESTRICTED* AREA. YOU MIND TELLING ME HOW YOU GOT PAST SECURITY?
PLEASE PUT YOUR HANDS OVER YOUR HEAD.
ARE YOU REALLY TRYING TO TELL *ME* WHAT TO DO?
CRAP!
ANOTHER LUNATIC WITH A SWORD!
BANG BANG BANG!
TNG! TNG! TNG!
WHAT THE HELL ARE YOU DOING?!
YOU MISSED AGENT KYLEN'S LAST MEETING. IF YOU SEE A SWORD, *YOU SHOOT!*
THAT STUPID SONOFA...
PLEASE PUT YOUR SWORD DOWN, MA'AM. I CAN--
NO!

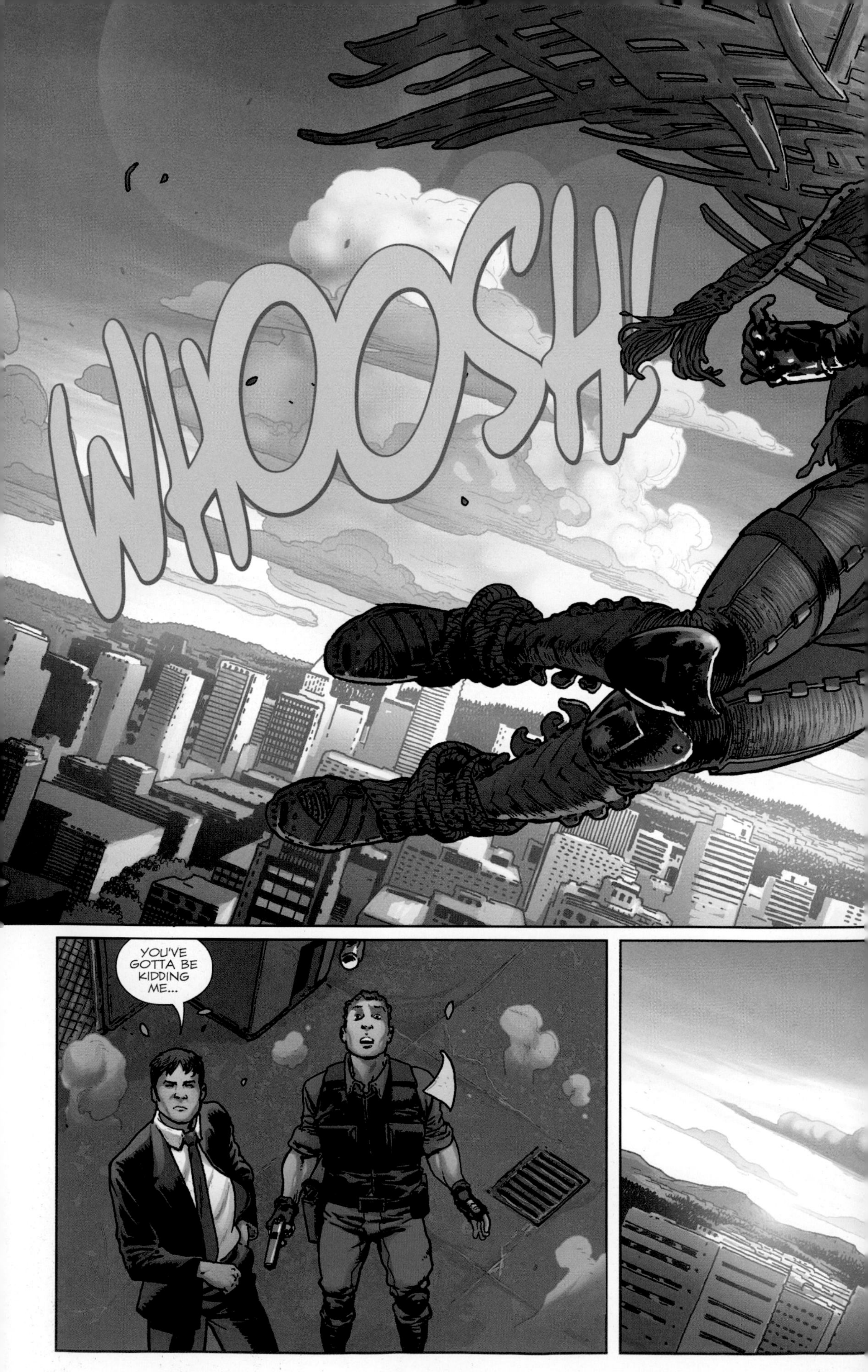
WHOOSH
YOU'VE GOTTA BE KIDDING ME...

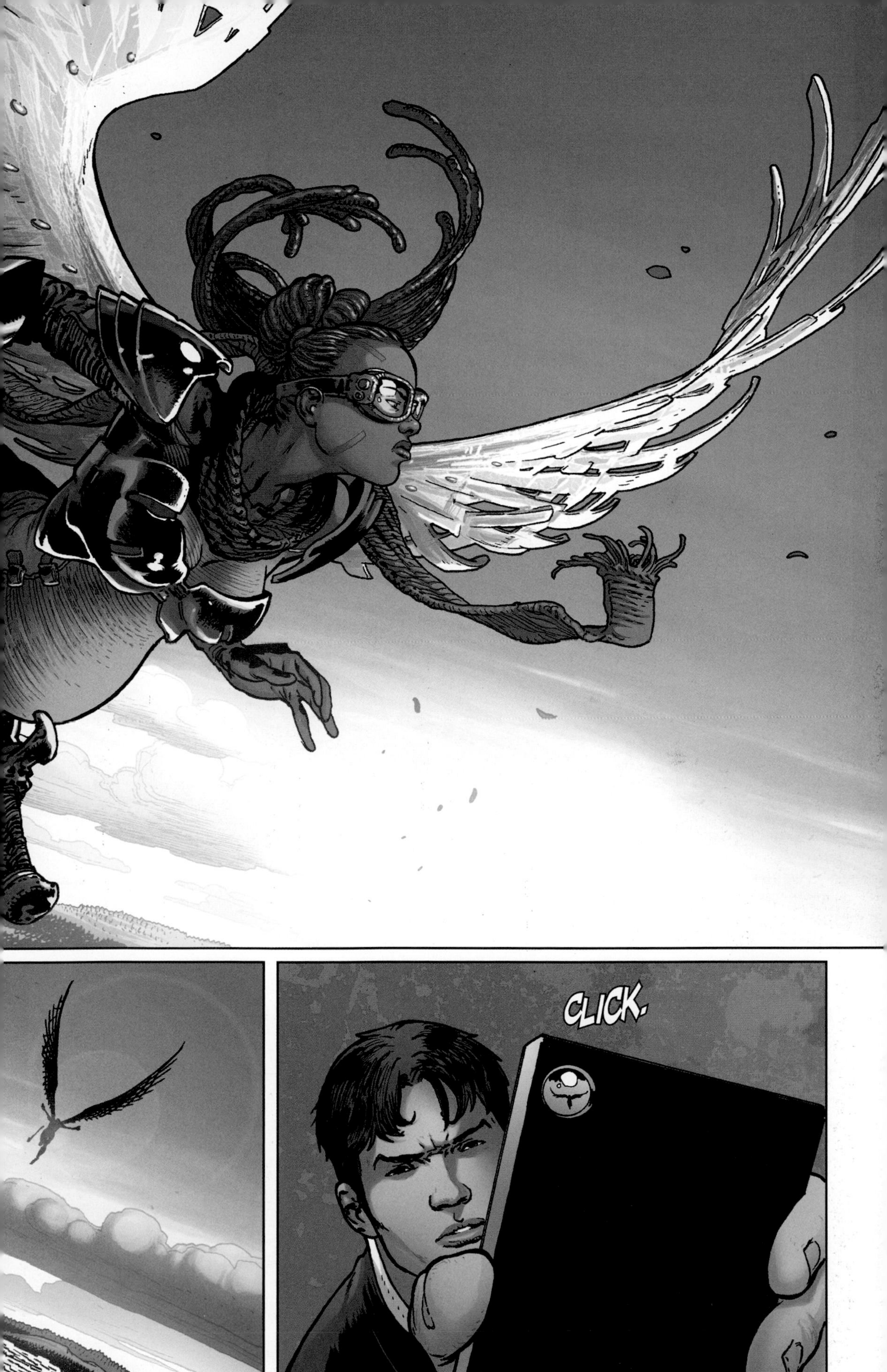
CLICK.

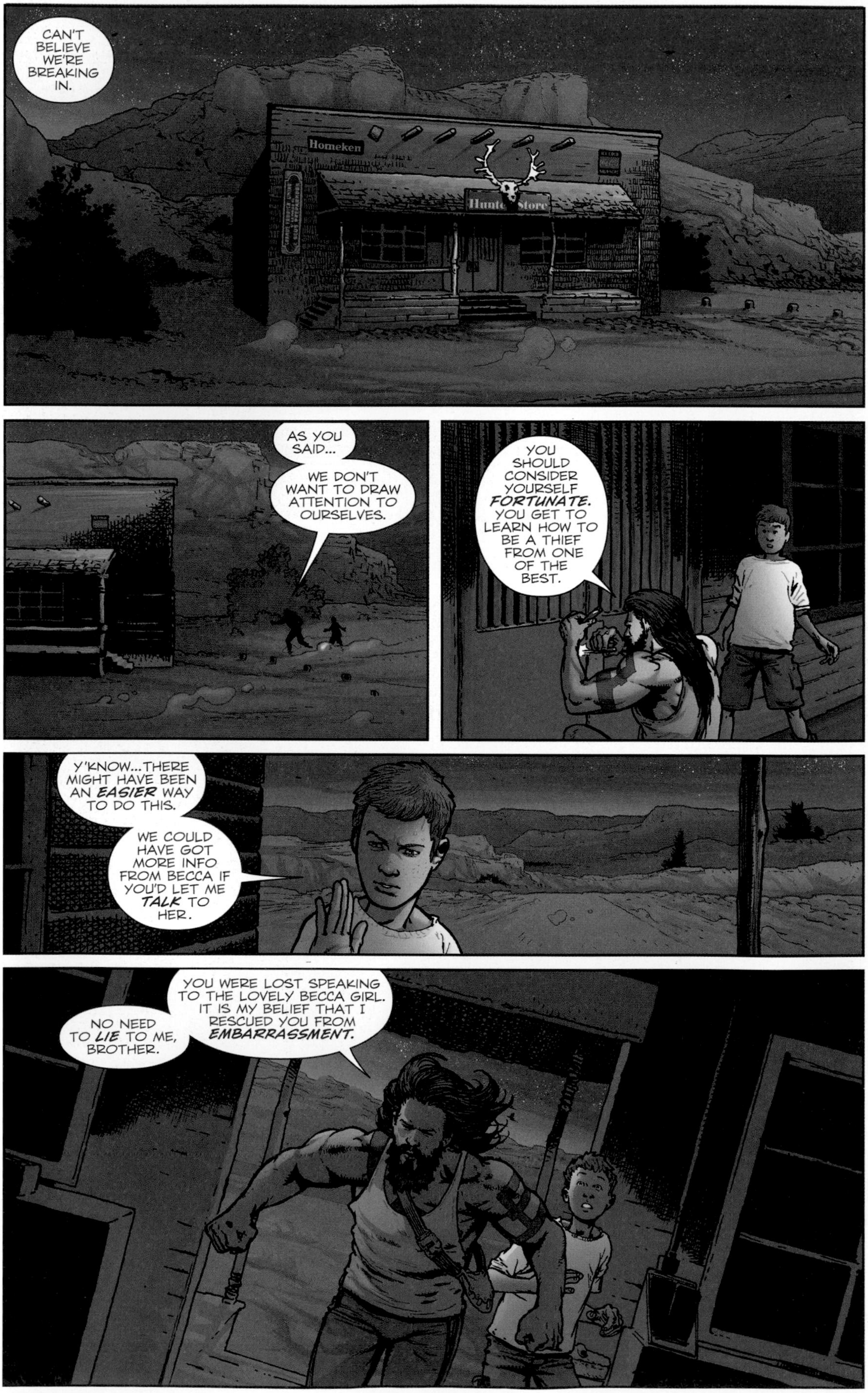
CAN'T BELIEVE WE'RE BREAKING IN.
Homeken
Hunter Store
AS YOU SAID...
WE DON'T WANT TO DRAW ATTENTION TO OURSELVES.
YOU SHOULD CONSIDER YOURSELF FORTUNATE. YOU GET TO LEARN HOW TO BE A THIEF FROM ONE OF THE BEST.
Y'KNOW...THERE MIGHT HAVE BEEN AN EASIER WAY TO DO THIS.
WE COULD HAVE GOT MORE INFO FROM BECCA IF YOU'D LET ME TALK TO HER.
NO NEED TO LIE TO ME, BROTHER.
YOU WERE LOST SPEAKING TO THE LOVELY BECCA GIRL. IT IS MY BELIEF THAT I RESCUED YOU FROM EMBARRASSMENT.

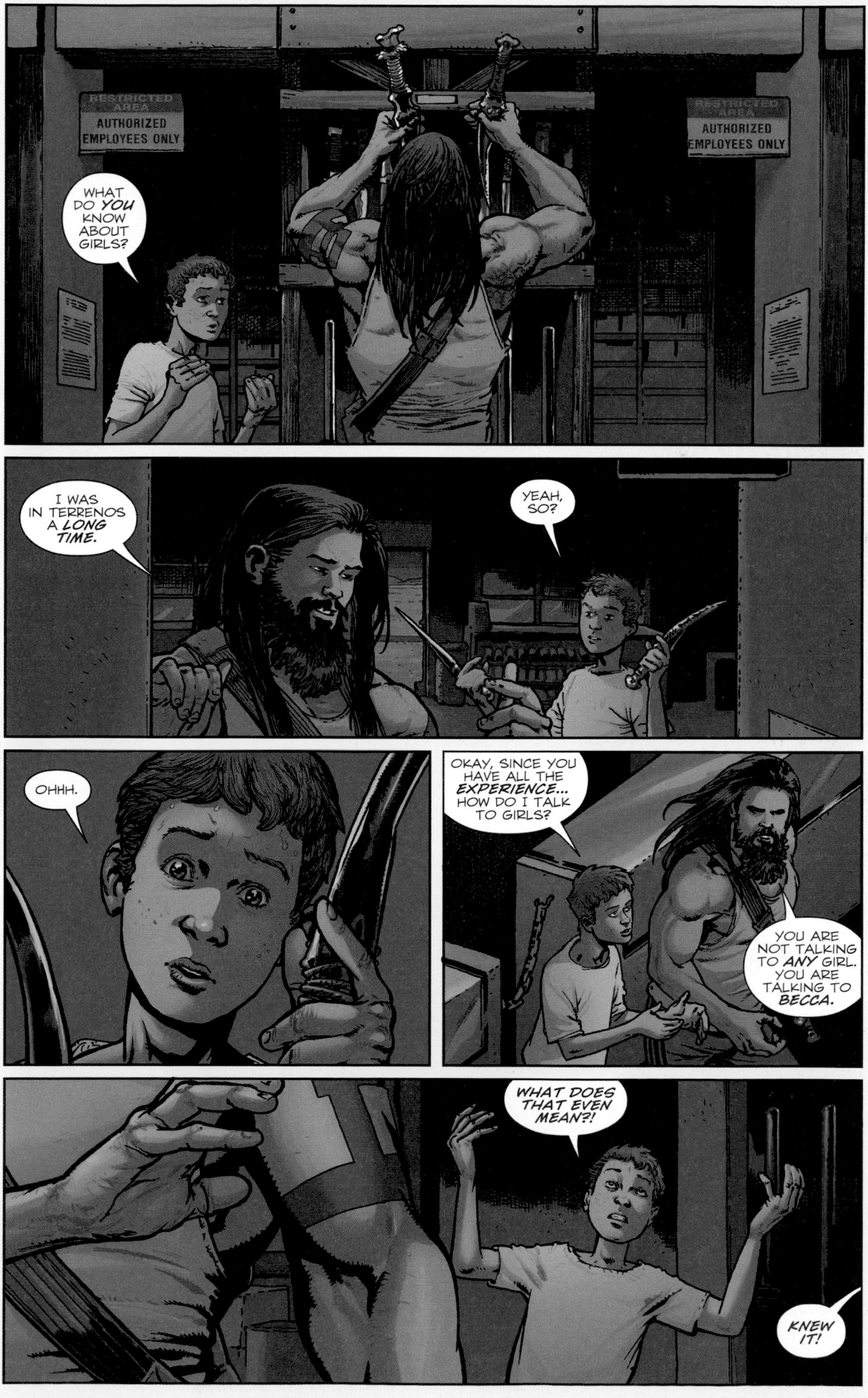
RESTRICTED AREA
AUTHORIZED EMPLOYEES ONLY
RESTRICTED AREA
AUTHORIZED EMPLOYEES ONLY
WHAT DO *YOU* KNOW ABOUT GIRLS?
I WAS IN TERRENOS A *LONG TIME.*
YEAH, SO?
OHHH.
OKAY, SINCE YOU HAVE ALL THE *EXPERIENCE...* HOW DO I TALK TO GIRLS?
YOU ARE NOT TALKING TO *ANY* GIRL. YOU ARE TALKING TO *BECCA.*
WHAT DOES THAT EVEN MEAN?!
KNEW IT!

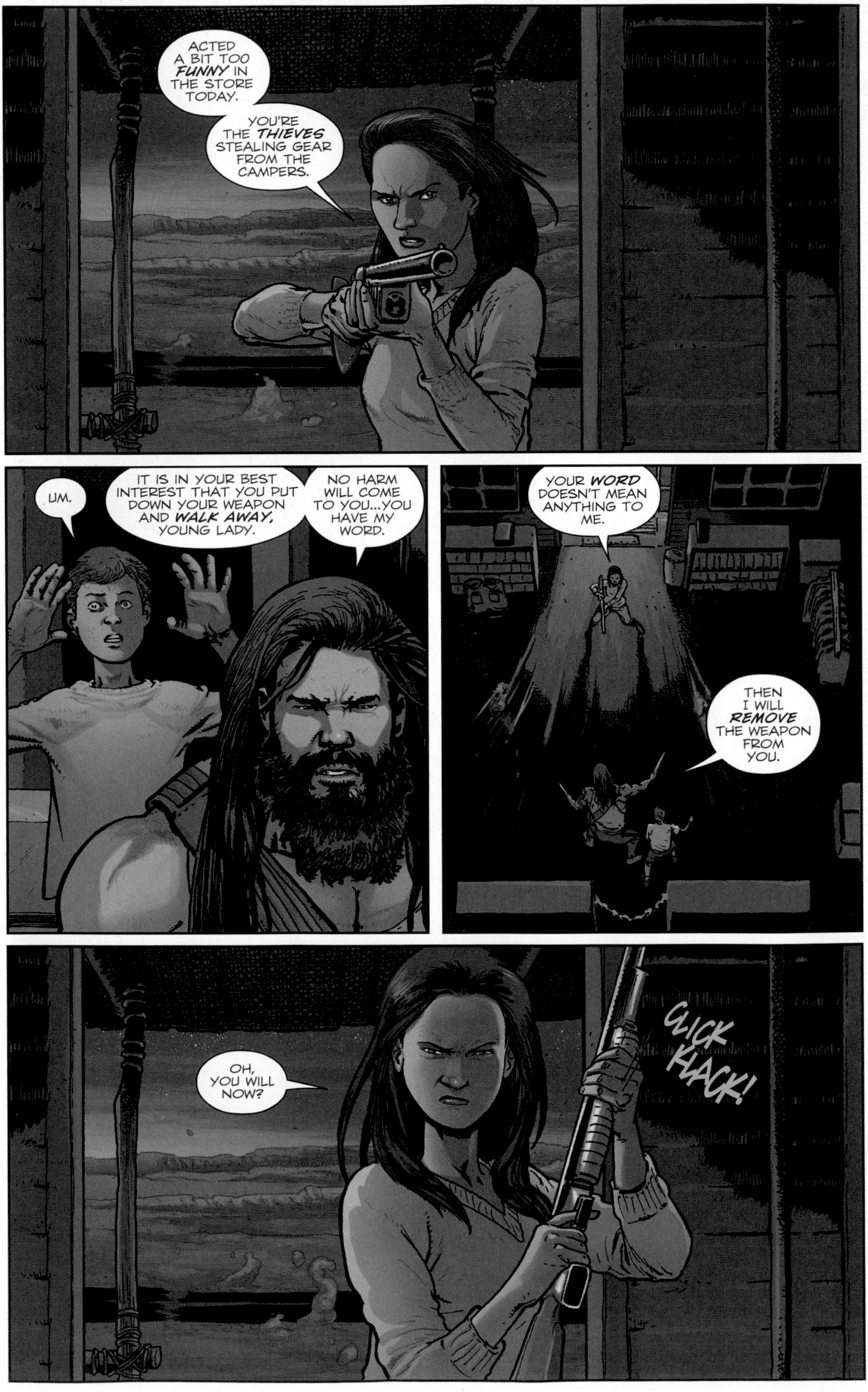
ACTED A BIT TOO FUNNY IN THE STORE TODAY.
YOU'RE THE THIEVES STEALING GEAR FROM THE CAMPERS.
UM.
IT IS IN YOUR BEST INTEREST THAT YOU PUT DOWN YOUR WEAPON AND WALK AWAY, YOUNG LADY.
NO HARM WILL COME TO YOU...YOU HAVE MY WORD.
YOUR WORD DOESN'T MEAN ANYTHING TO ME.
THEN I WILL REMOVE THE WEAPON FROM YOU.
OH, YOU WILL NOW?
CLICK KLACK!

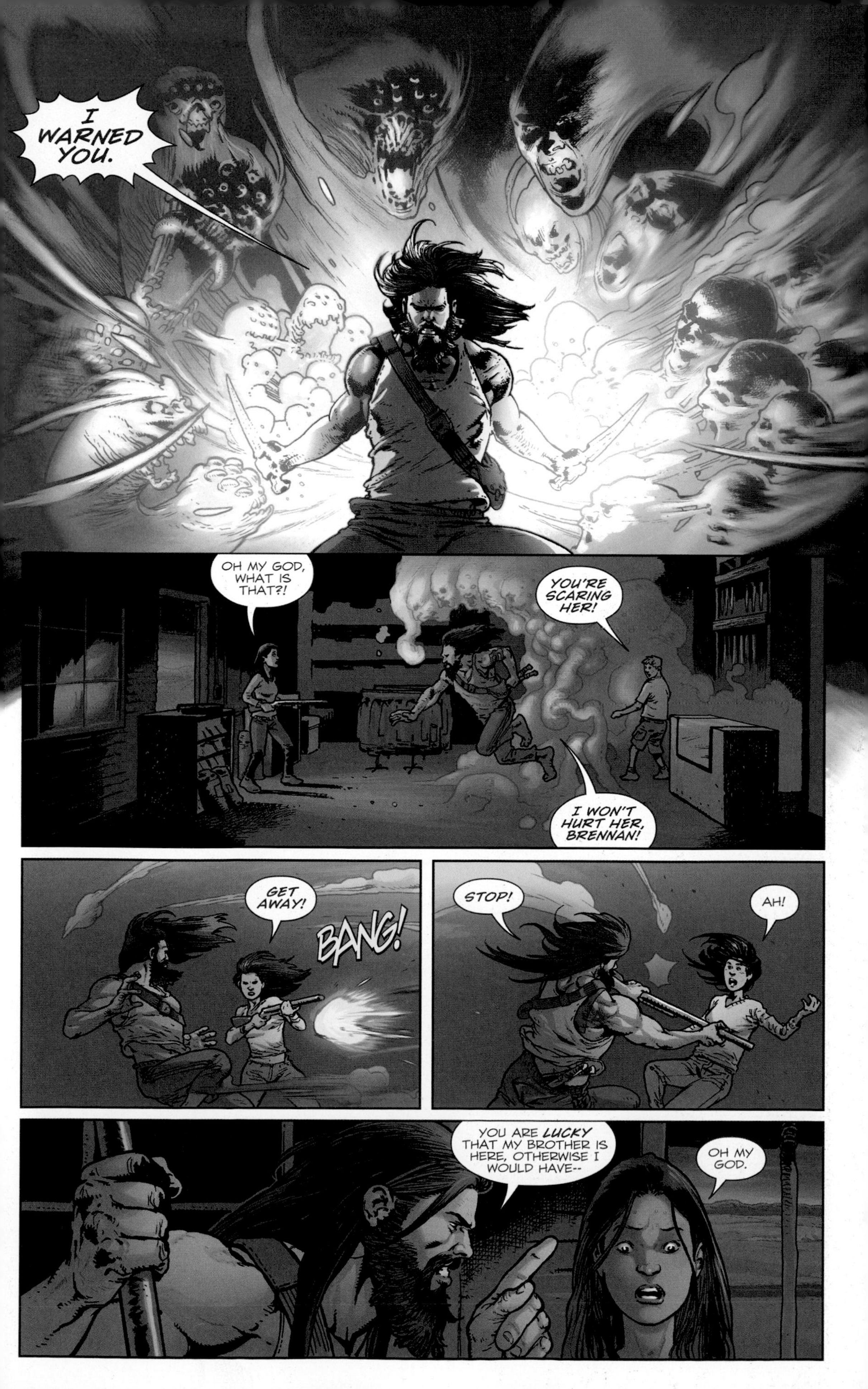
I WARNED YOU.
OH MY GOD, WHAT IS THAT?!
YOU'RE SCARING HER!
I WON'T HURT HER, BRENNAN!
GET AWAY!
BANG!
STOP!
AH!
YOU ARE LUCKY THAT MY BROTHER IS HERE, OTHERWISE I WOULD HAVE--
OH MY GOD.

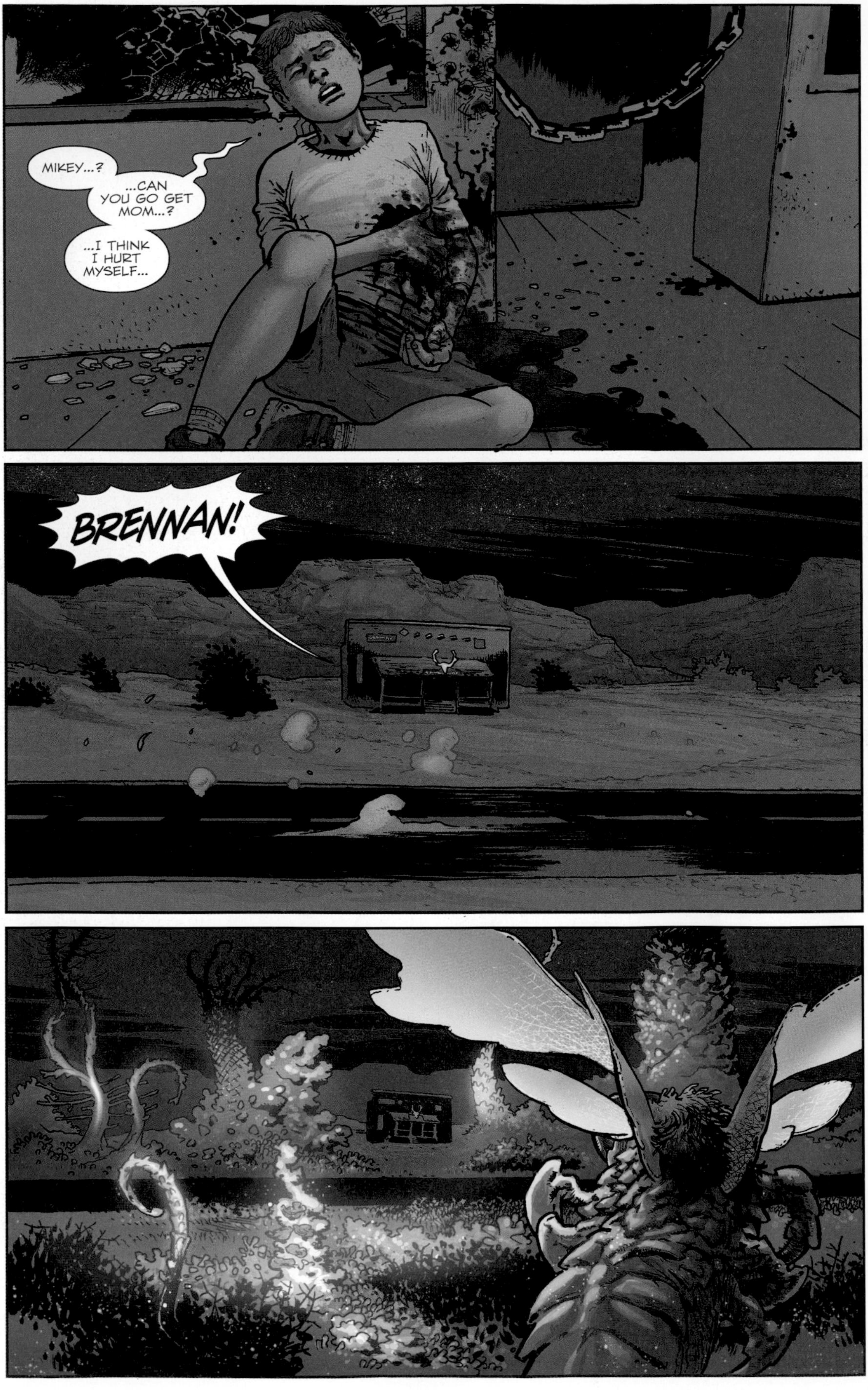
MIKEY...?
...CAN YOU GO GET MOM...?
...I THINK I HURT MYSELF...
BRENNAN!

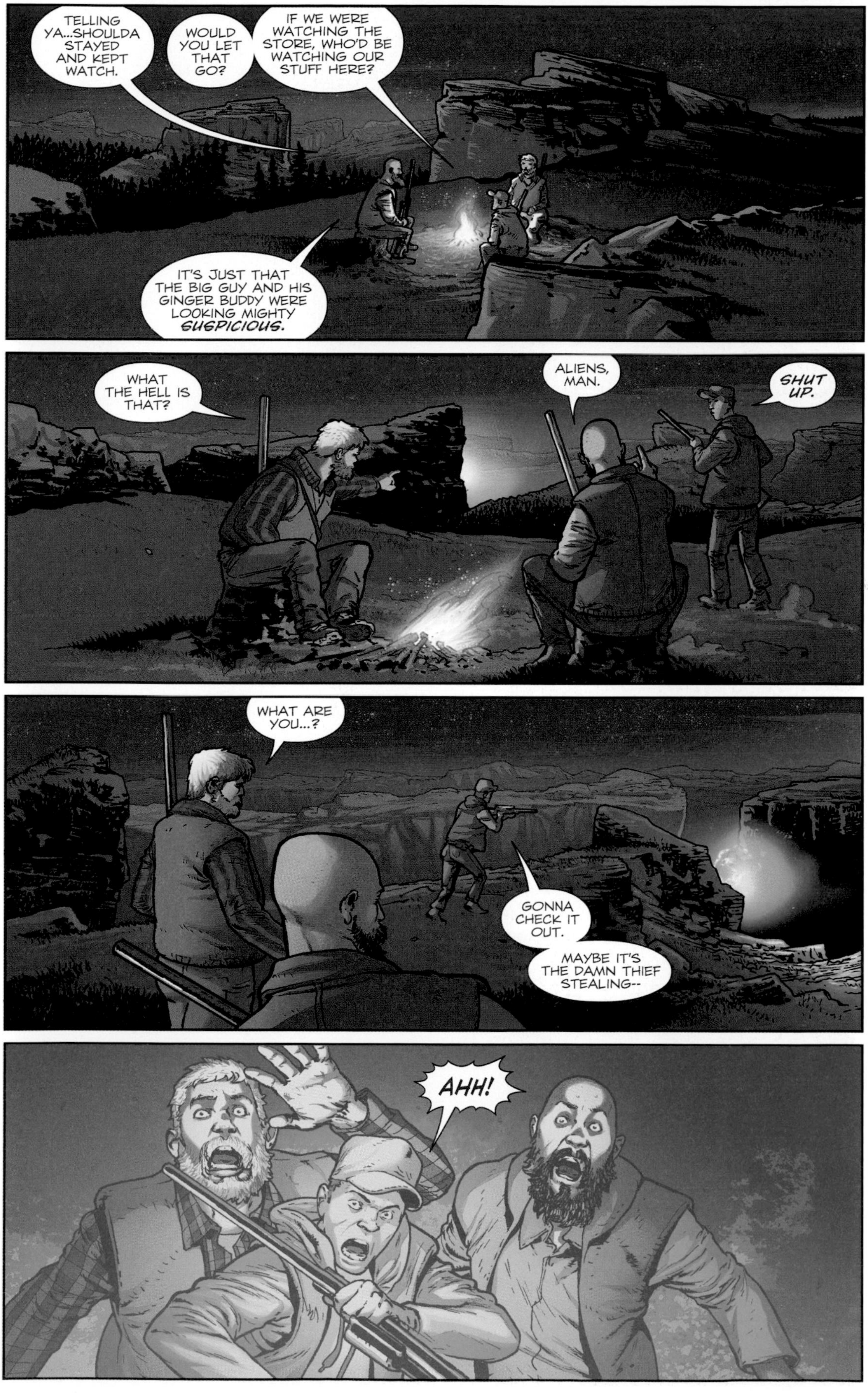
TELLING YA...SHOULDA STAYED AND KEPT WATCH.
WOULD YOU LET THAT GO?
IF WE WERE WATCHING THE STORE, WHO'D BE WATCHING OUR STUFF HERE?
IT'S JUST THAT THE BIG GUY AND HIS GINGER BUDDY WERE LOOKING MIGHTY *SUSPICIOUS.*
WHAT THE HELL IS THAT?
ALIENS, MAN.
SHUT UP.
WHAT ARE YOU...?
GONNA CHECK IT OUT.
MAYBE IT'S THE DAMN THIEF STEALING--
AHH!

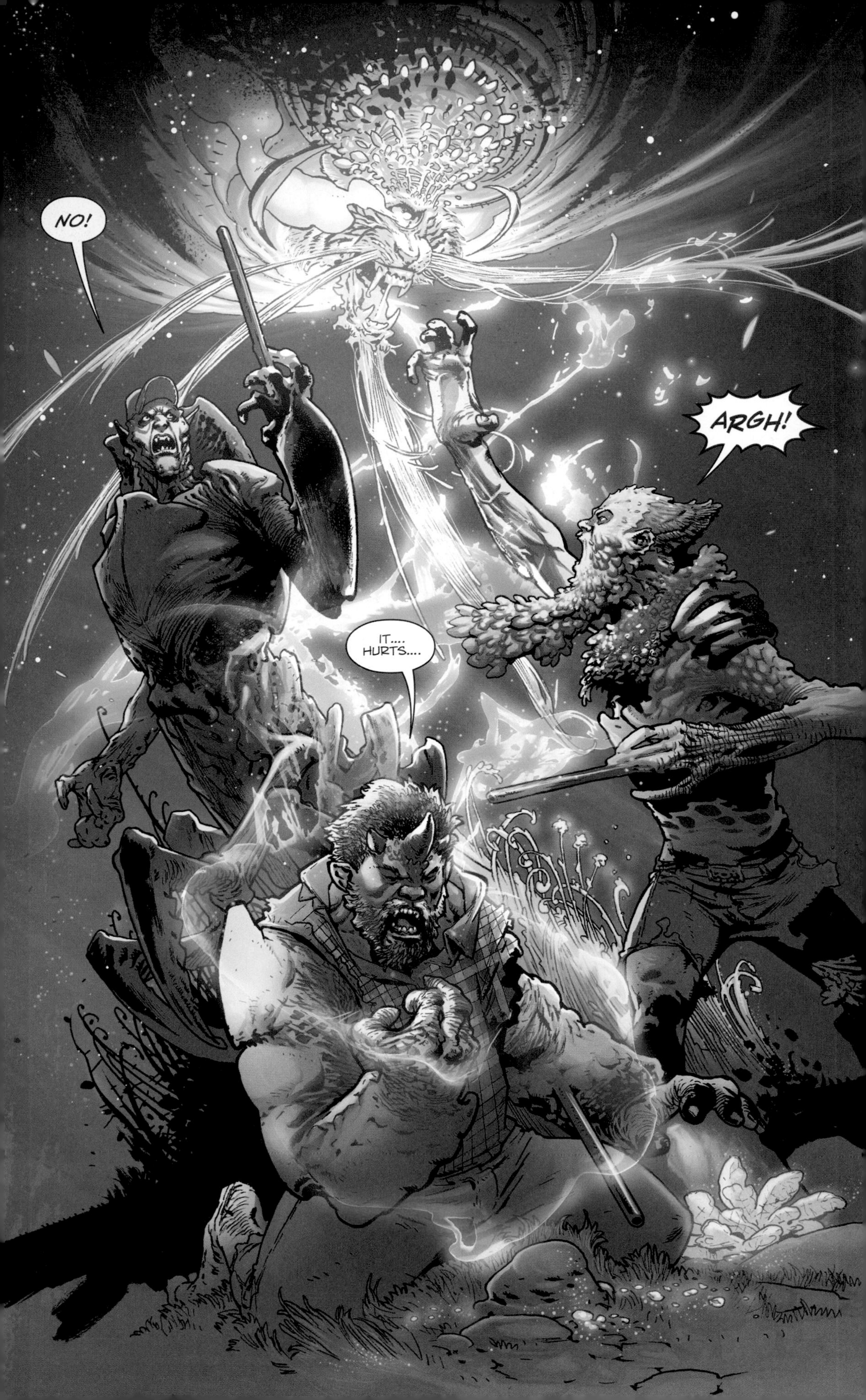
NO!
ARGH!
IT.... HURTS....

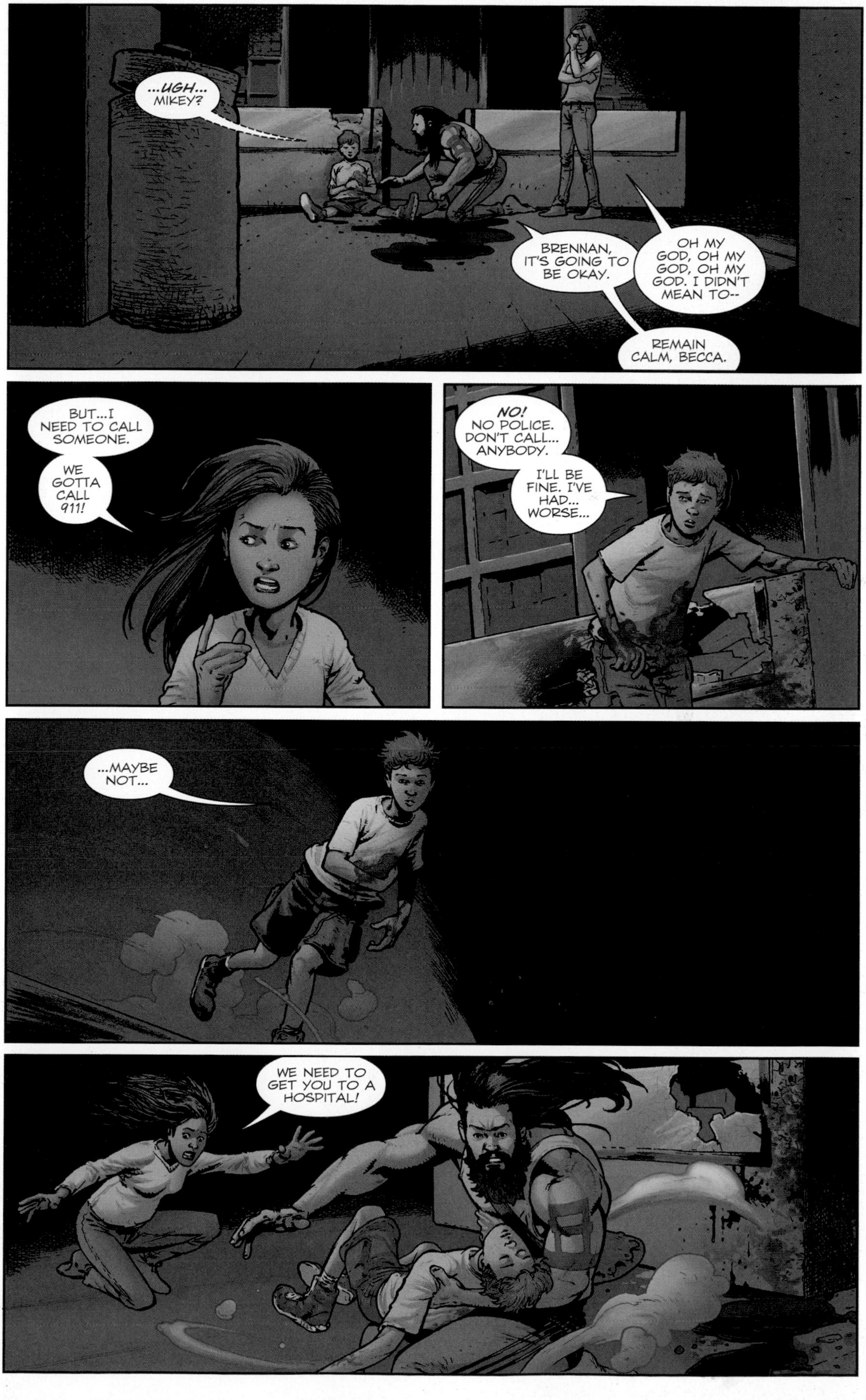
...UGH... MIKEY?
BRENNAN, IT'S GOING TO BE OKAY.
OH MY GOD, OH MY GOD, OH MY GOD. I DIDN'T MEAN TO--
REMAIN CALM, BECCA.
BUT...I NEED TO CALL SOMEONE.
WE GOTTA CALL 911!
NO! NO POLICE. DON'T CALL... ANYBODY.
I'LL BE FINE. I'VE HAD... WORSE...
...MAYBE NOT...
WE NEED TO GET YOU TO A HOSPITAL!

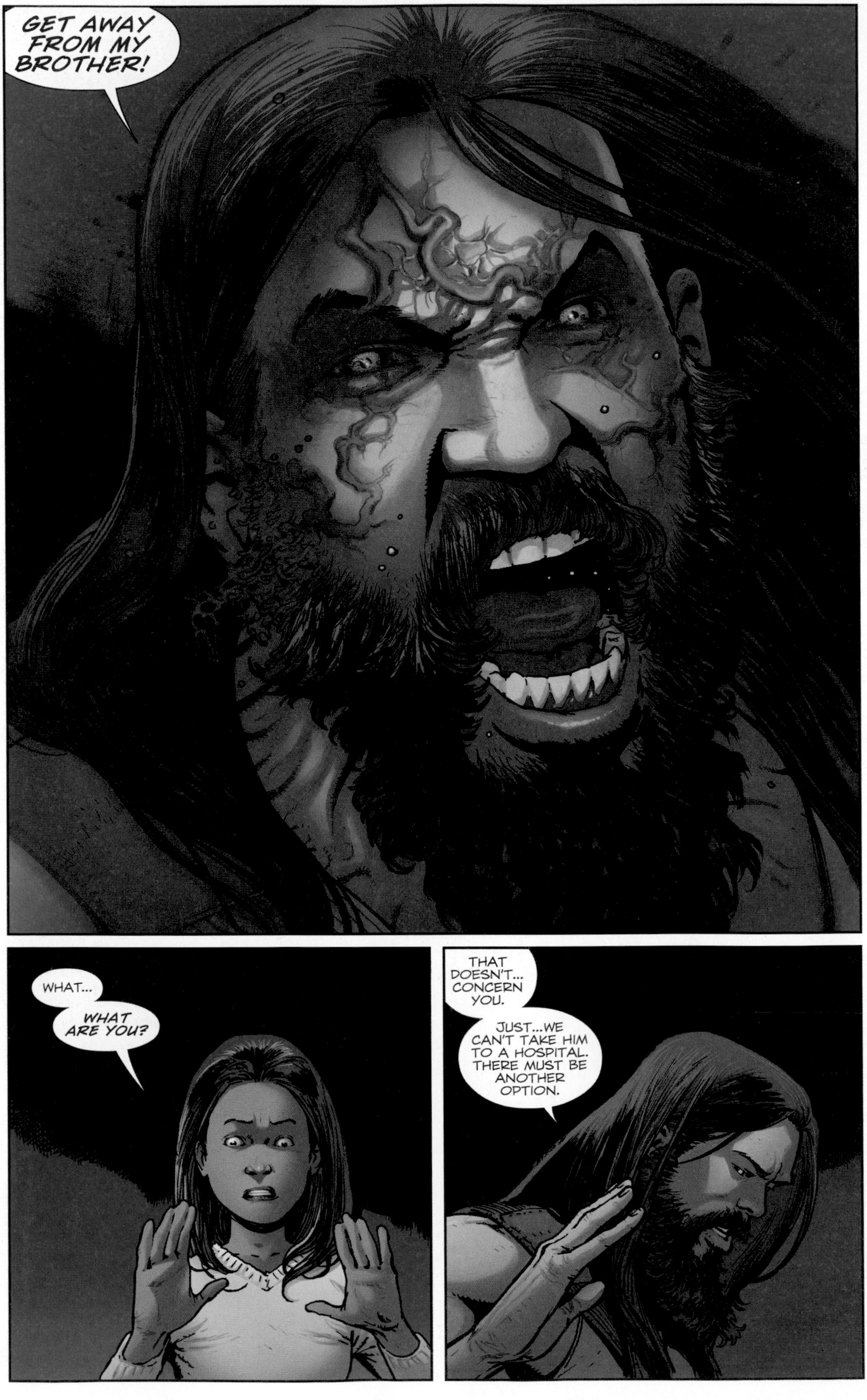
GET AWAY FROM MY BROTHER!
WHAT...
WHAT ARE YOU?
THAT DOESN'T... CONCERN YOU.
JUST...WE CAN'T TAKE HIM TO A HOSPITAL. THERE MUST BE ANOTHER OPTION.

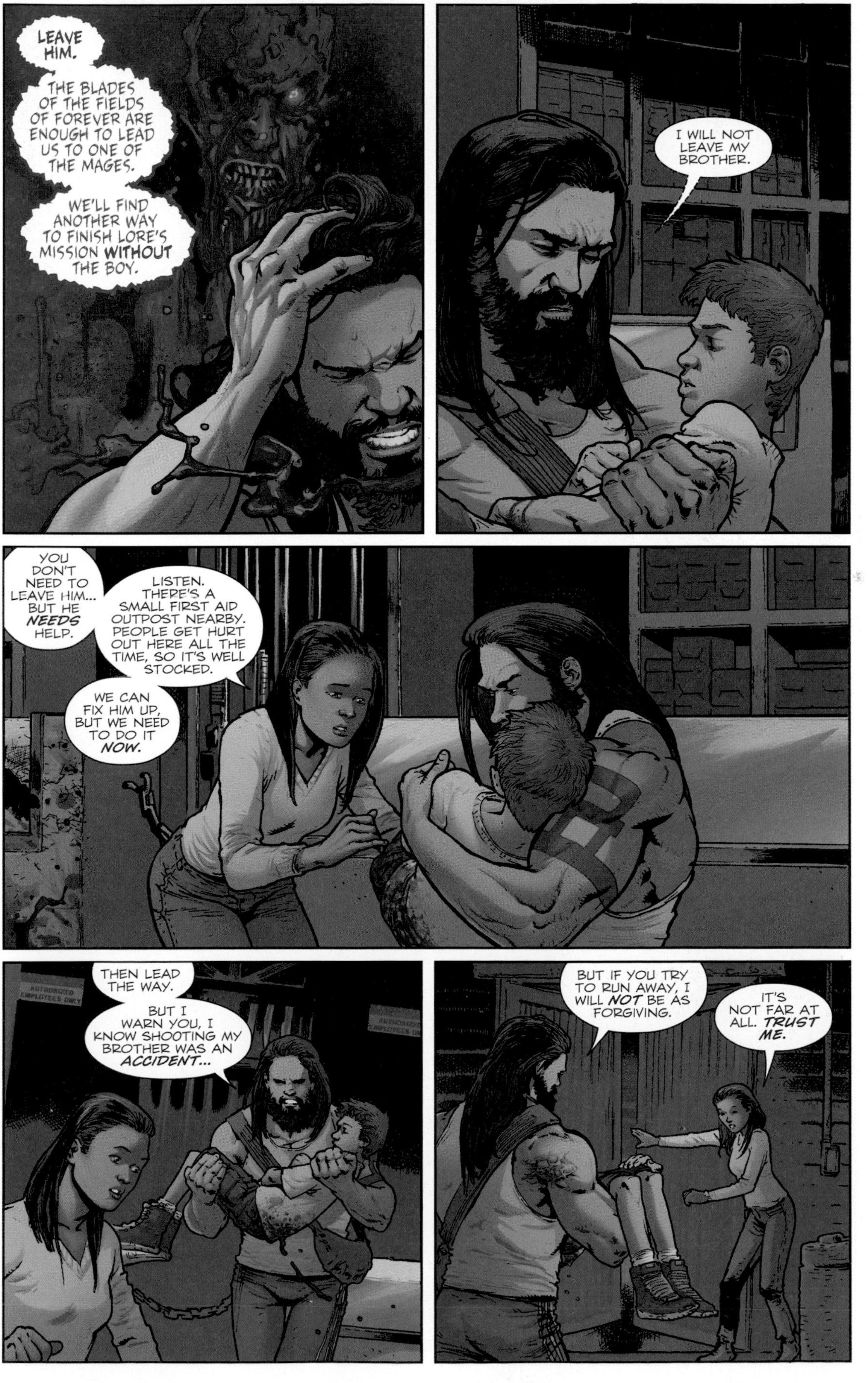

LEAVE HIM.
THE BLADES OF THE FIELDS OF FOREVER ARE ENOUGH TO LEAD US TO ONE OF THE MAGES.
WE'LL FIND ANOTHER WAY TO FINISH LORE'S MISSION **WITHOUT** THE BOY.
I WILL NOT LEAVE MY BROTHER.
YOU DON'T NEED TO LEAVE HIM... BUT HE ***NEEDS*** HELP.
LISTEN. THERE'S A SMALL FIRST AID OUTPOST NEARBY. PEOPLE GET HURT OUT HERE ALL THE TIME, SO IT'S WELL STOCKED.
WE CAN FIX HIM UP, BUT WE NEED TO DO IT ***NOW.***
THEN LEAD THE WAY.
BUT I WARN YOU, I KNOW SHOOTING MY BROTHER WAS AN ***ACCIDENT...***
BUT IF YOU TRY TO RUN AWAY, I WILL ***NOT*** BE AS FORGIVING.
IT'S NOT FAR AT ALL. ***TRUST ME.***

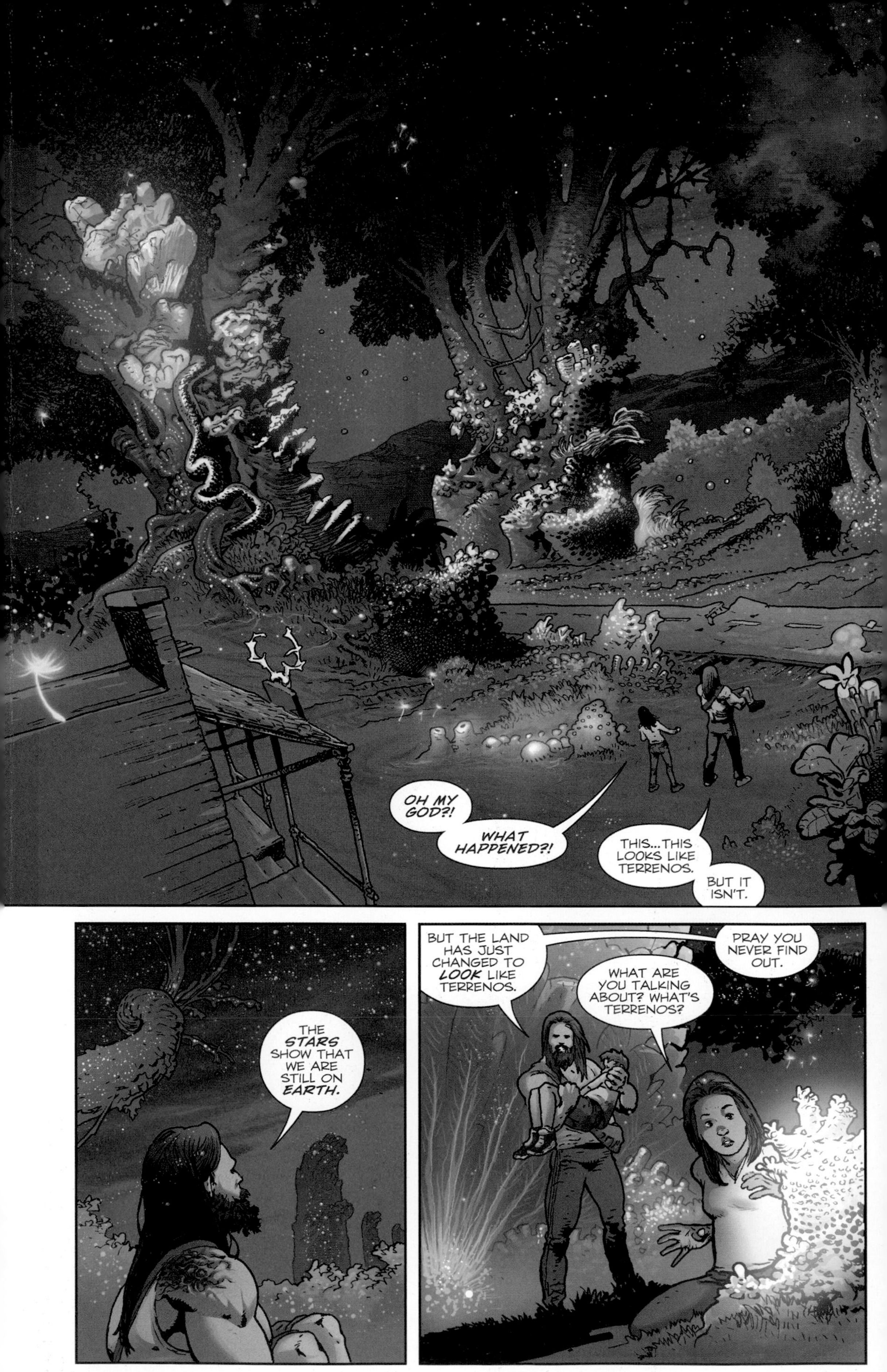
OH MY GOD?!
WHAT HAPPENED?!
THIS...THIS LOOKS LIKE TERRENOS.
BUT IT ISN'T.
THE STARS SHOW THAT WE ARE STILL ON EARTH.
BUT THE LAND HAS JUST CHANGED TO LOOK LIKE TERRENOS.
WHAT ARE YOU TALKING ABOUT? WHAT'S TERRENOS?
PRAY YOU NEVER FIND OUT.

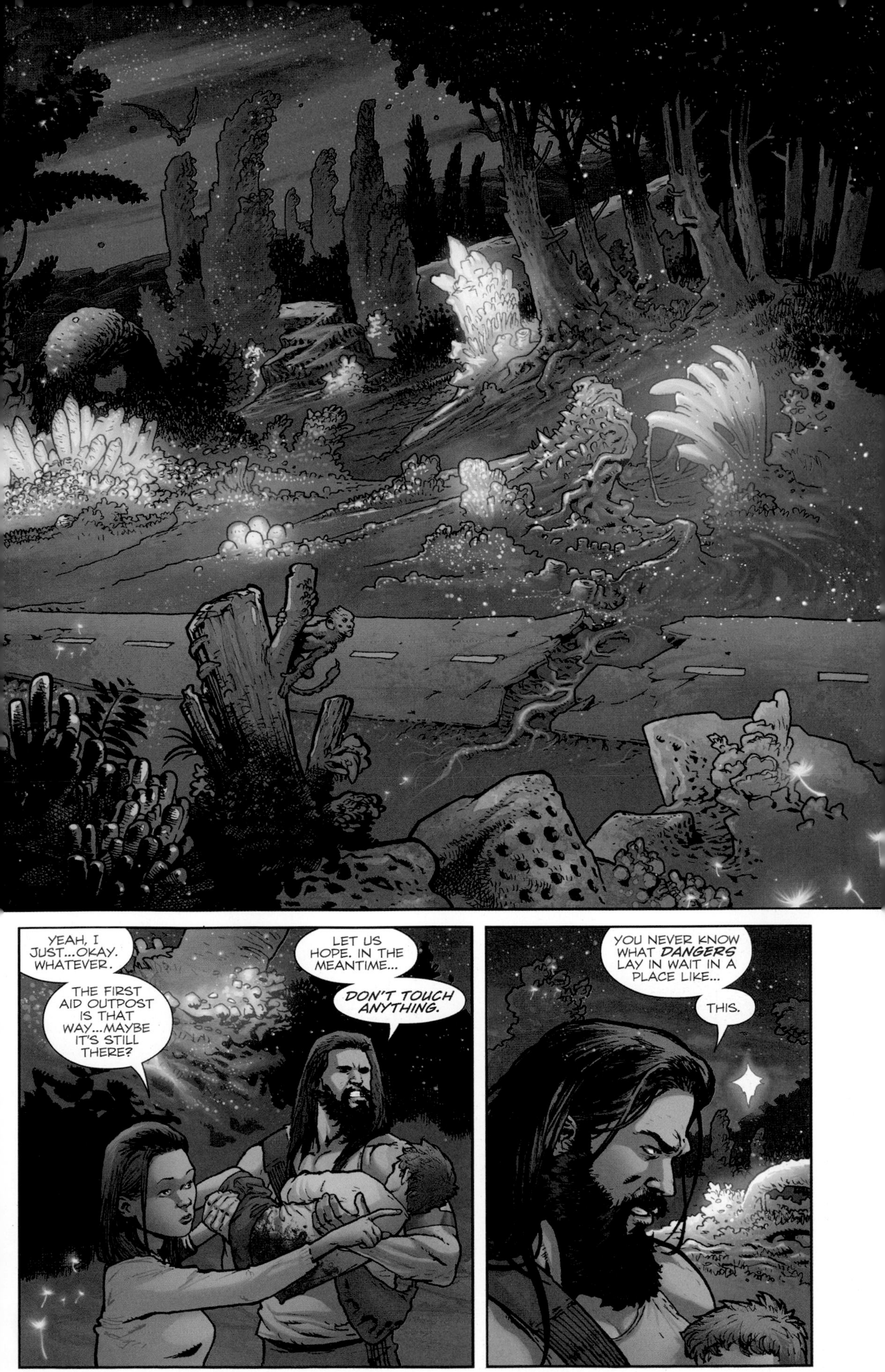
YEAH, I JUST...OKAY. WHATEVER.
THE FIRST AID OUTPOST IS THAT WAY...MAYBE IT'S STILL THERE?
LET US HOPE. IN THE MEANTIME...
DON'T TOUCH ANYTHING.
YOU NEVER KNOW WHAT DANGERS LAY IN WAIT IN A PLACE LIKE...
THIS.

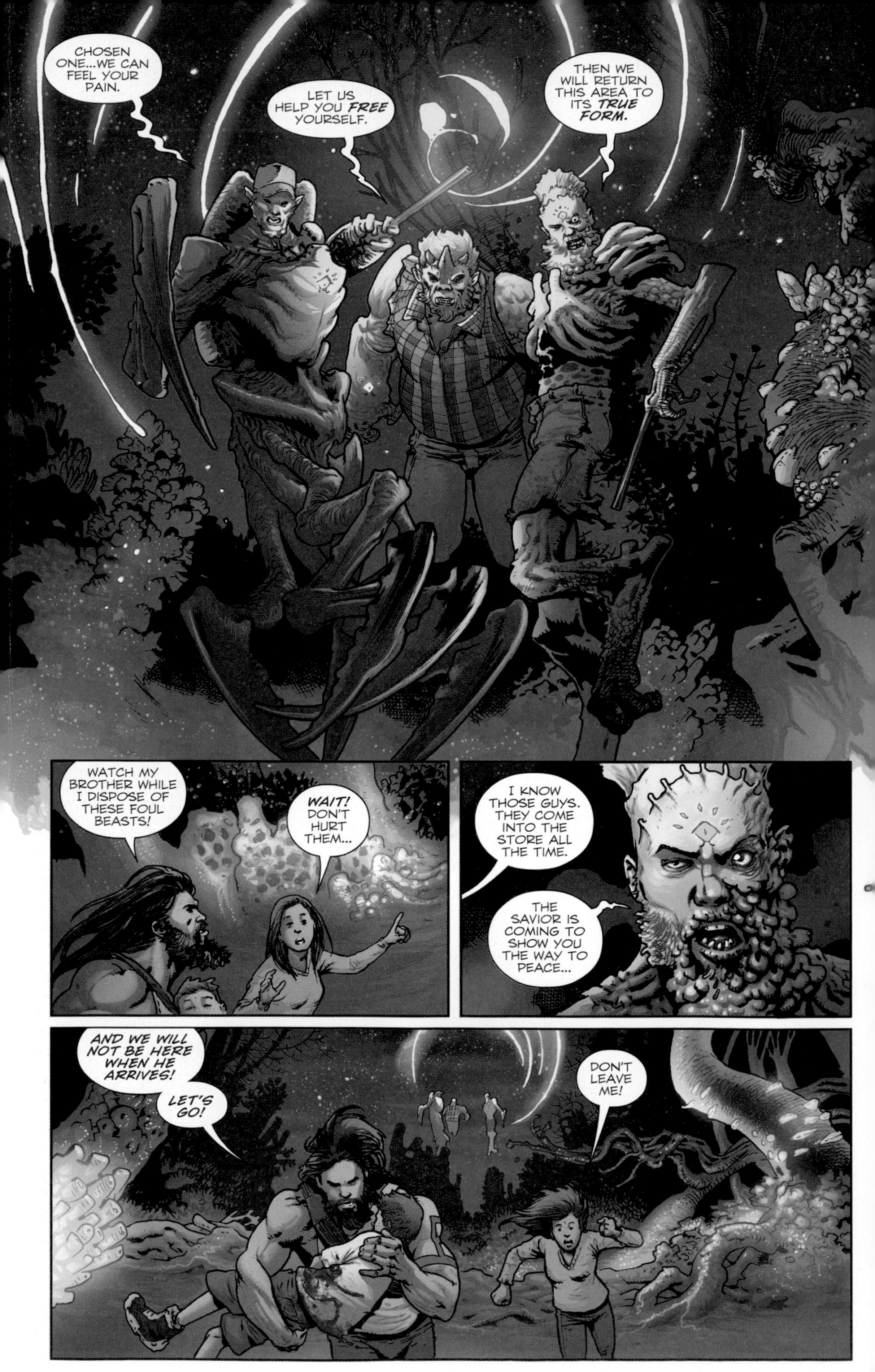
CHOSEN ONE...WE CAN FEEL YOUR PAIN.
LET US HELP YOU FREE YOURSELF.
THEN WE WILL RETURN THIS AREA TO ITS TRUE FORM.
WATCH MY BROTHER WHILE I DISPOSE OF THESE FOUL BEASTS!
WAIT! DON'T HURT THEM...
I KNOW THOSE GUYS. THEY COME INTO THE STORE ALL THE TIME.
THE SAVIOR IS COMING TO SHOW YOU THE WAY TO PEACE...
AND WE WILL NOT BE HERE WHEN HE ARRIVES!
LET'S GO!
DON'T LEAVE ME!

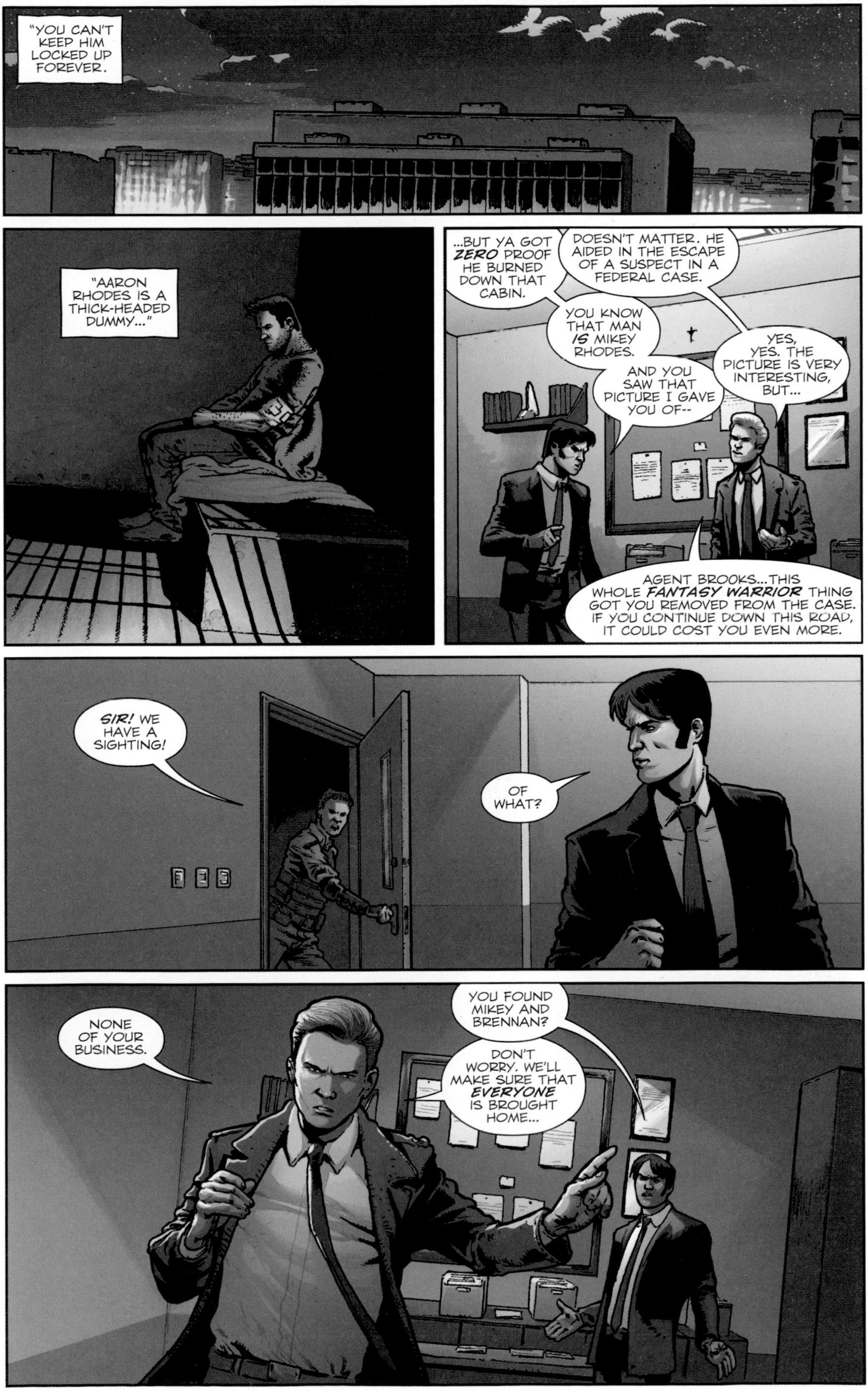
"YOU CAN'T KEEP HIM LOCKED UP FOREVER.
"AARON RHODES IS A THICK-HEADED DUMMY..."
...BUT YA GOT *ZERO* PROOF HE BURNED DOWN THAT CABIN.
DOESN'T MATTER. HE AIDED IN THE ESCAPE OF A SUSPECT IN A FEDERAL CASE.
YOU KNOW THAT MAN *IS* MIKEY RHODES.
AND YOU SAW THAT PICTURE I GAVE YOU OF--
YES, YES. THE PICTURE IS VERY INTERESTING, BUT...
AGENT BROOKS...THIS WHOLE *FANTASY WARRIOR* THING GOT YOU REMOVED FROM THE CASE. IF YOU CONTINUE DOWN THIS ROAD, IT COULD COST YOU EVEN MORE.
SIR! WE HAVE A SIGHTING!
OF WHAT?
NONE OF YOUR BUSINESS.
YOU FOUND MIKEY AND BRENNAN?
DON'T WORRY. WE'LL MAKE SURE THAT *EVERYONE* IS BROUGHT HOME...

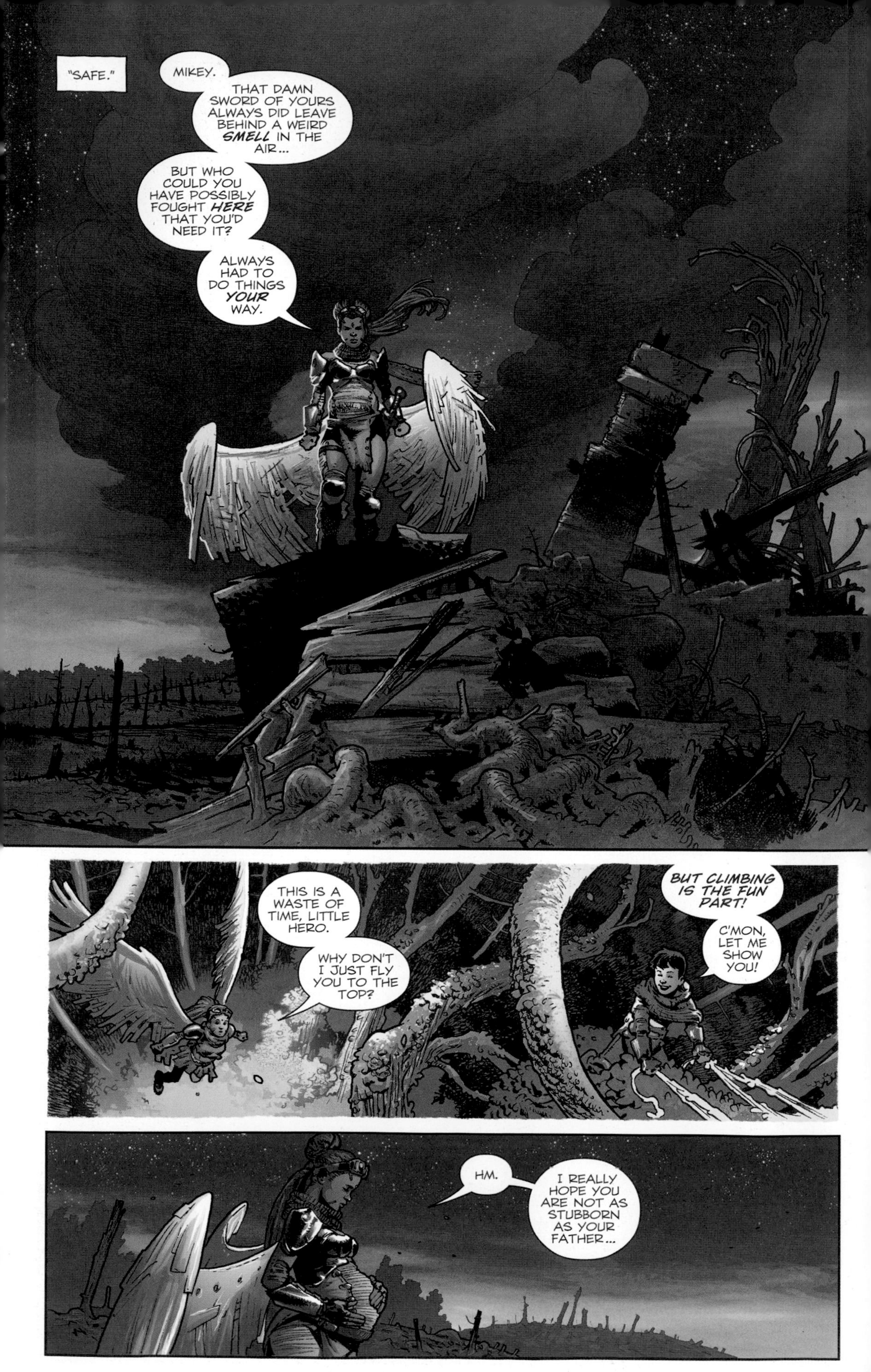
"SAFE."
MIKEY.
THAT DAMN SWORD OF YOURS ALWAYS DID LEAVE BEHIND A WEIRD SMELL IN THE AIR...
BUT WHO COULD YOU HAVE POSSIBLY FOUGHT HERE THAT YOU'D NEED IT?
ALWAYS HAD TO DO THINGS YOUR WAY.
THIS IS A WASTE OF TIME, LITTLE HERO.
WHY DON'T I JUST FLY YOU TO THE TOP?
BUT CLIMBING IS THE FUN PART!
C'MON, LET ME SHOW YOU!
HM.
I REALLY HOPE YOU ARE NOT AS STUBBORN AS YOUR FATHER...

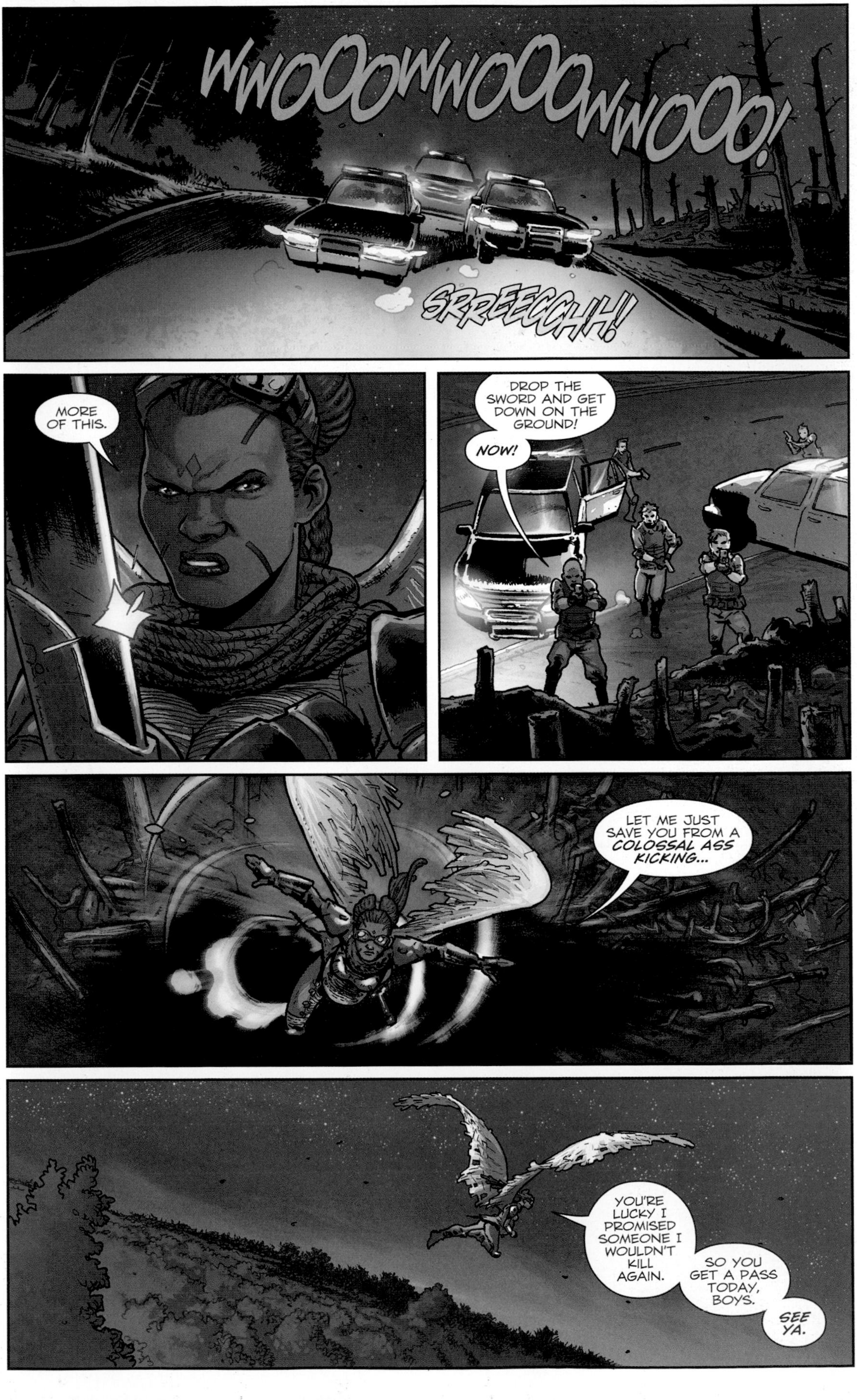
WWOOOWWOOOWWOOO!
SRREECCHH!
MORE OF THIS.
DROP THE SWORD AND GET DOWN ON THE GROUND!
NOW!
LET ME JUST SAVE YOU FROM A COLOSSAL ASS KICKING...
YOU'RE LUCKY I PROMISED SOMEONE I WOULDN'T KILL AGAIN.
SO YOU GET A PASS TODAY, BOYS.
SEE YA.

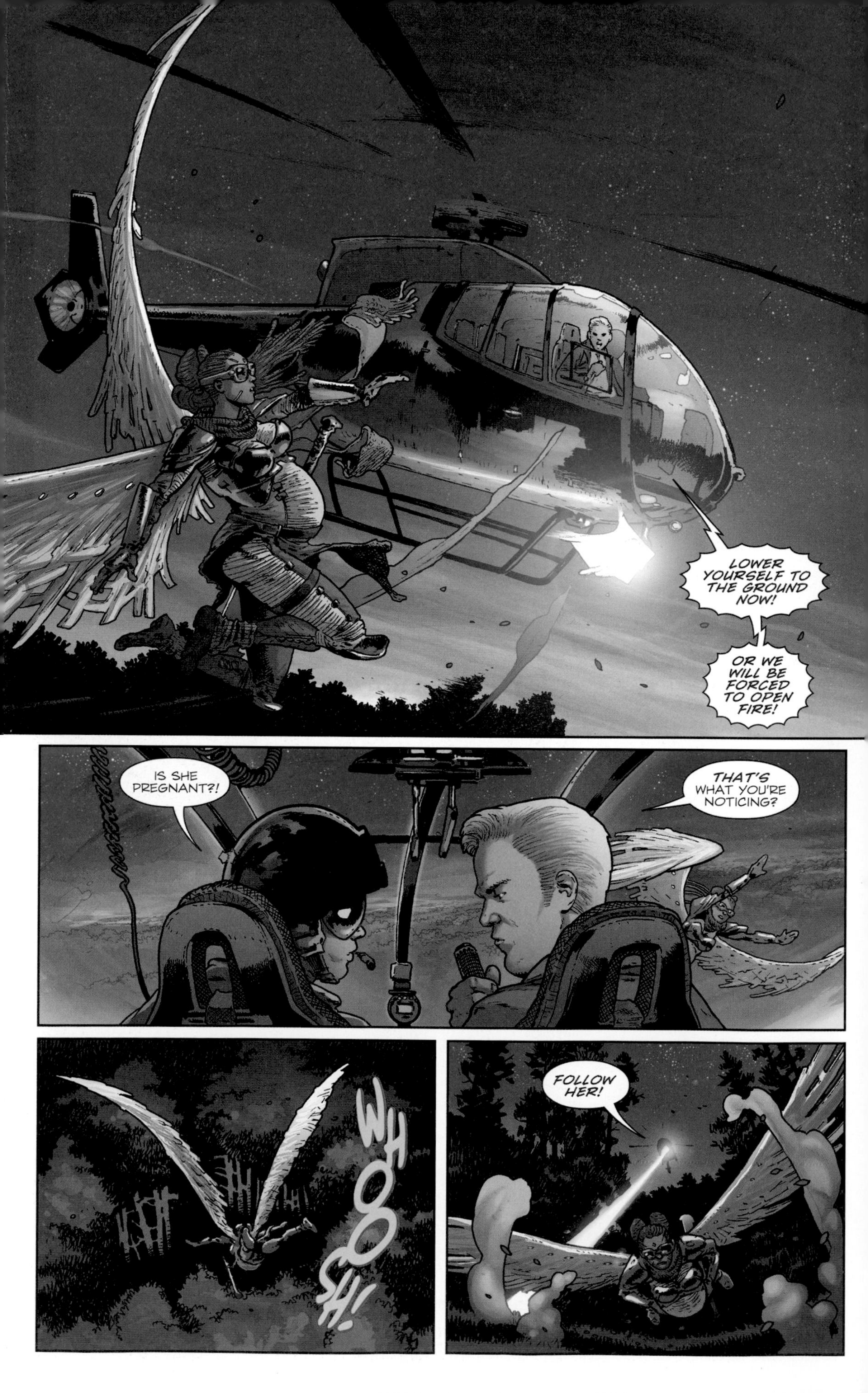
LOWER YOURSELF TO THE GROUND NOW!
OR WE WILL BE FORCED TO OPEN FIRE!
IS SHE PREGNANT?!
THAT'S WHAT YOU'RE NOTICING?
WHOOSH!
FOLLOW HER!

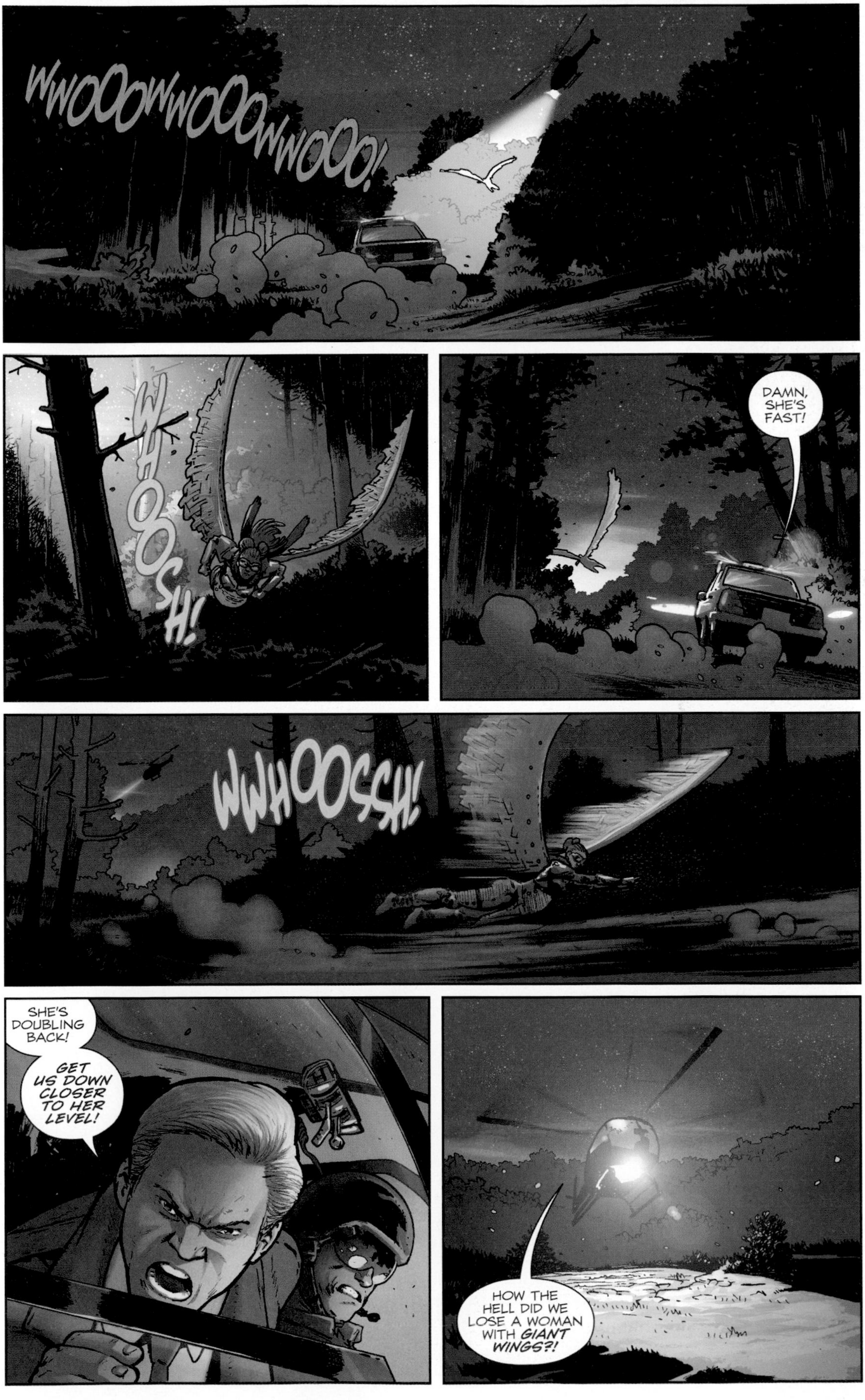
WWOOOWWOOOWWOOO!
WHOOOSH!
DAMN, SHE'S FAST!
WWHOOSSH!
SHE'S DOUBLING BACK!
GET US DOWN CLOSER TO HER LEVEL!
HOW THE HELL DID WE LOSE A WOMAN WITH GIANT WINGS?!

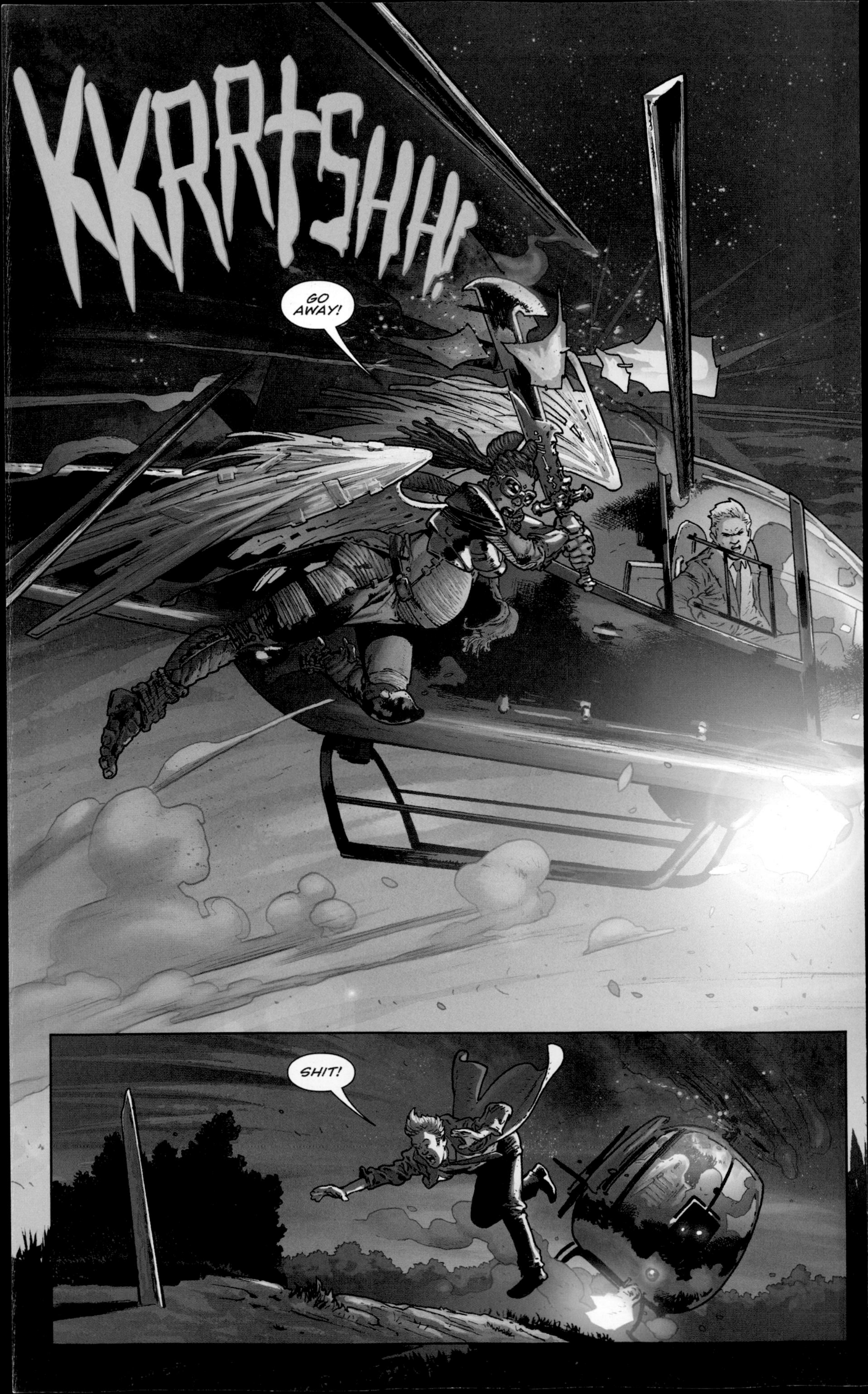
KKRRTSHH!
GO AWAY!
SHIT!

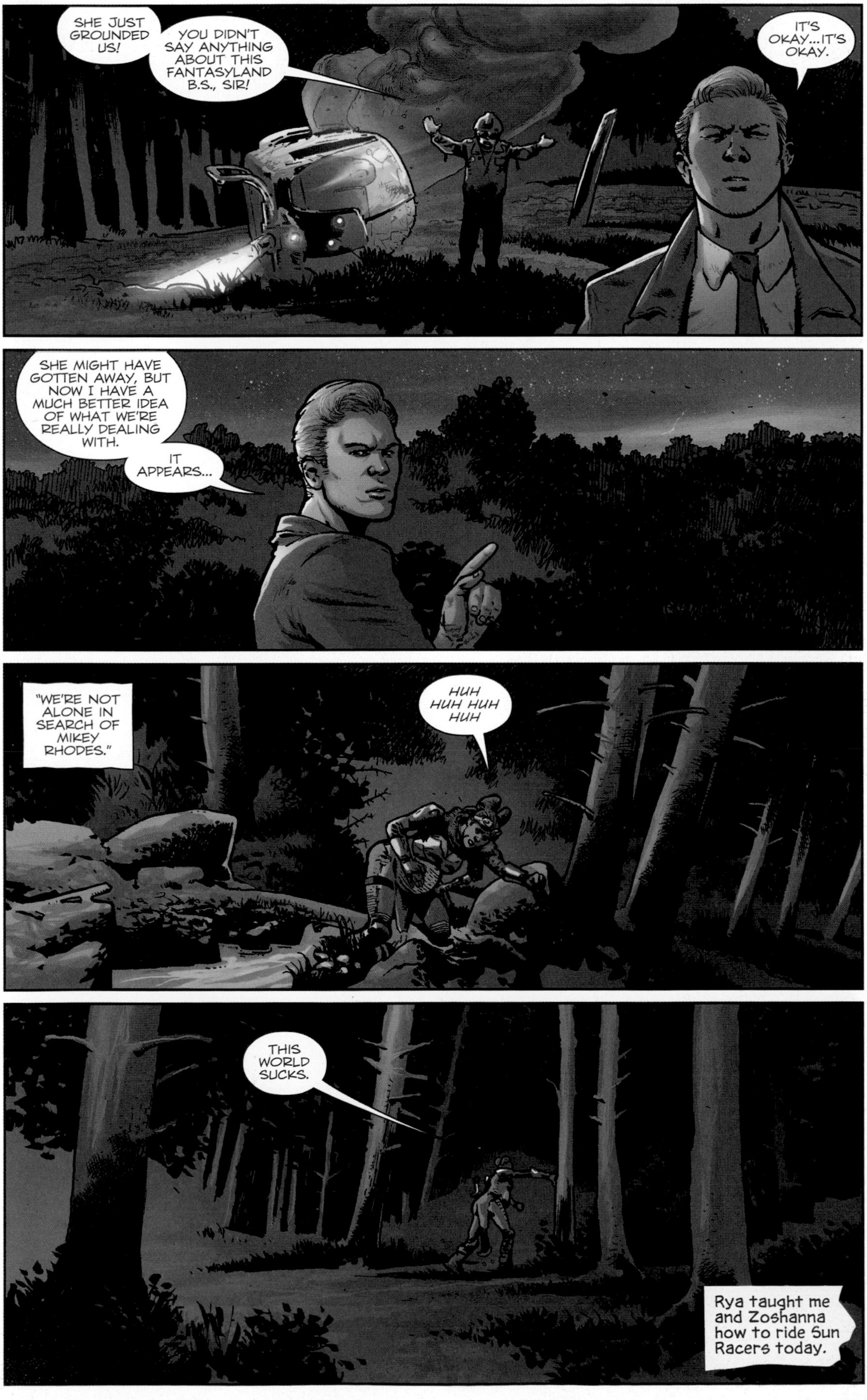
SHE JUST GROUNDED US!
YOU DIDN'T SAY ANYTHING ABOUT THIS FANTASYLAND B.S., SIR!
IT'S OKAY...IT'S OKAY.
SHE MIGHT HAVE GOTTEN AWAY, BUT NOW I HAVE A MUCH BETTER IDEA OF WHAT WE'RE REALLY DEALING WITH.
IT APPEARS...
"WE'RE NOT ALONE IN SEARCH OF MIKEY RHODES."
HUH HUH HUH HUH
THIS WORLD SUCKS.
Rya taught me and Zoshanna how to ride Sun Racers today.

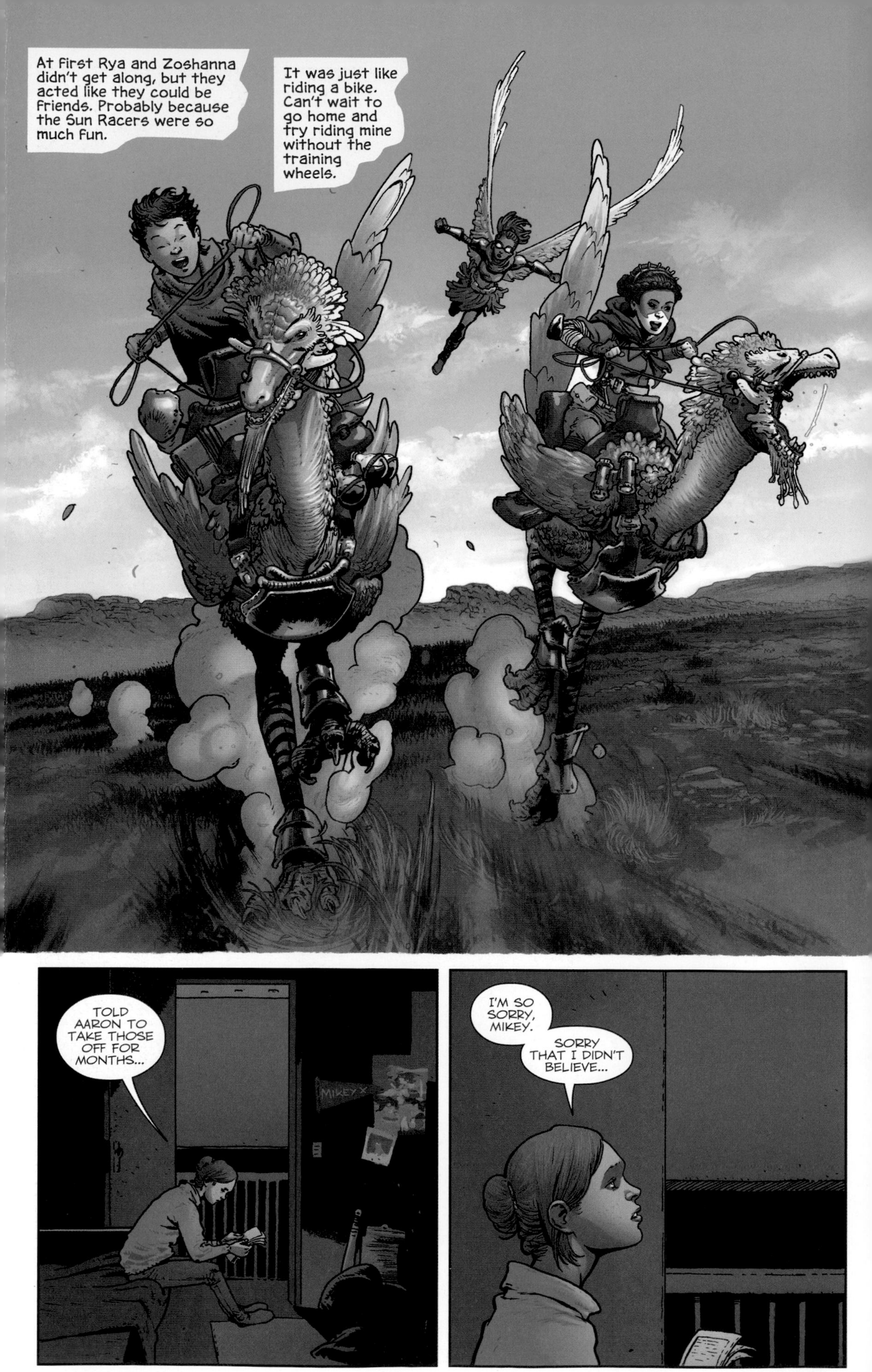

At first Rya and Zoshanna didn't get along, but they acted like they could be friends. Probably because the Sun Racers were so much fun.
It was just like riding a bike. Can't wait to go home and try riding mine without the training wheels.
TOLD AARON TO TAKE THOSE OFF FOR MONTHS...
MIKEY
I'M SO SORRY, MIKEY.
SORRY THAT I DIDN'T BELIEVE...

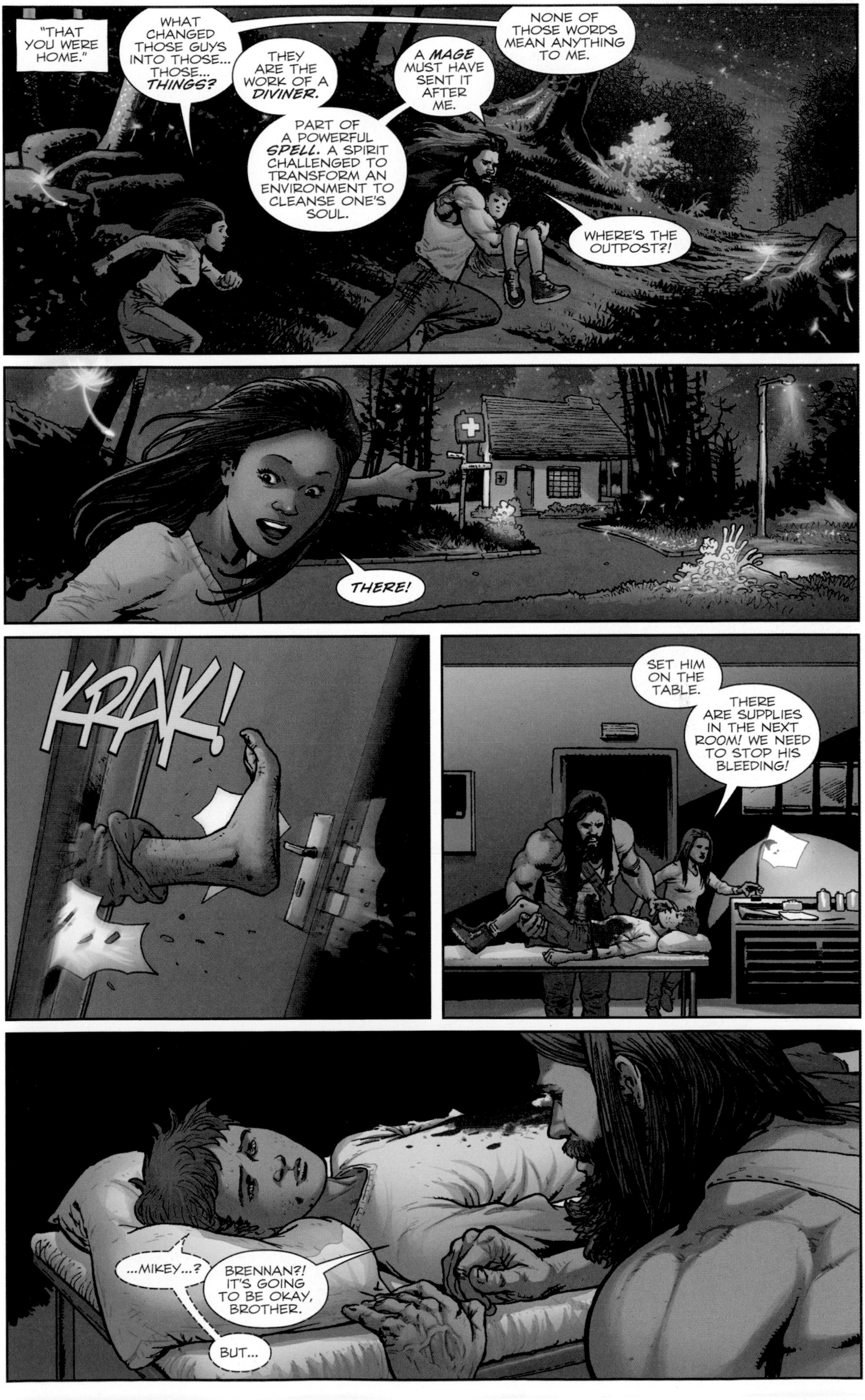
"THAT YOU WERE HOME."
WHAT CHANGED THOSE GUYS INTO THOSE... THOSE... THINGS?
THEY ARE THE WORK OF A DIVINER.
A MAGE MUST HAVE SENT IT AFTER ME.
NONE OF THOSE WORDS MEAN ANYTHING TO ME.
PART OF A POWERFUL SPELL. A SPIRIT CHALLENGED TO TRANSFORM AN ENVIRONMENT TO CLEANSE ONE'S SOUL.
WHERE'S THE OUTPOST?!
THERE!
KRAK!
SET HIM ON THE TABLE.
THERE ARE SUPPLIES IN THE NEXT ROOM! WE NEED TO STOP HIS BLEEDING!
...MIKEY...?
BRENNAN?! IT'S GOING TO BE OKAY, BROTHER.
BUT...

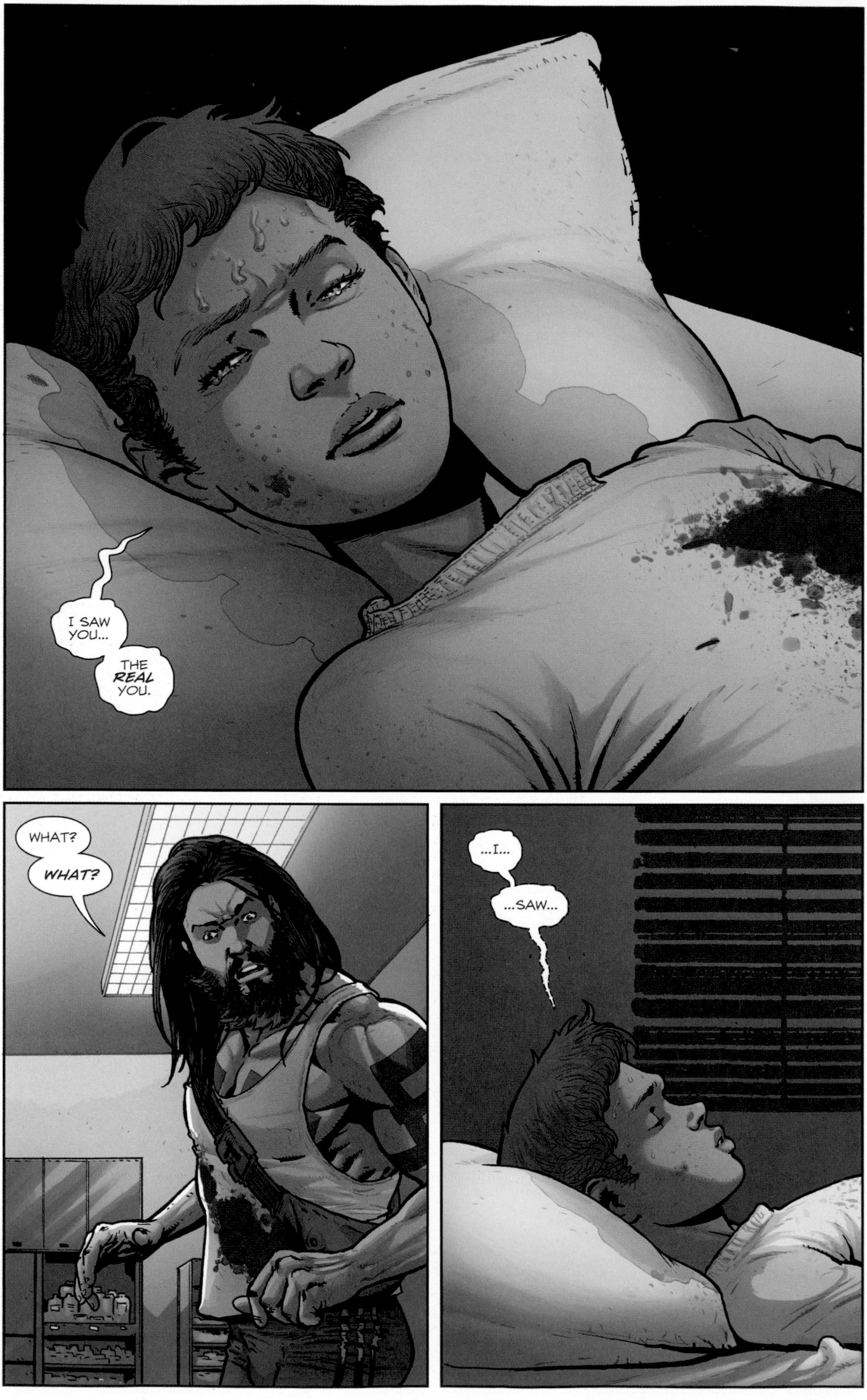
I SAW YOU...
THE REAL YOU.
WHAT?
WHAT?
...I...
...SAW...

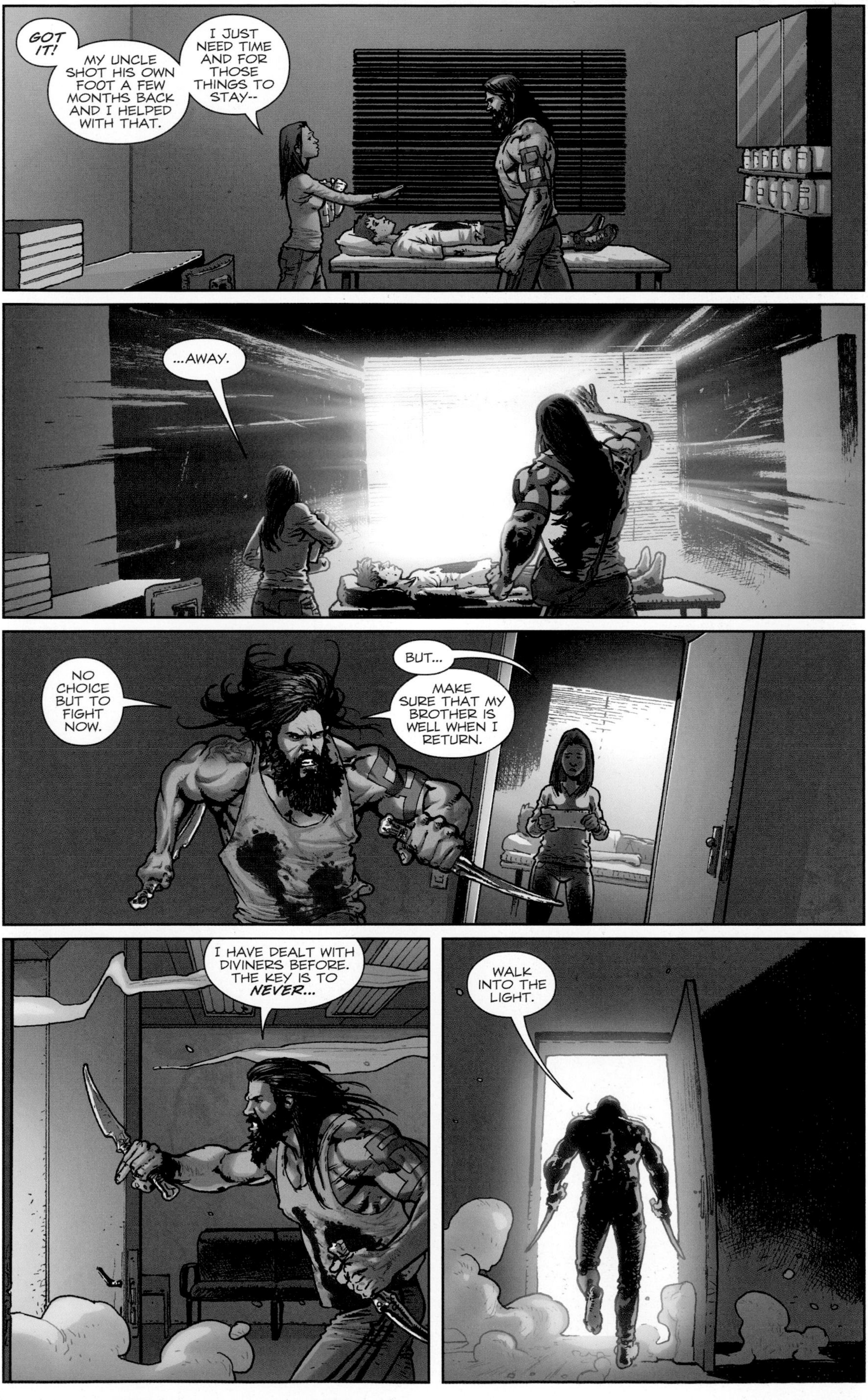
GOT IT!
MY UNCLE SHOT HIS OWN FOOT A FEW MONTHS BACK AND I HELPED WITH THAT.
I JUST NEED TIME AND FOR THOSE THINGS TO STAY--
...AWAY.
NO CHOICE BUT TO FIGHT NOW.
BUT...
MAKE SURE THAT MY BROTHER IS WELL WHEN I RETURN.
I HAVE DEALT WITH DIVINERS BEFORE. THE KEY IS TO *NEVER*...
WALK INTO THE LIGHT.

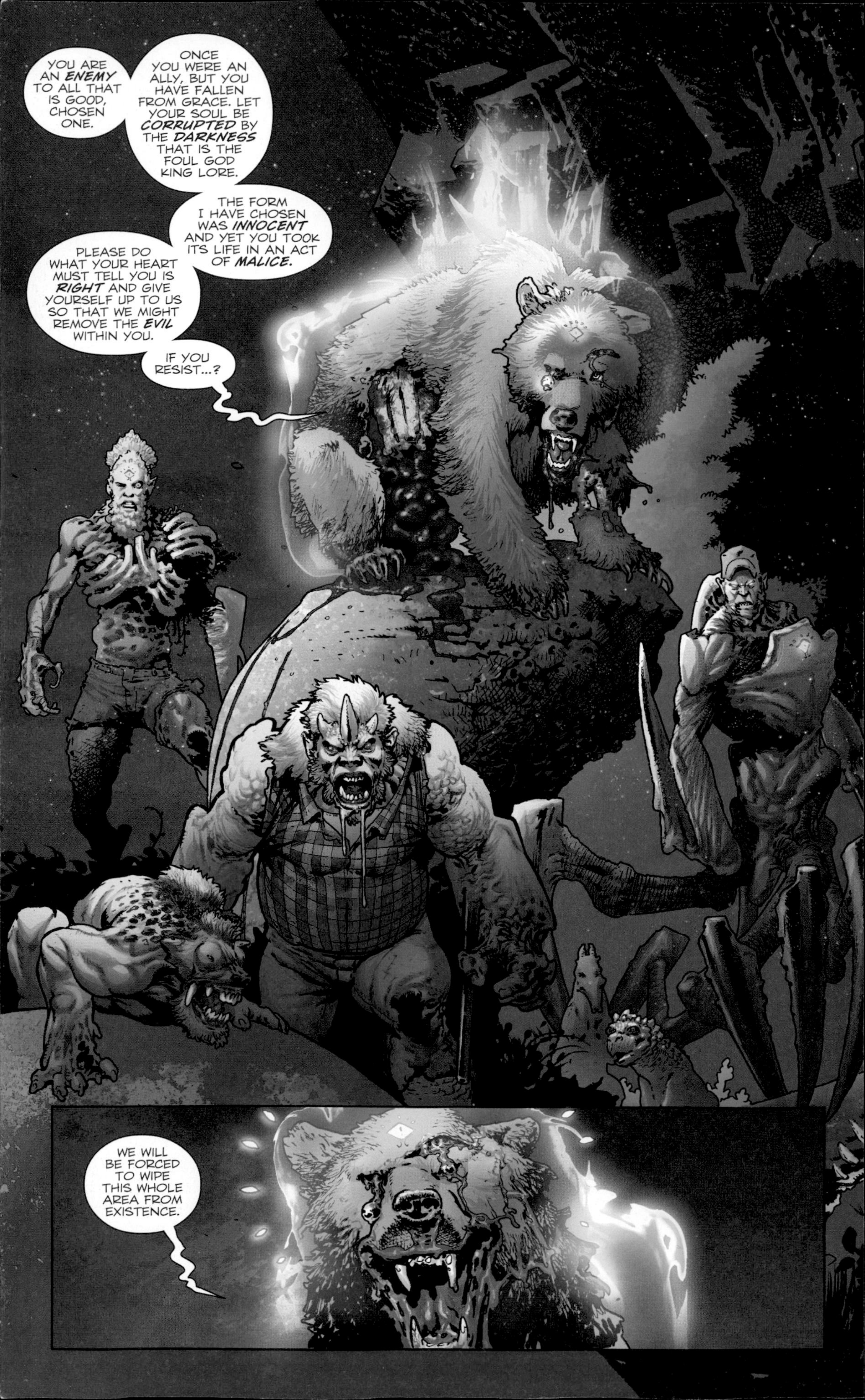
YOU ARE AN *ENEMY* TO ALL THAT IS GOOD, CHOSEN ONE.
ONCE YOU WERE AN ALLY, BUT YOU HAVE FALLEN FROM GRACE. LET YOUR SOUL BE ***CORRUPTED*** BY THE ***DARKNESS*** THAT IS THE FOUL GOD KING LORE.
THE FORM I HAVE CHOSEN WAS ***INNOCENT*** AND YET YOU TOOK ITS LIFE IN AN ACT OF ***MALICE.***
PLEASE DO WHAT YOUR HEART MUST TELL YOU IS ***RIGHT*** AND GIVE YOURSELF UP TO US SO THAT WE MIGHT REMOVE THE ***EVIL*** WITHIN YOU.
IF YOU RESIST...?
WE WILL BE FORCED TO WIPE THIS WHOLE AREA FROM EXISTENCE.

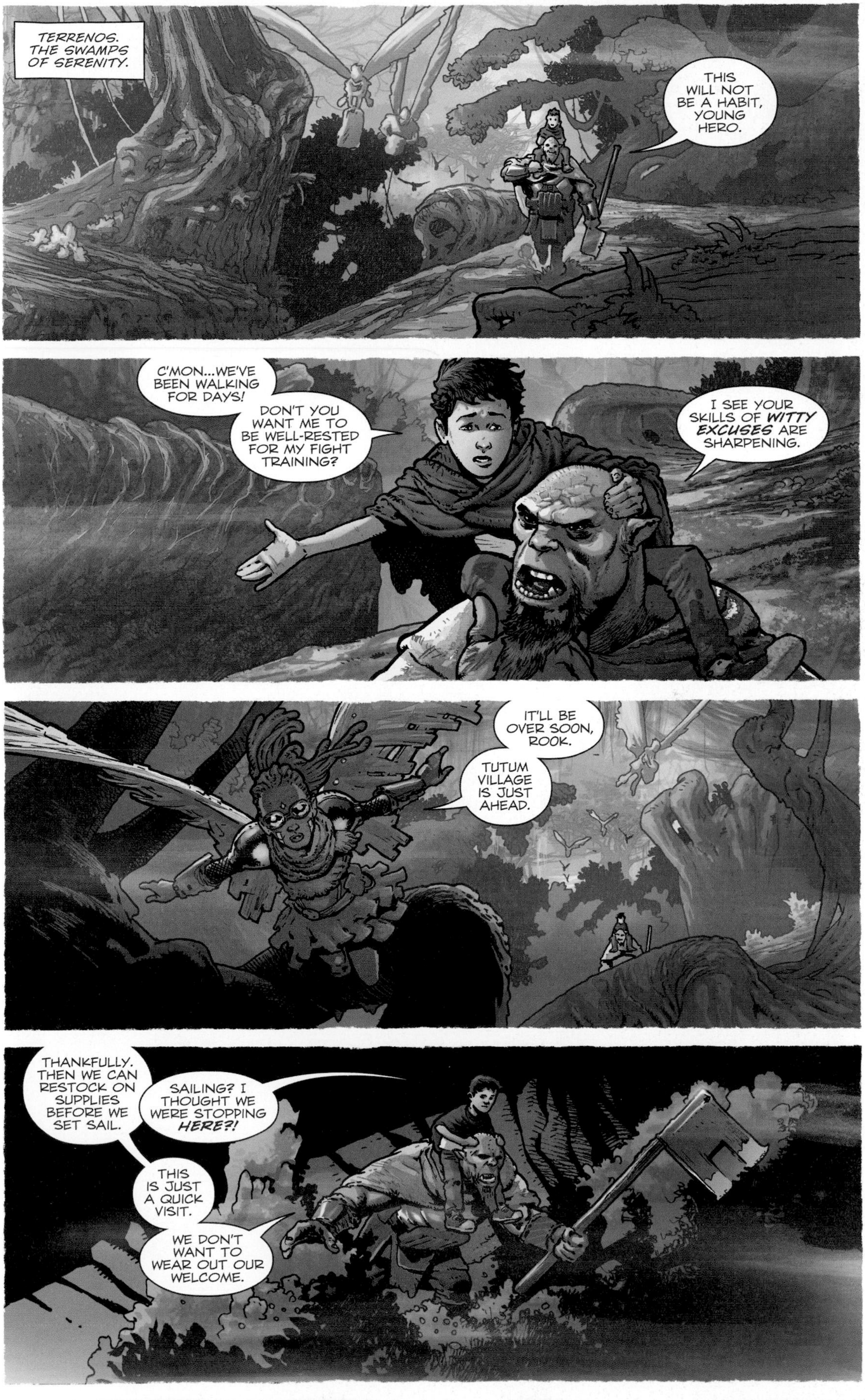
TERRENOS. THE SWAMPS OF SERENITY.
THIS WILL NOT BE A HABIT, YOUNG HERO.
C'MON...WE'VE BEEN WALKING FOR DAYS!
DON'T YOU WANT ME TO BE WELL-RESTED FOR MY FIGHT TRAINING?
I SEE YOUR SKILLS OF WITTY EXCUSES ARE SHARPENING.
IT'LL BE OVER SOON, ROOK.
TUTUM VILLAGE IS JUST AHEAD.
THANKFULLY. THEN WE CAN RESTOCK ON SUPPLIES BEFORE WE SET SAIL.
SAILING? I THOUGHT WE WERE STOPPING HERE?!
THIS IS JUST A QUICK VISIT.
WE DON'T WANT TO WEAR OUT OUR WELCOME.

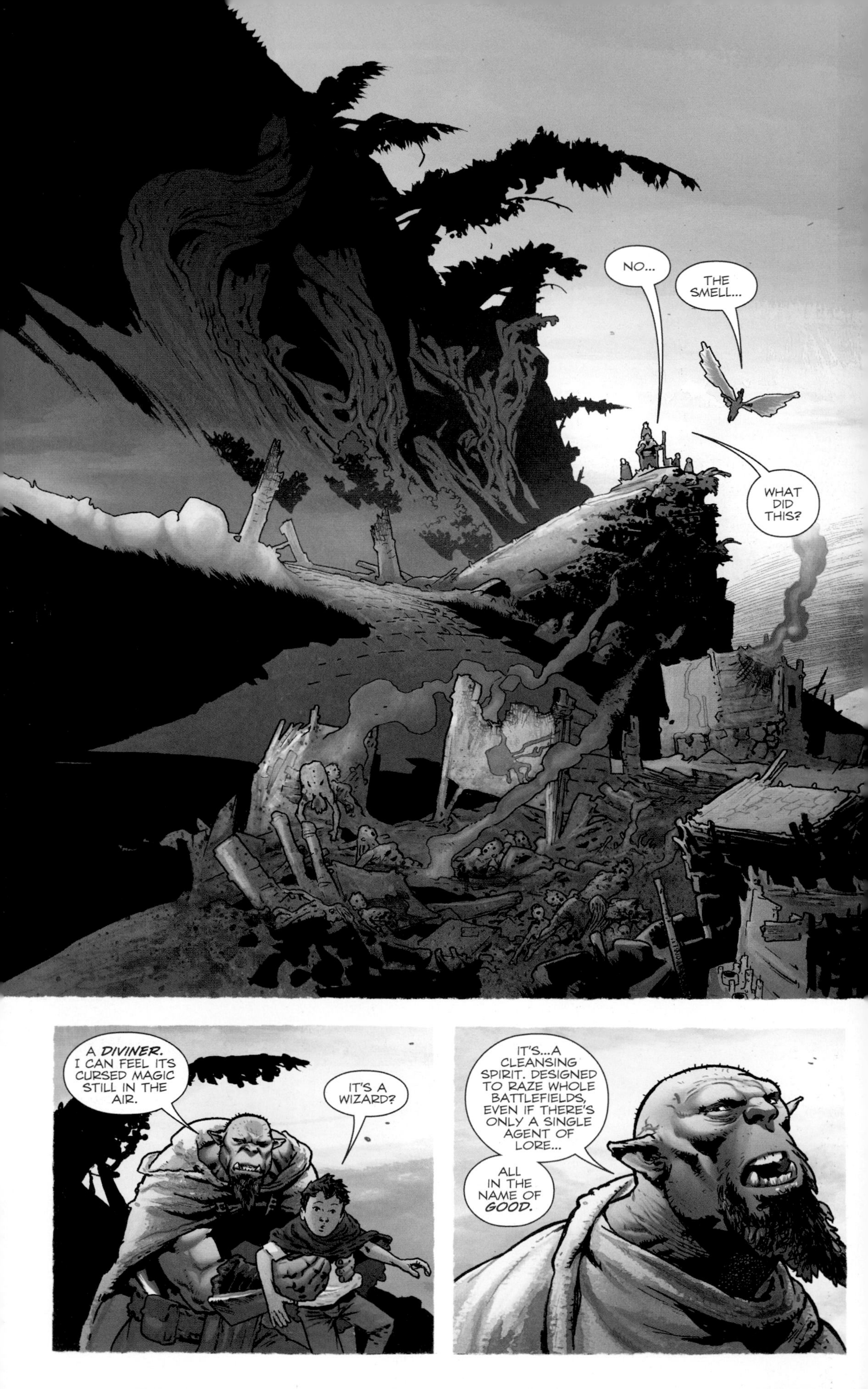
NO...
THE SMELL...
WHAT DID THIS?
A DIVINER. I CAN FEEL ITS CURSED MAGIC STILL IN THE AIR.
IT'S A WIZARD?
IT'S...A CLEANSING SPIRIT. DESIGNED TO RAZE WHOLE BATTLEFIELDS, EVEN IF THERE'S ONLY A SINGLE AGENT OF LORE...
ALL IN THE NAME OF GOOD.

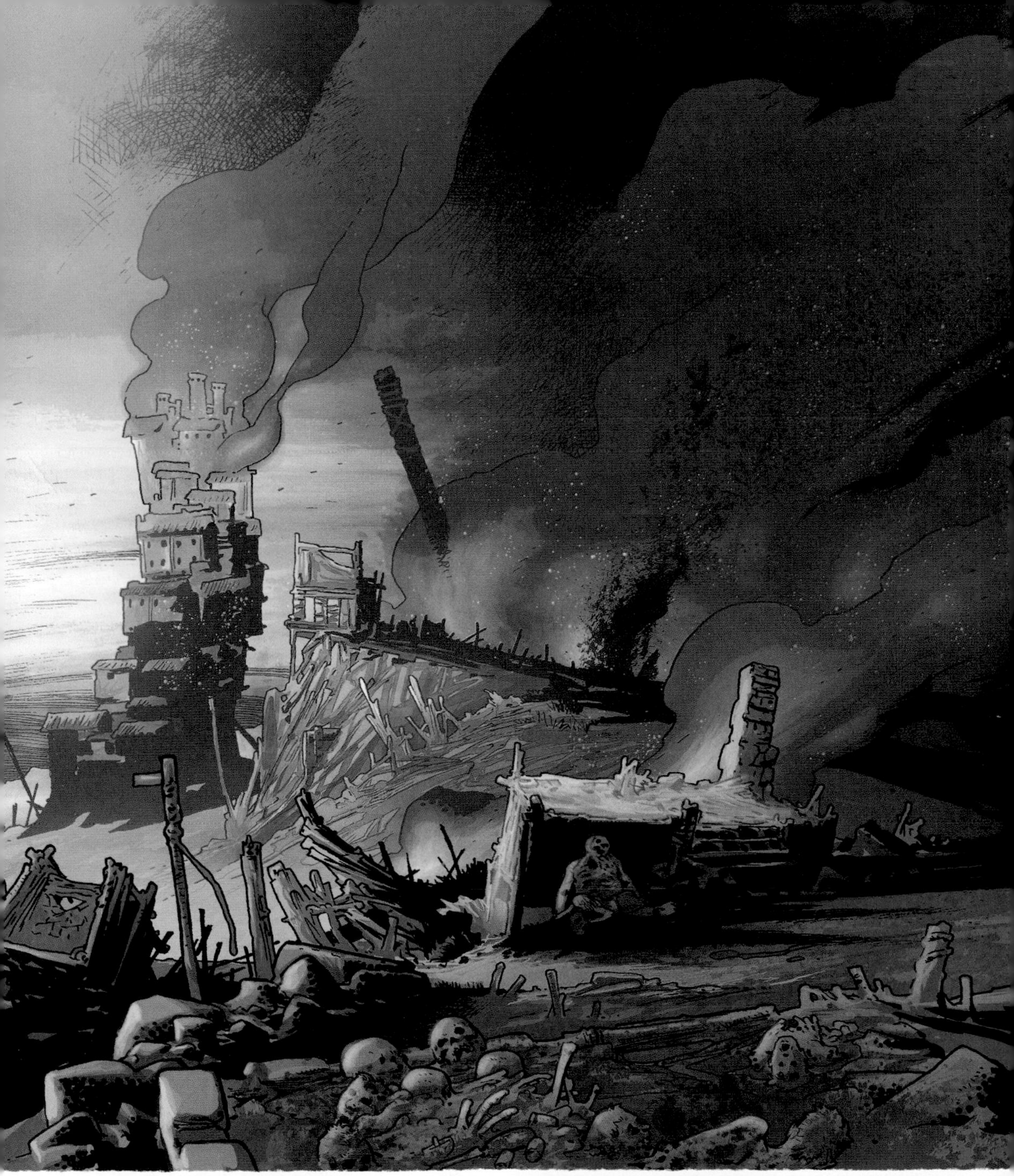

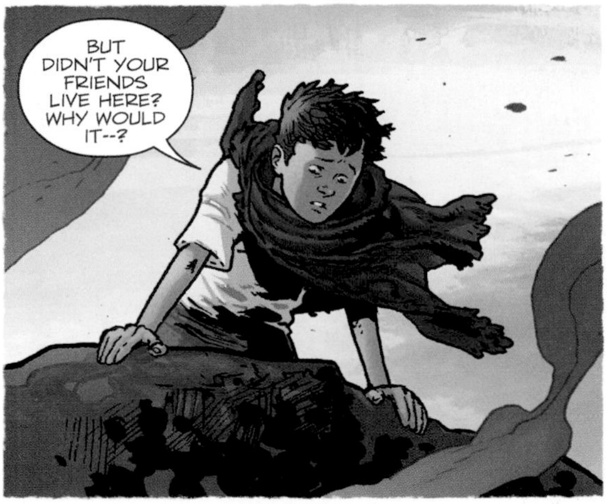
BUT DIDN'T YOUR FRIENDS LIVE HERE? WHY WOULD IT--?

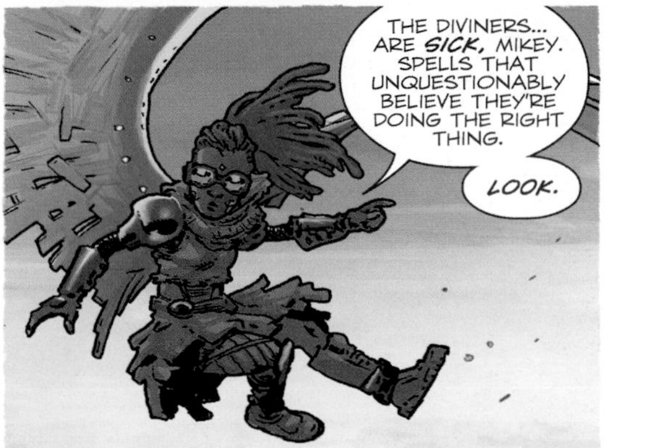
THE DIVINERS... ARE SICK, MIKEY. SPELLS THAT UNQUESTIONABLY BELIEVE THEY'RE DOING THE RIGHT THING.
LOOK.

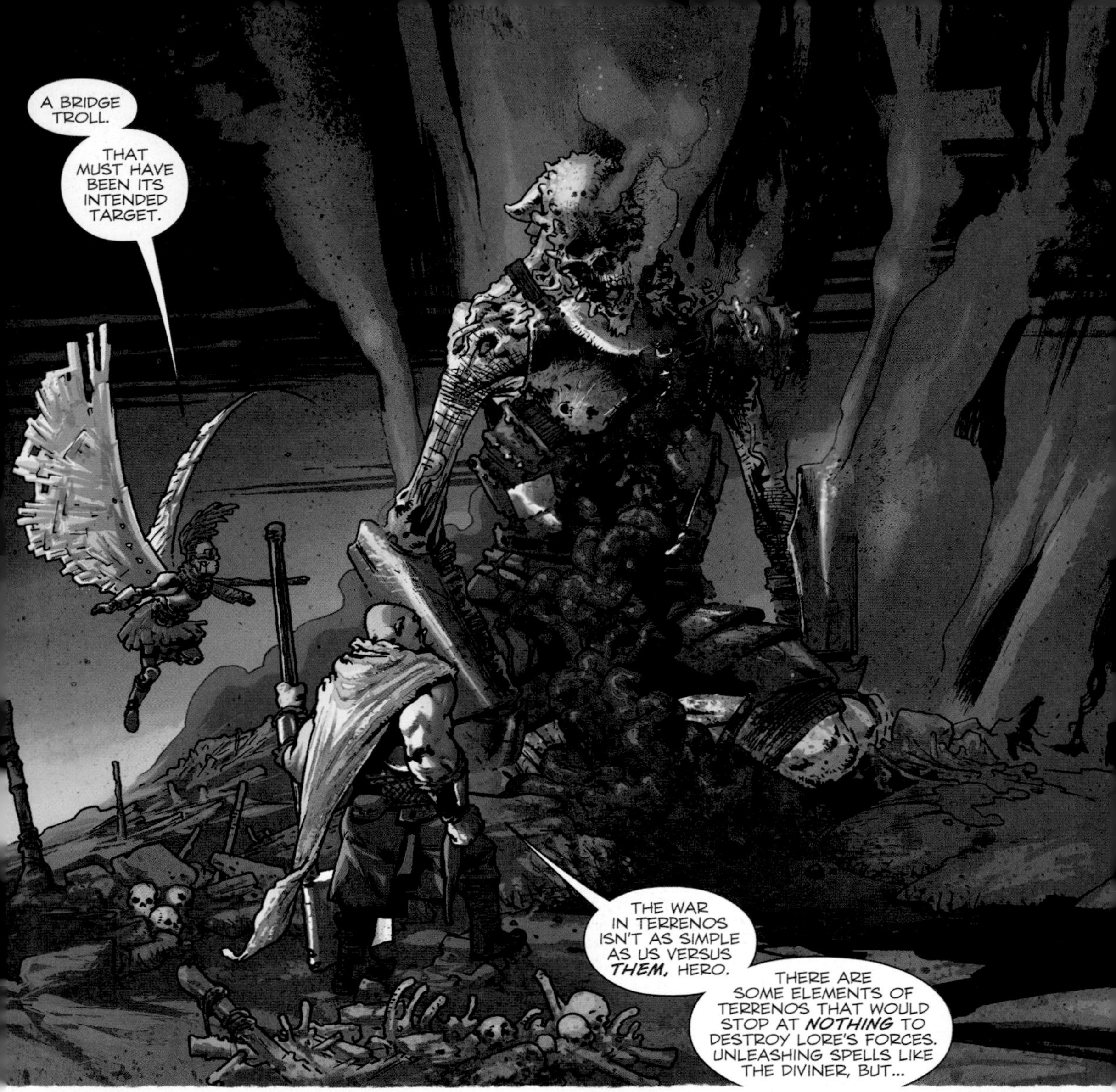
A BRIDGE TROLL.
THAT MUST HAVE BEEN ITS INTENDED TARGET.
THE WAR IN TERRENOS ISN'T AS SIMPLE AS US VERSUS *THEM,* HERO.
THERE ARE SOME ELEMENTS OF TERRENOS THAT WOULD STOP AT *NOTHING* TO DESTROY LORE'S FORCES. UNLEASHING SPELLS LIKE THE DIVINER, BUT...

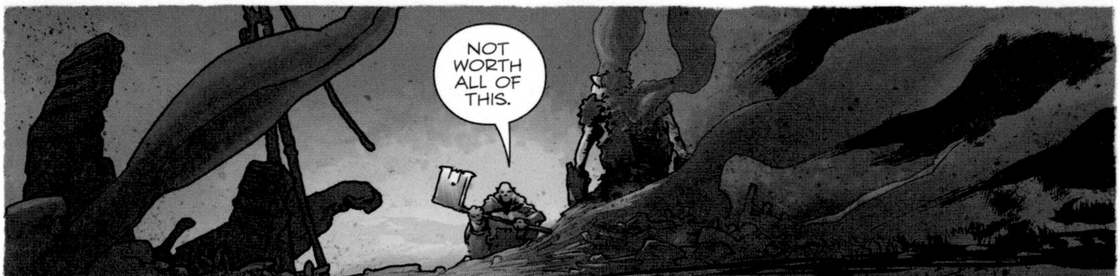
NOT WORTH ALL OF THIS.

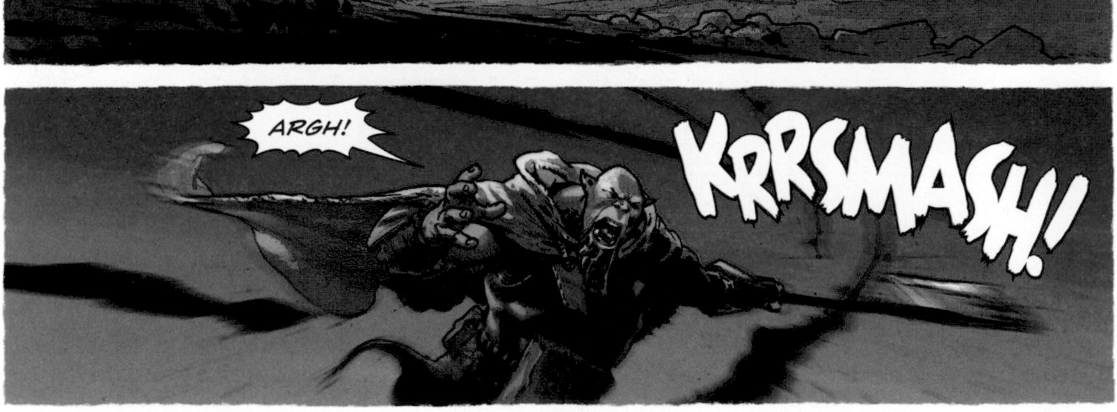
ARGH!
KRRSMASH!

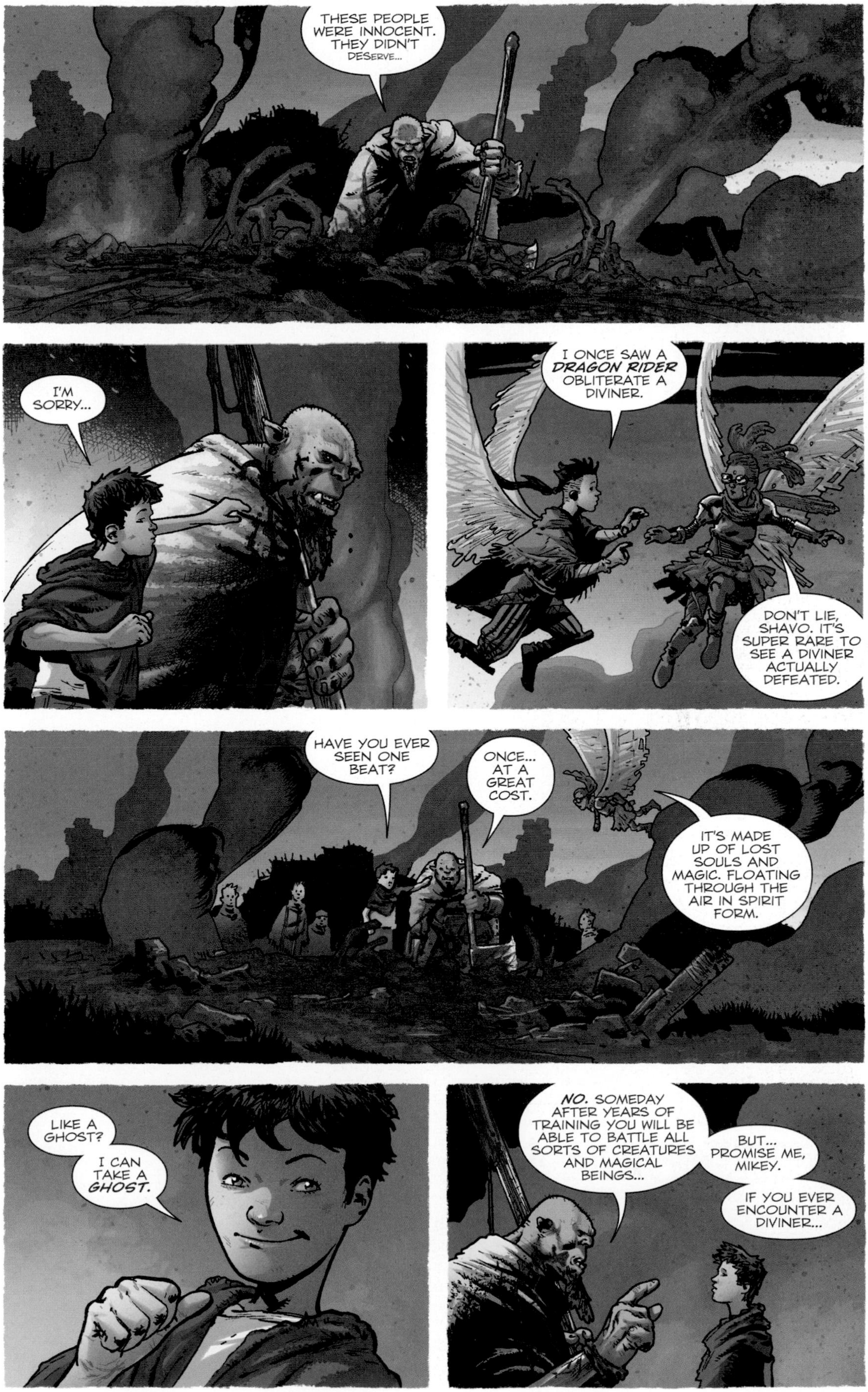
THESE PEOPLE WERE INNOCENT. THEY DIDN'T DESERVE...
I'M SORRY...
I ONCE SAW A DRAGON RIDER OBLITERATE A DIVINER.
DON'T LIE, SHAVO. IT'S SUPER RARE TO SEE A DIVINER ACTUALLY DEFEATED.
HAVE YOU EVER SEEN ONE BEAT?
ONCE... AT A GREAT COST.
IT'S MADE UP OF LOST SOULS AND MAGIC. FLOATING THROUGH THE AIR IN SPIRIT FORM.
LIKE A GHOST?
I CAN TAKE A GHOST.
NO. SOMEDAY AFTER YEARS OF TRAINING YOU WILL BE ABLE TO BATTLE ALL SORTS OF CREATURES AND MAGICAL BEINGS...
BUT... PROMISE ME, MIKEY.
IF YOU EVER ENCOUNTER A DIVINER...

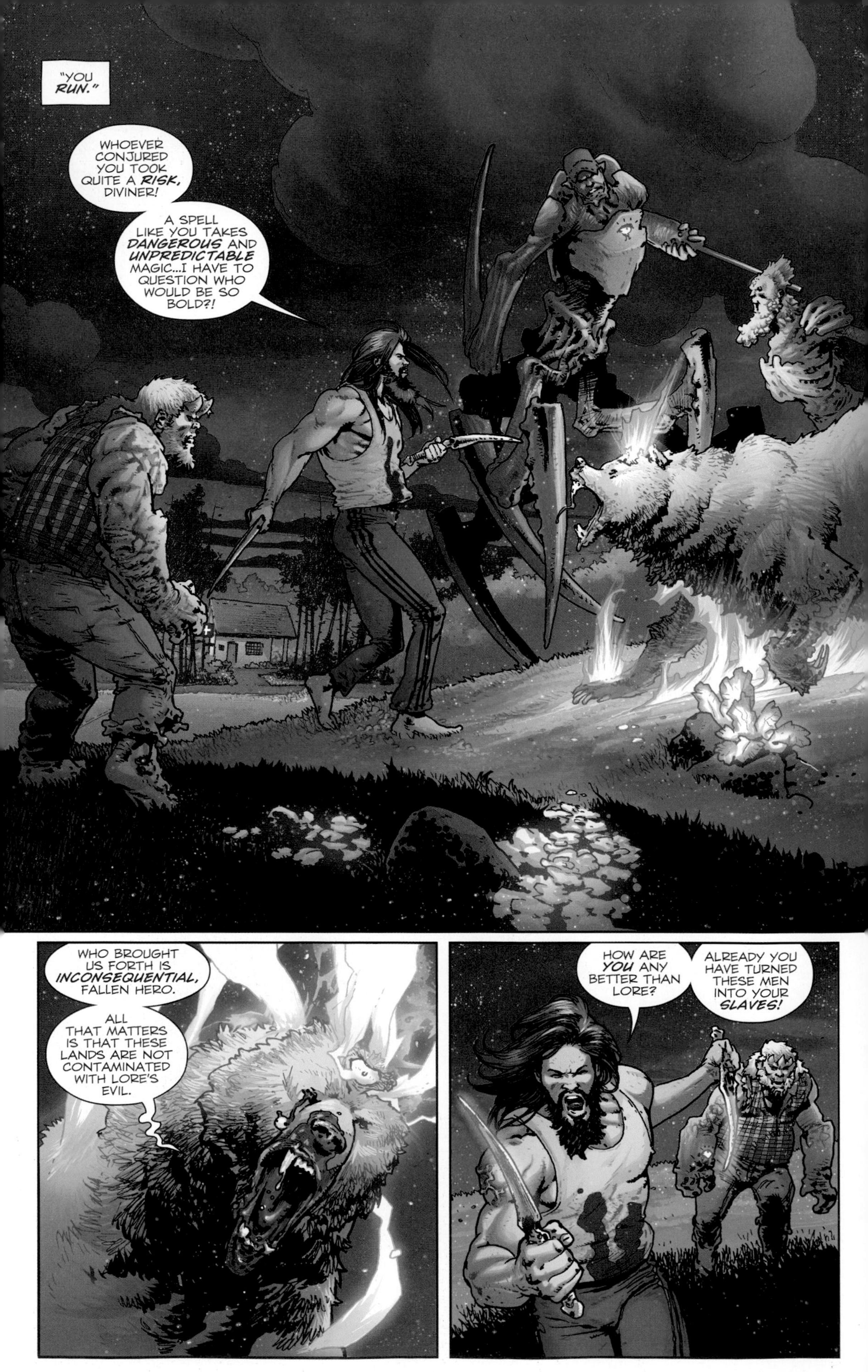
"YOU RUN."
WHOEVER CONJURED YOU TOOK QUITE A RISK, DIVINER!
A SPELL LIKE YOU TAKES DANGEROUS AND UNPREDICTABLE MAGIC...I HAVE TO QUESTION WHO WOULD BE SO BOLD?!
WHO BROUGHT US FORTH IS INCONSEQUENTIAL, FALLEN HERO.
ALL THAT MATTERS IS THAT THESE LANDS ARE NOT CONTAMINATED WITH LORE'S EVIL.
HOW ARE YOU ANY BETTER THAN LORE?
ALREADY YOU HAVE TURNED THESE MEN INTO YOUR SLAVES!

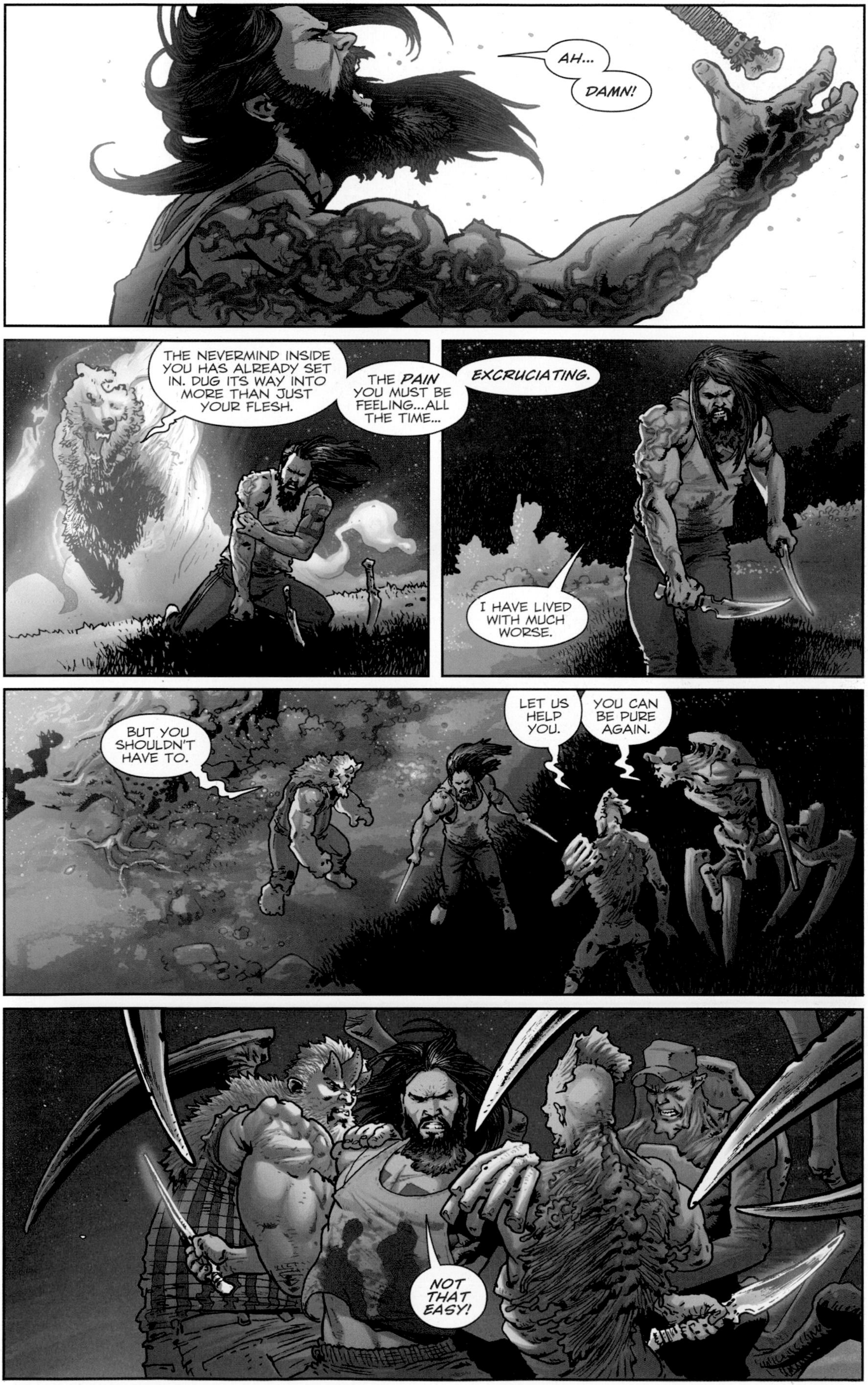
AH...
DAMN!
THE NEVERMIND INSIDE YOU HAS ALREADY SET IN. DUG ITS WAY INTO MORE THAN JUST YOUR FLESH.
THE PAIN YOU MUST BE FEELING...ALL THE TIME...
EXCRUCIATING.
I HAVE LIVED WITH MUCH WORSE.
BUT YOU SHOULDN'T HAVE TO.
LET US HELP YOU.
YOU CAN BE PURE AGAIN.
NOT THAT EASY!

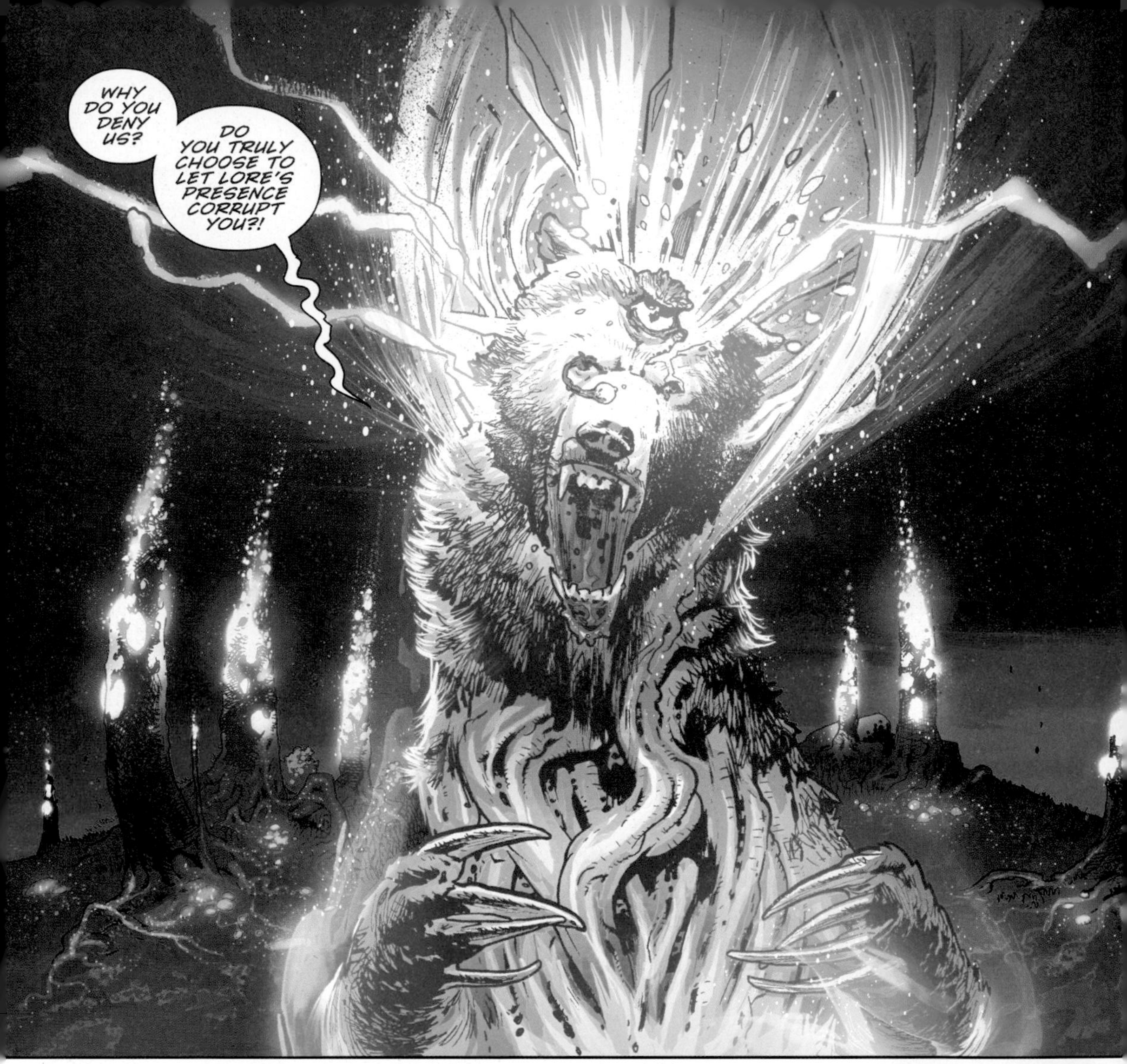
WHY DO YOU DENY US?
DO YOU TRULY CHOOSE TO LET LORE'S PRESENCE CORRUPT YOU?!

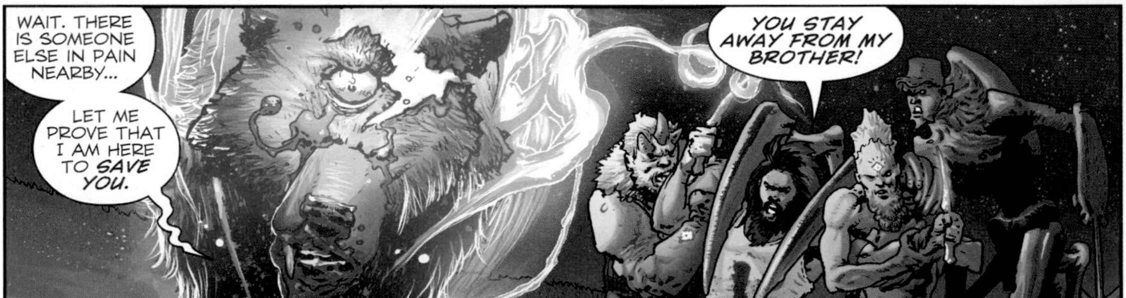
WAIT. THERE IS SOMEONE ELSE IN PAIN NEARBY...
LET ME PROVE THAT I AM HERE TO *SAVE YOU.*
YOU STAY AWAY FROM MY BROTHER!

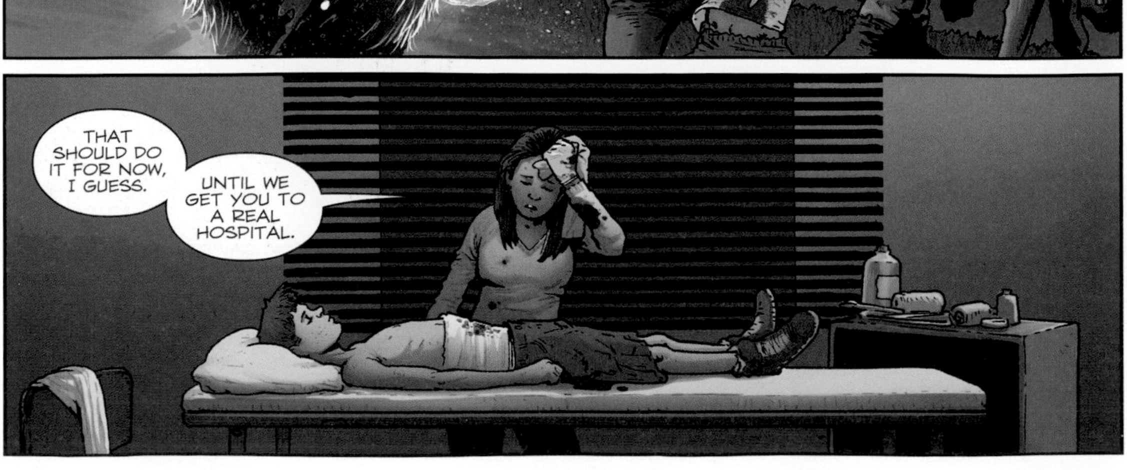
THAT SHOULD DO IT FOR NOW, I GUESS.
UNTIL WE GET YOU TO A REAL HOSPITAL.

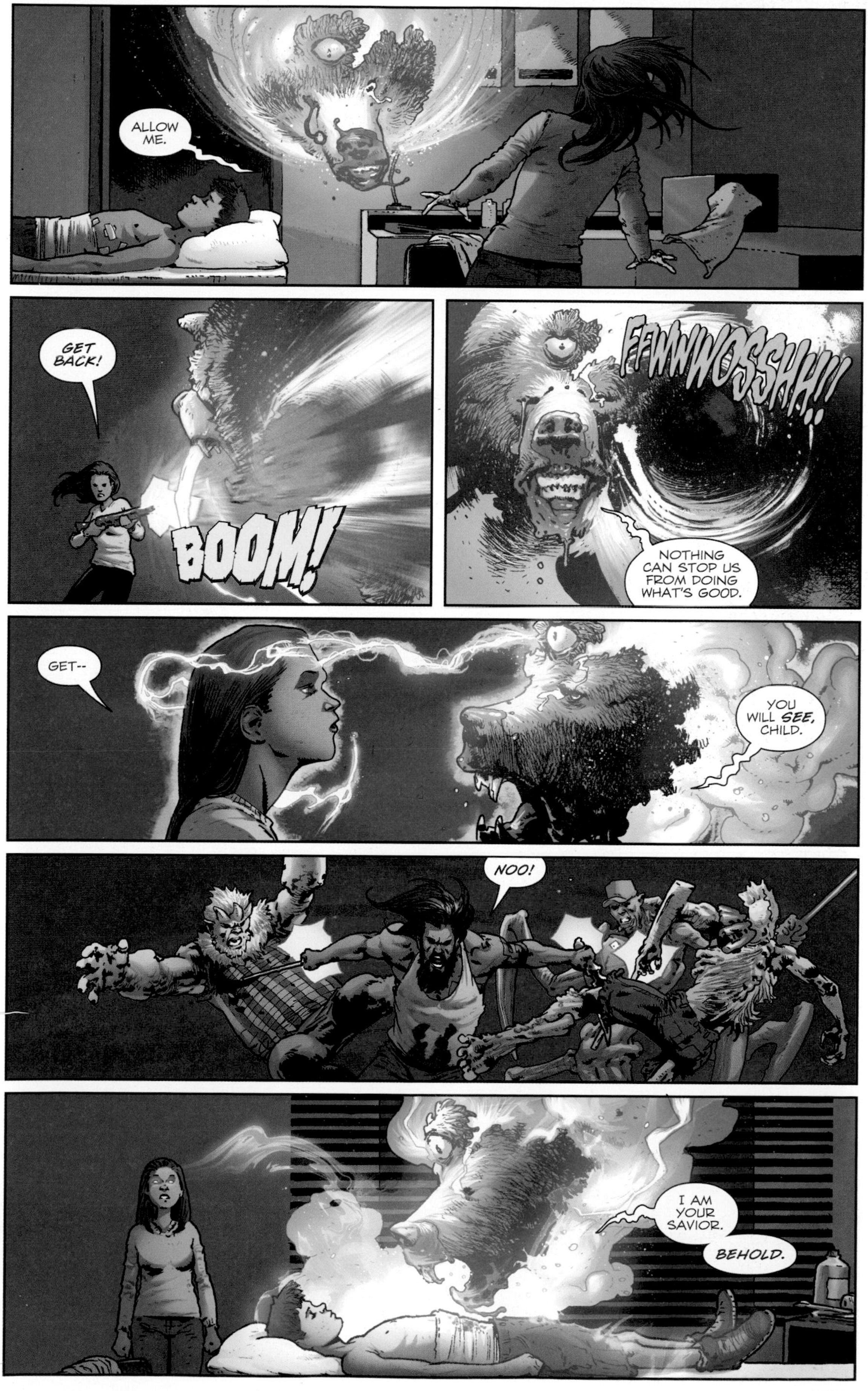
ALLOW ME.
GET BACK!
BOOM!
FFWWWOSSHH!!
NOTHING CAN STOP US FROM DOING WHAT'S GOOD.
GET--
YOU WILL SEE, CHILD.
NOO!
I AM YOUR SAVIOR.
BEHOLD.

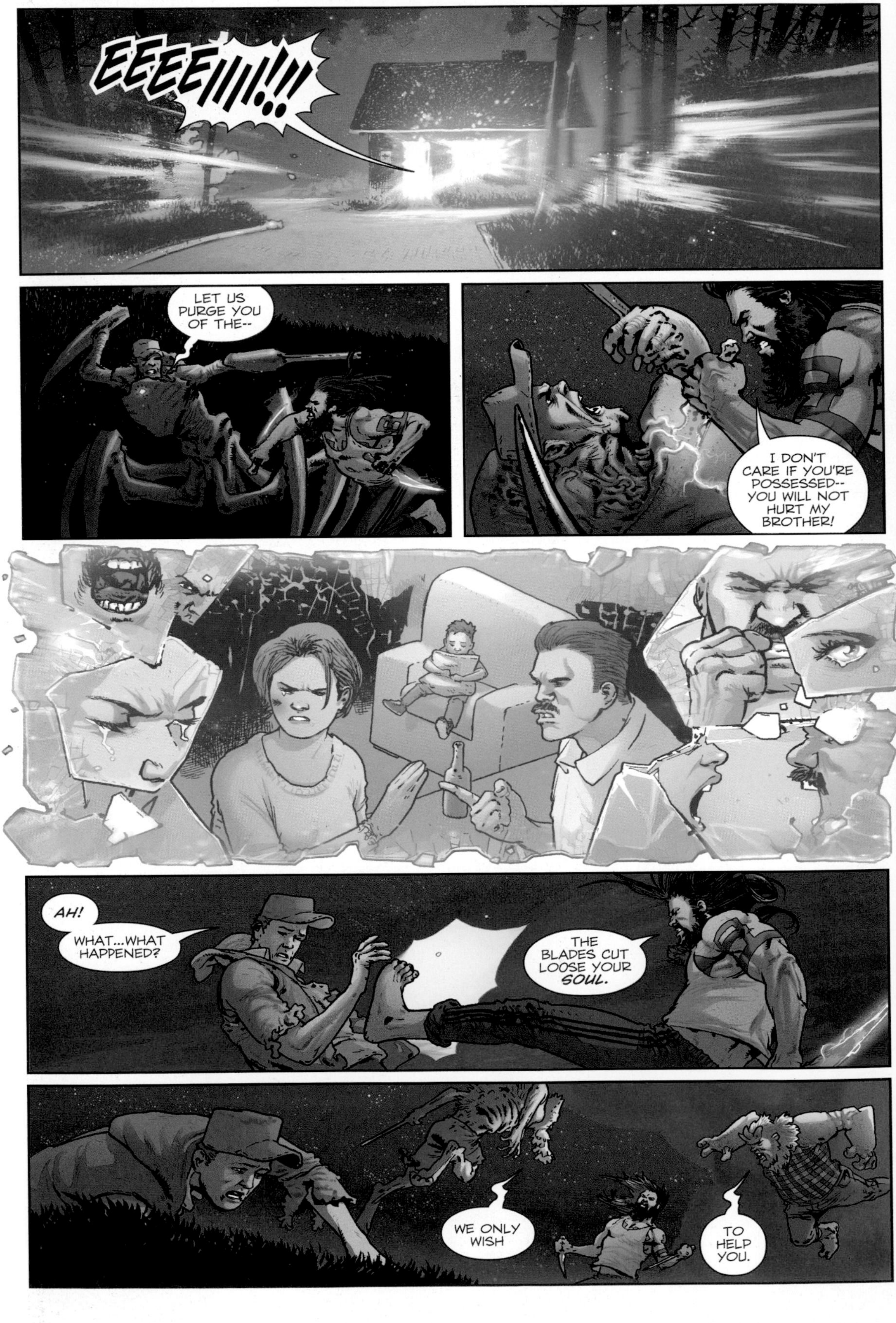
EEEE!!!!!!!
LET US PURGE YOU OF THE--
I DON'T CARE IF YOU'RE POSSESSED-- YOU WILL NOT HURT MY BROTHER!
AH!
WHAT...WHAT HAPPENED?
THE BLADES CUT LOOSE YOUR SOUL.
WE ONLY WISH
TO HELP YOU.

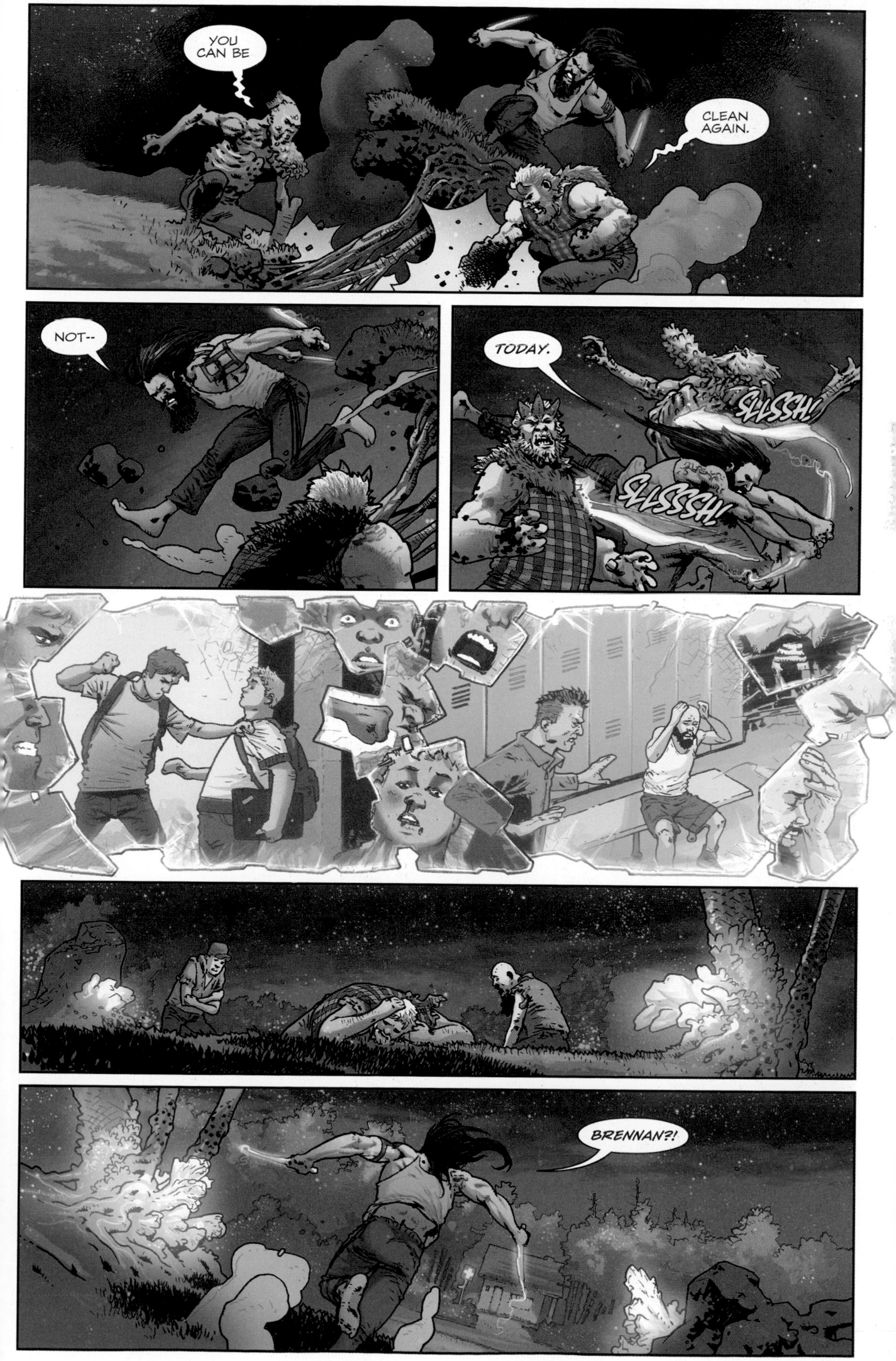

YOU CAN BE
CLEAN AGAIN.
NOT--
TODAY.
SLISSSH!
SLISSSH!
BRENNAN?!

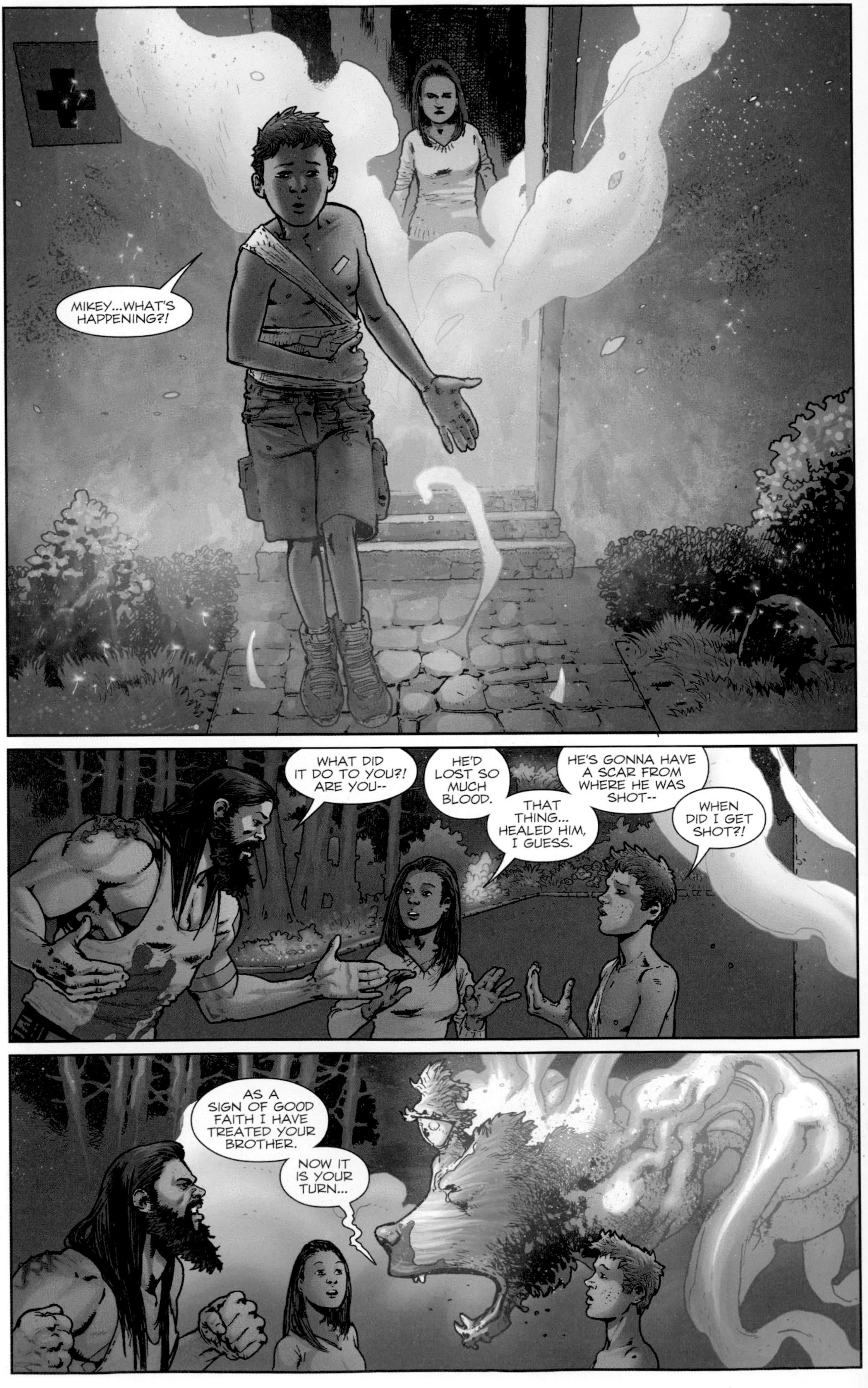

MIKEY...WHAT'S HAPPENING?!
WHAT DID IT DO TO YOU?! ARE YOU--
HE'D LOST SO MUCH BLOOD.
THAT THING... HEALED HIM, I GUESS.
HE'S GONNA HAVE A SCAR FROM WHERE HE WAS SHOT--
WHEN DID I GET SHOT?!
AS A SIGN OF GOOD FAITH I HAVE TREATED YOUR BROTHER.
NOW IT IS YOUR TURN...

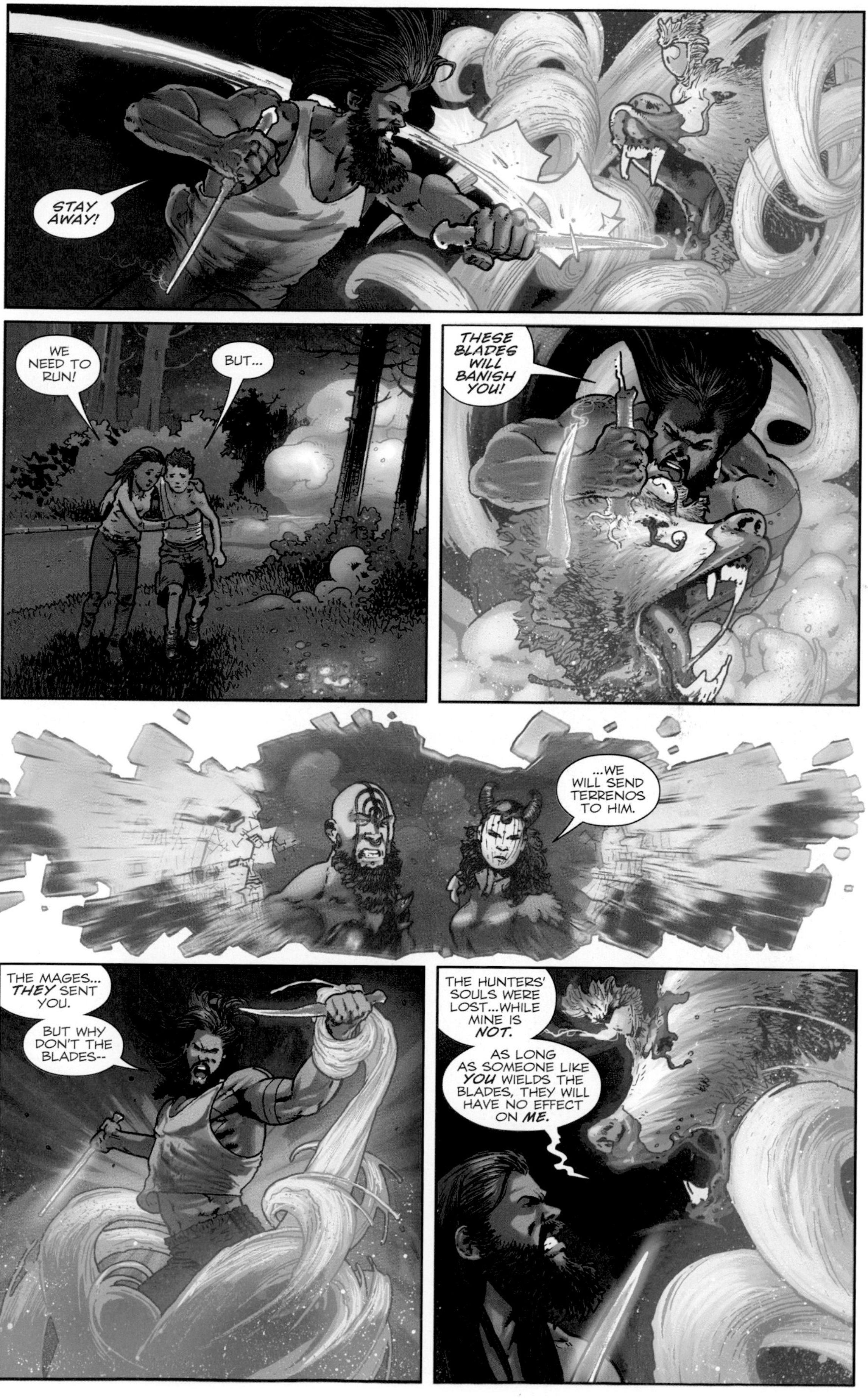
STAY AWAY!
WE NEED TO RUN!
BUT...
THESE BLADES WILL BANISH YOU!
...WE WILL SEND TERRENOS TO HIM.
THE MAGES... THEY SENT YOU.
BUT WHY DON'T THE BLADES--
THE HUNTERS' SOULS WERE LOST...WHILE MINE IS NOT.
AS LONG AS SOMEONE LIKE YOU WIELDS THE BLADES, THEY WILL HAVE NO EFFECT ON ME.

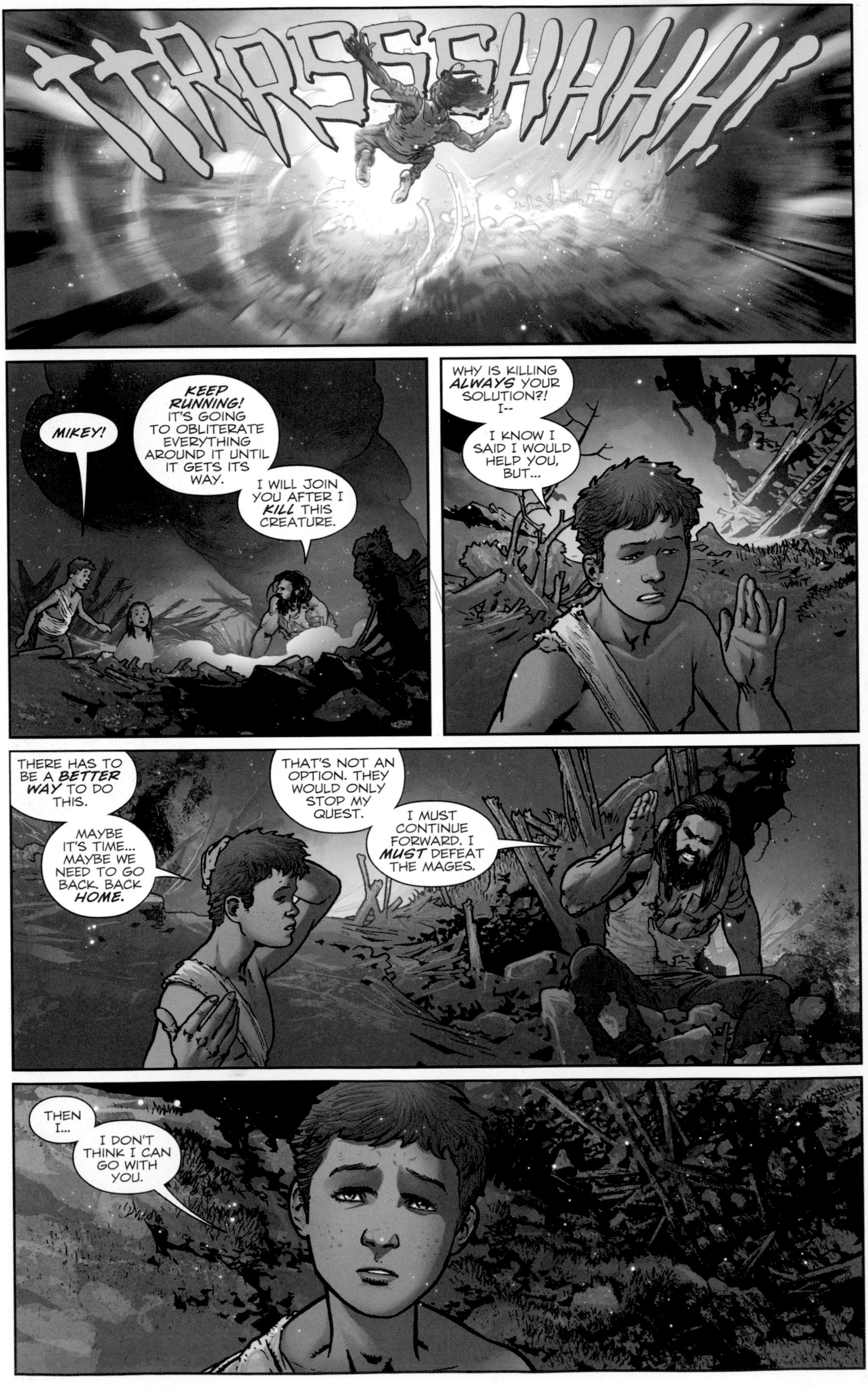
TTRRSSSHHHH!
MIKEY!
KEEP RUNNING! IT'S GOING TO OBLITERATE EVERYTHING AROUND IT UNTIL IT GETS ITS WAY.
I WILL JOIN YOU AFTER I KILL THIS CREATURE.
WHY IS KILLING ALWAYS YOUR SOLUTION?! I--
I KNOW I SAID I WOULD HELP YOU, BUT...
THERE HAS TO BE A BETTER WAY TO DO THIS.
MAYBE IT'S TIME... MAYBE WE NEED TO GO BACK. BACK HOME.
THAT'S NOT AN OPTION. THEY WOULD ONLY STOP MY QUEST.
I MUST CONTINUE FORWARD. I MUST DEFEAT THE MAGES.
THEN I...
I DON'T THINK I CAN GO WITH YOU.

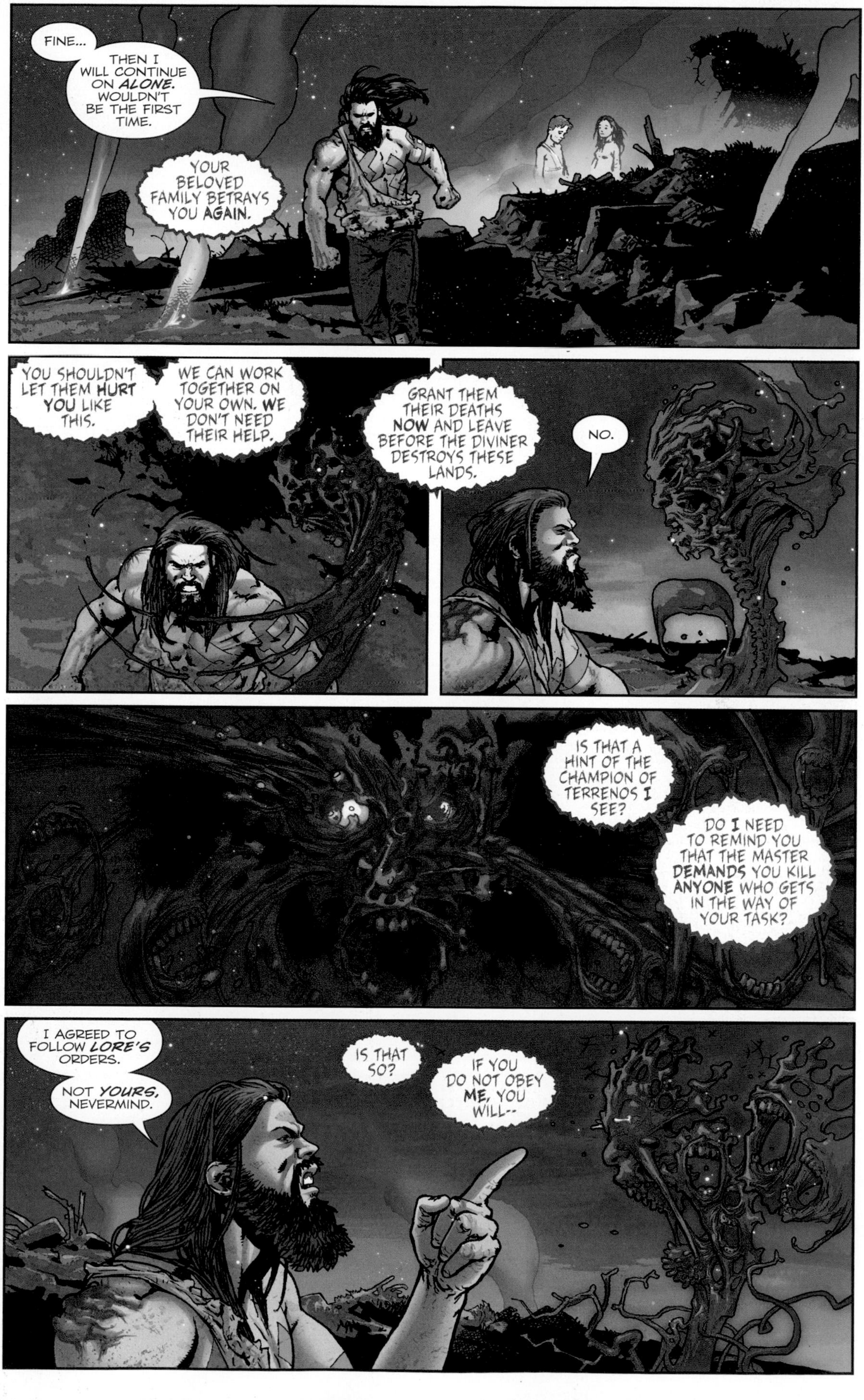
FINE...
THEN I WILL CONTINUE ON ALONE. WOULDN'T BE THE FIRST TIME.
YOUR BELOVED FAMILY BETRAYS YOU AGAIN.
YOU SHOULDN'T LET THEM HURT YOU LIKE THIS.
WE CAN WORK TOGETHER ON YOUR OWN. WE DON'T NEED THEIR HELP.
GRANT THEM THEIR DEATHS NOW AND LEAVE BEFORE THE DIVINER DESTROYS THESE LANDS.
NO.
IS THAT A HINT OF THE CHAMPION OF TERRENOS I SEE?
DO I NEED TO REMIND YOU THAT THE MASTER DEMANDS YOU KILL ANYONE WHO GETS IN THE WAY OF YOUR TASK?
I AGREED TO FOLLOW LORE'S ORDERS.
NOT YOURS, NEVERMIND.
IS THAT SO?
IF YOU DO NOT OBEY ME, YOU WILL--

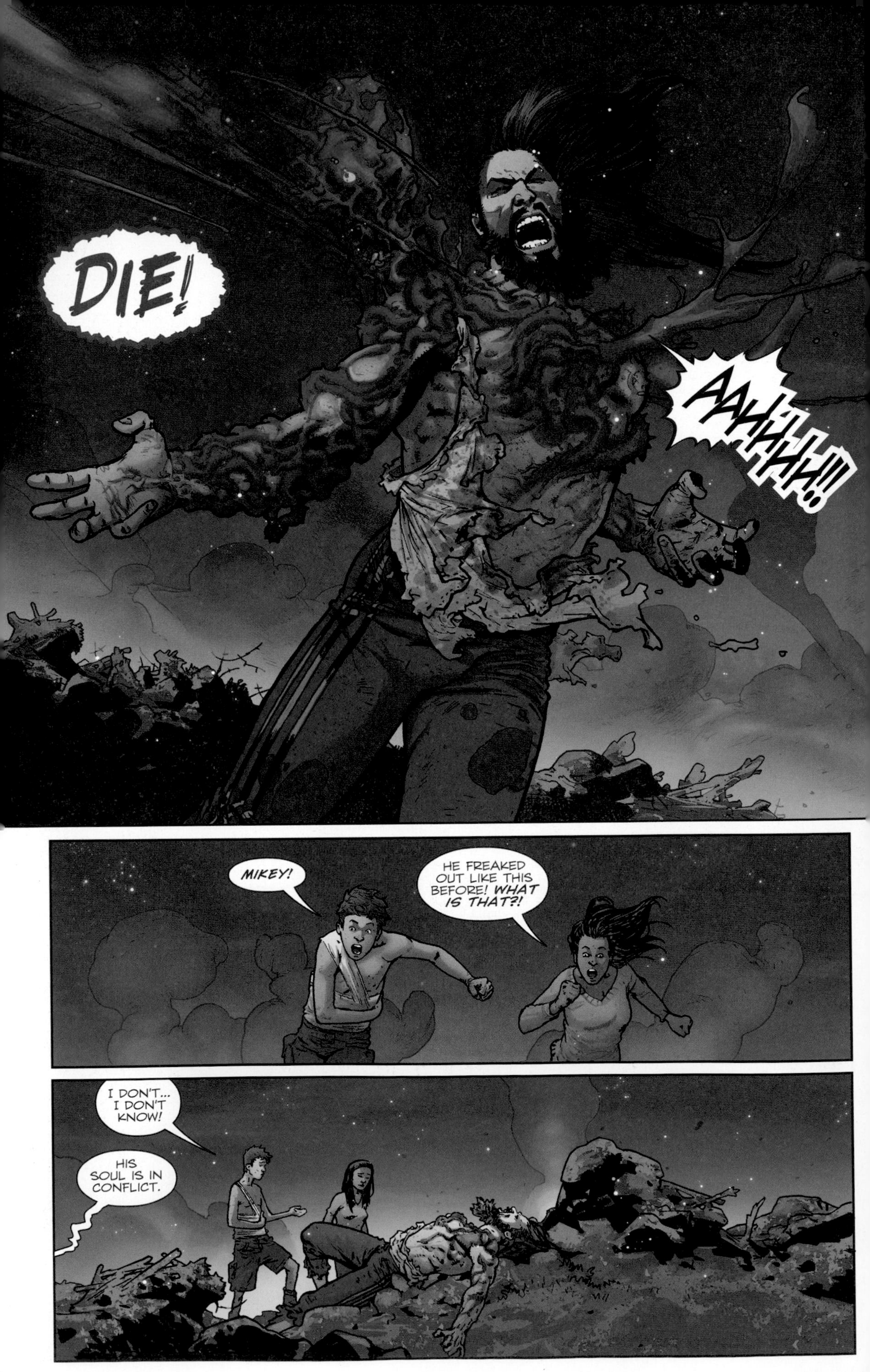
DIE!
AAHHHH!!
MIKEY!
HE FREAKED OUT LIKE THIS BEFORE! WHAT IS THAT?!
I DON'T... I DON'T KNOW!
HIS SOUL IS IN CONFLICT.

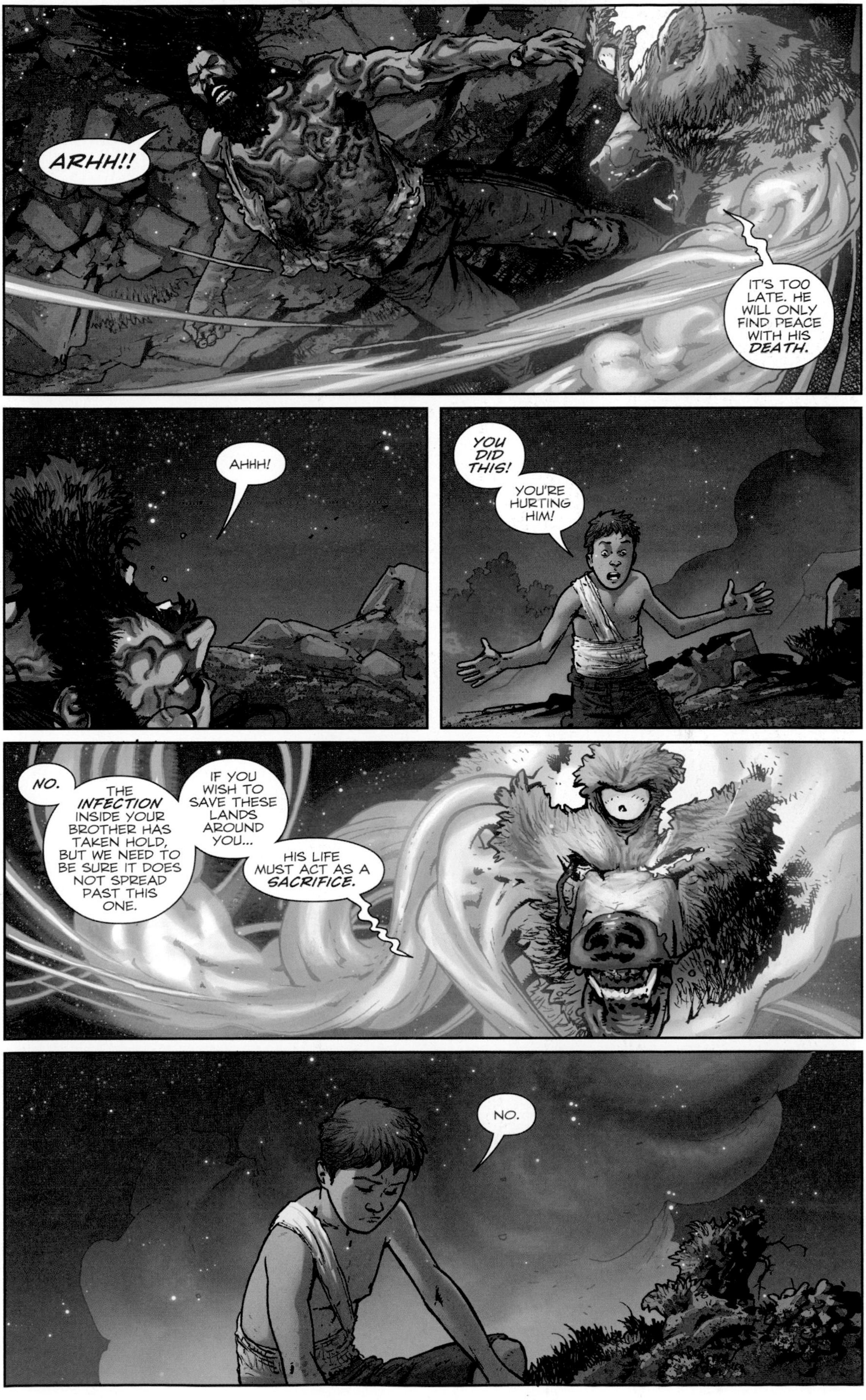
ARHH!!
IT'S TOO LATE. HE WILL ONLY FIND PEACE WITH HIS *DEATH.*
AHHH!
YOU DID THIS!
YOU'RE HURTING HIM!
NO.
THE *INFECTION* INSIDE YOUR BROTHER HAS TAKEN HOLD, BUT WE NEED TO BE SURE IT DOES NOT SPREAD PAST THIS ONE.
IF YOU WISH TO SAVE THESE LANDS AROUND YOU...
HIS LIFE MUST ACT AS A *SACRIFICE.*
NO.

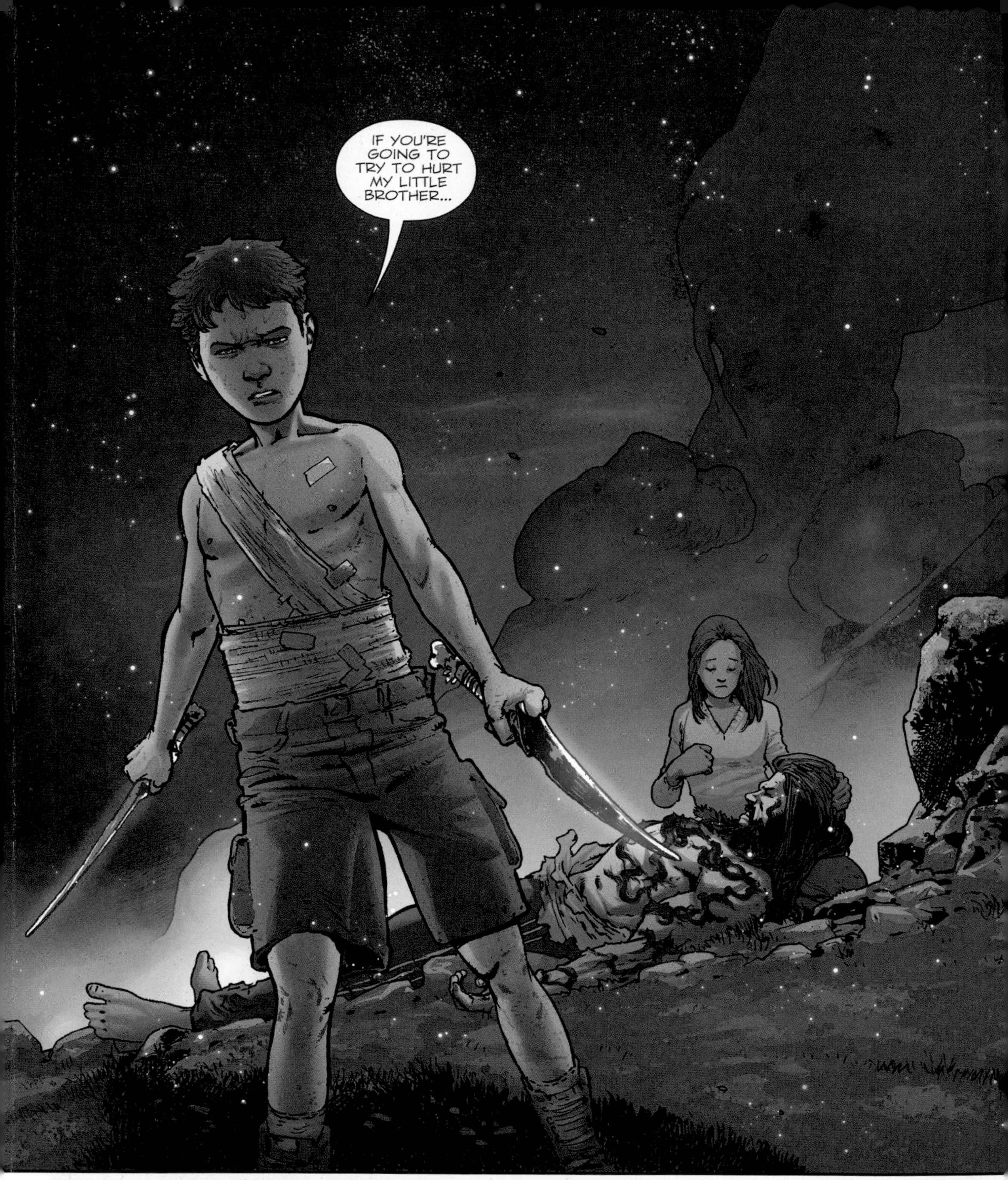
IF YOU'RE GOING TO TRY TO HURT MY LITTLE BROTHER...

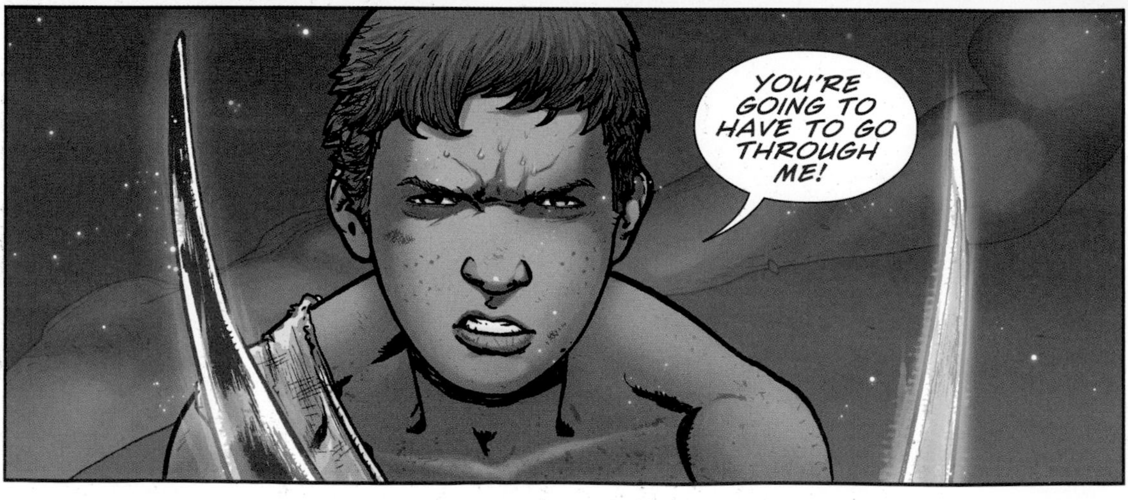
YOU'RE GOING TO HAVE TO GO THROUGH ME!

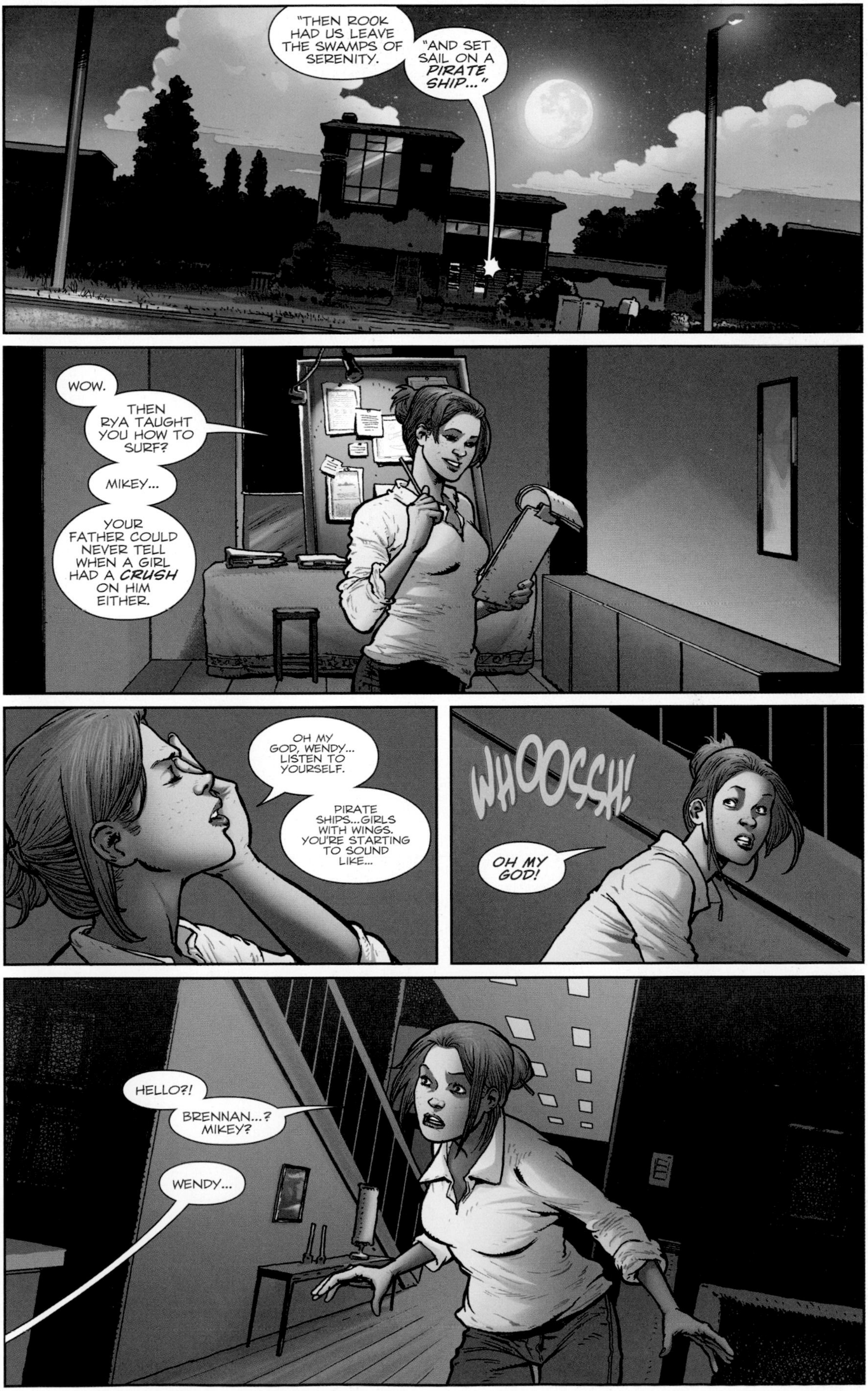
"THEN ROOK HAD US LEAVE THE SWAMPS OF SERENITY.
"AND SET SAIL ON A PIRATE SHIP..."
WOW.
THEN RYA TAUGHT YOU HOW TO SURF?
MIKEY...
YOUR FATHER COULD NEVER TELL WHEN A GIRL HAD A CRUSH ON HIM EITHER.
OH MY GOD, WENDY... LISTEN TO YOURSELF.
PIRATE SHIPS...GIRLS WITH WINGS. YOU'RE STARTING TO SOUND LIKE...
WHOOSSH!
OH MY GOD!
HELLO?!
BRENNAN...? MIKEY?
WENDY...

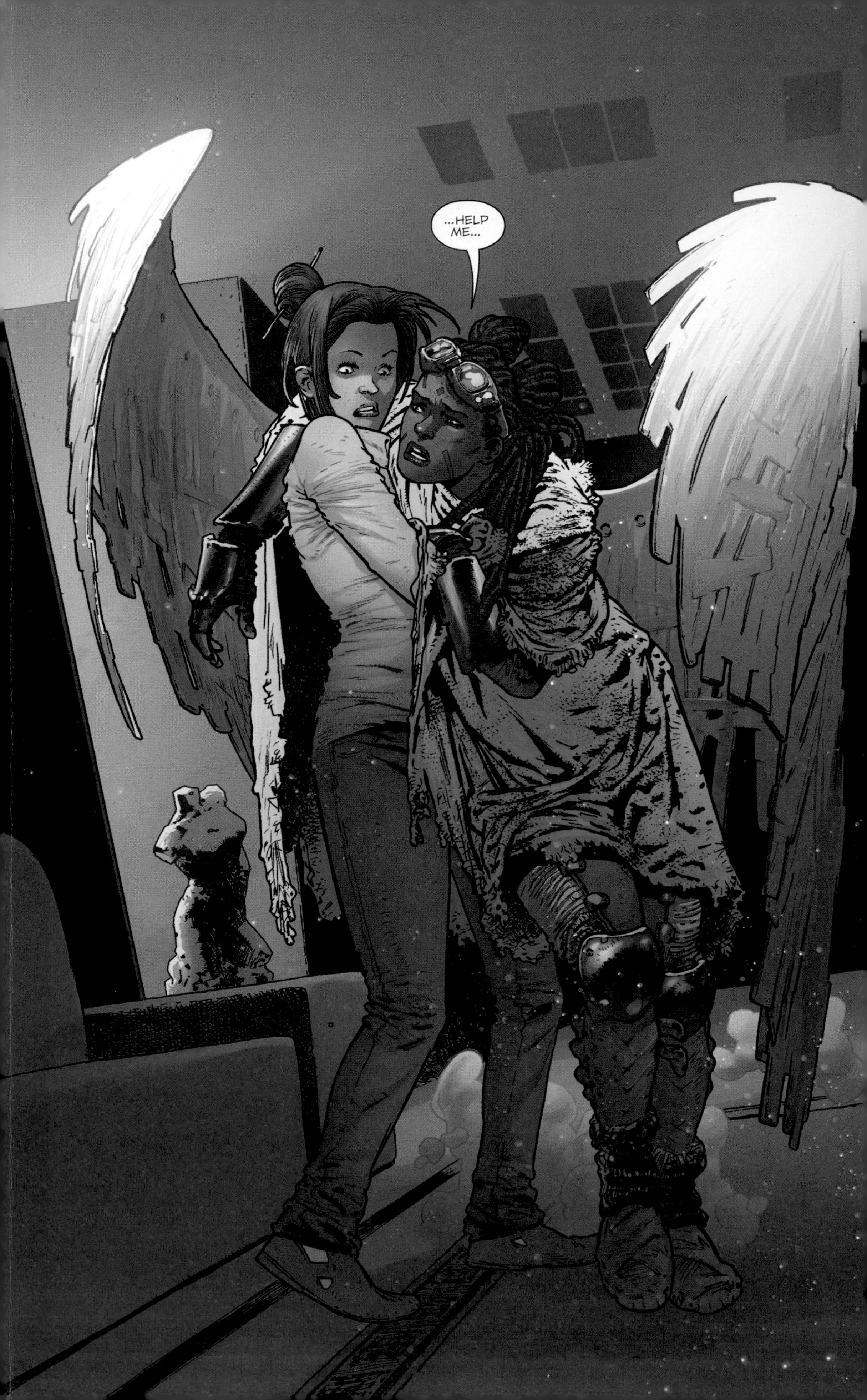
...HELP ME...

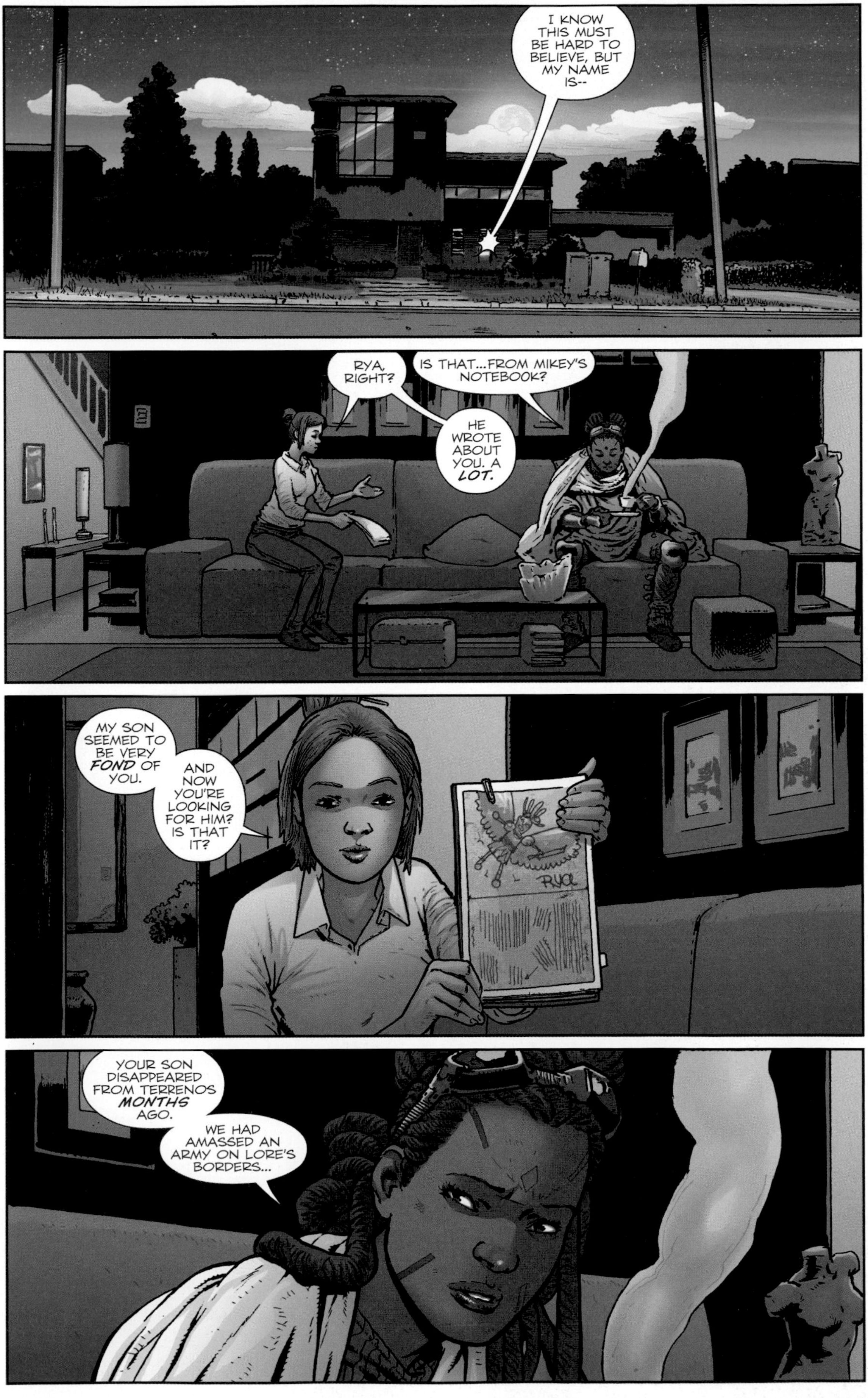
I KNOW THIS MUST BE HARD TO BELIEVE, BUT MY NAME IS--
RYA, RIGHT?
IS THAT...FROM MIKEY'S NOTEBOOK?
HE WROTE ABOUT YOU. A LOT.
MY SON SEEMED TO BE VERY FOND OF YOU.
AND NOW YOU'RE LOOKING FOR HIM? IS THAT IT?
RYA
YOUR SON DISAPPEARED FROM TERRENOS MONTHS AGO.
WE HAD AMASSED AN ARMY ON LORE'S BORDERS...

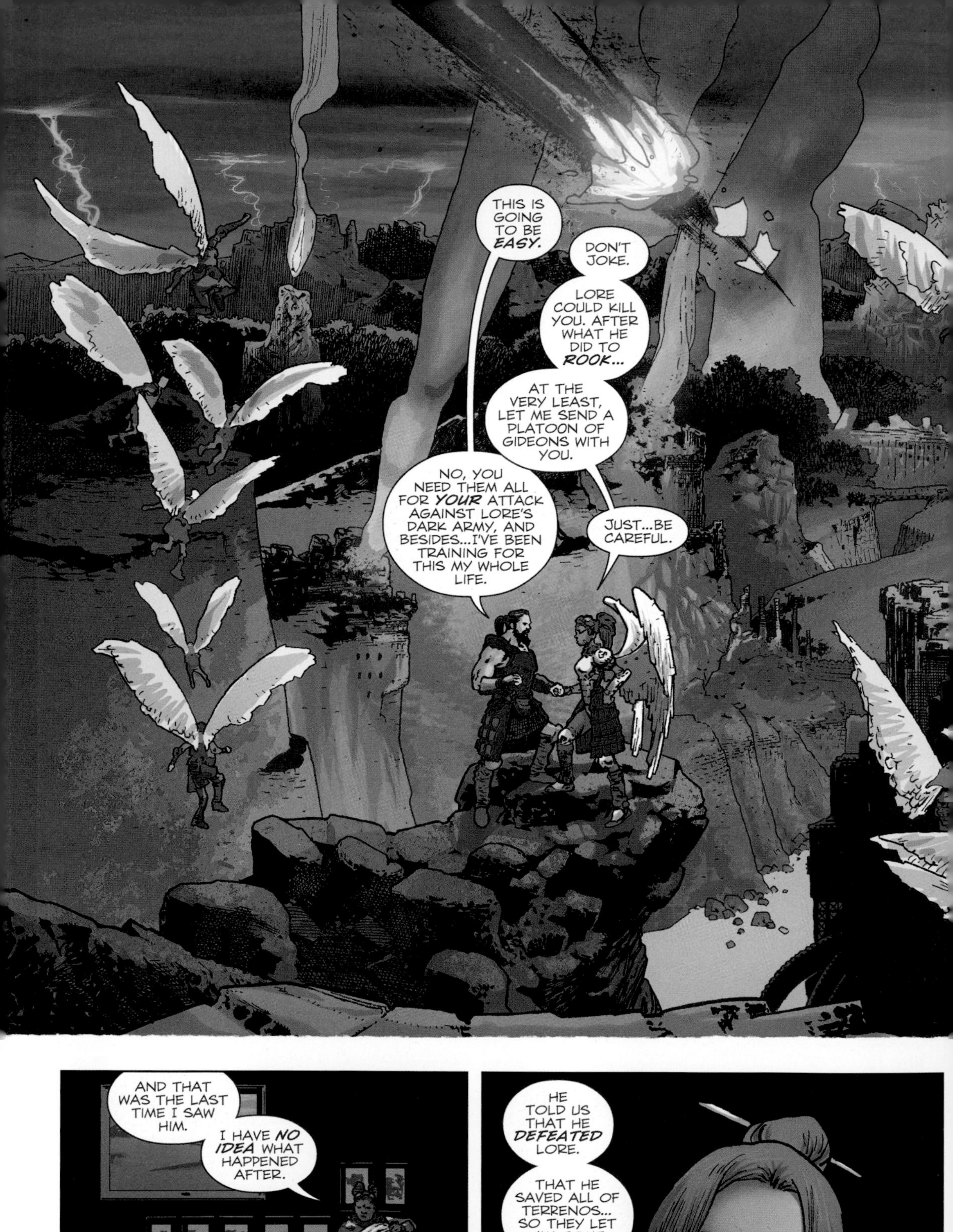
THIS IS GOING TO BE EASY.
DON'T JOKE.
LORE COULD KILL YOU. AFTER WHAT HE DID TO ROOK...
AT THE VERY LEAST, LET ME SEND A PLATOON OF GIDEONS WITH YOU.
NO, YOU NEED THEM ALL FOR YOUR ATTACK AGAINST LORE'S DARK ARMY, AND BESIDES...I'VE BEEN TRAINING FOR THIS MY WHOLE LIFE.
JUST...BE CAREFUL.

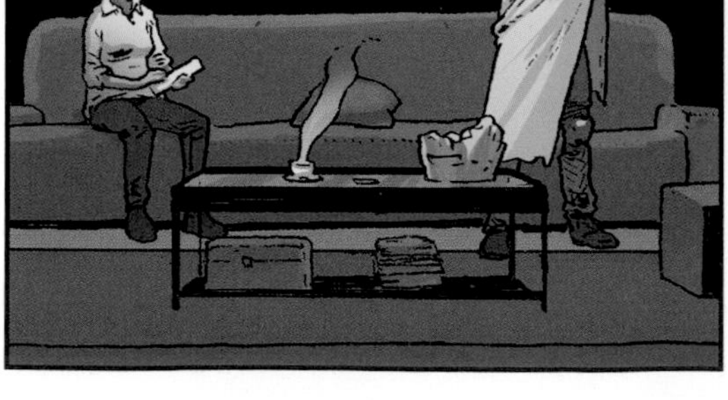
AND THAT WAS THE LAST TIME I SAW HIM.
I HAVE NO IDEA WHAT HAPPENED AFTER.

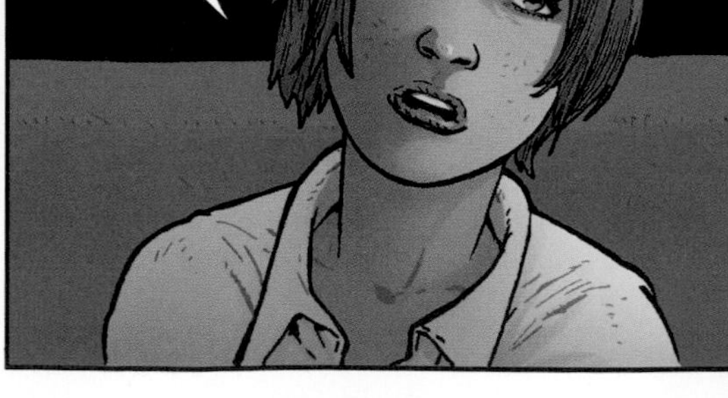
HE TOLD US THAT HE DEFEATED LORE.
THAT HE SAVED ALL OF TERRENOS... SO THEY LET HIM COME HOME.

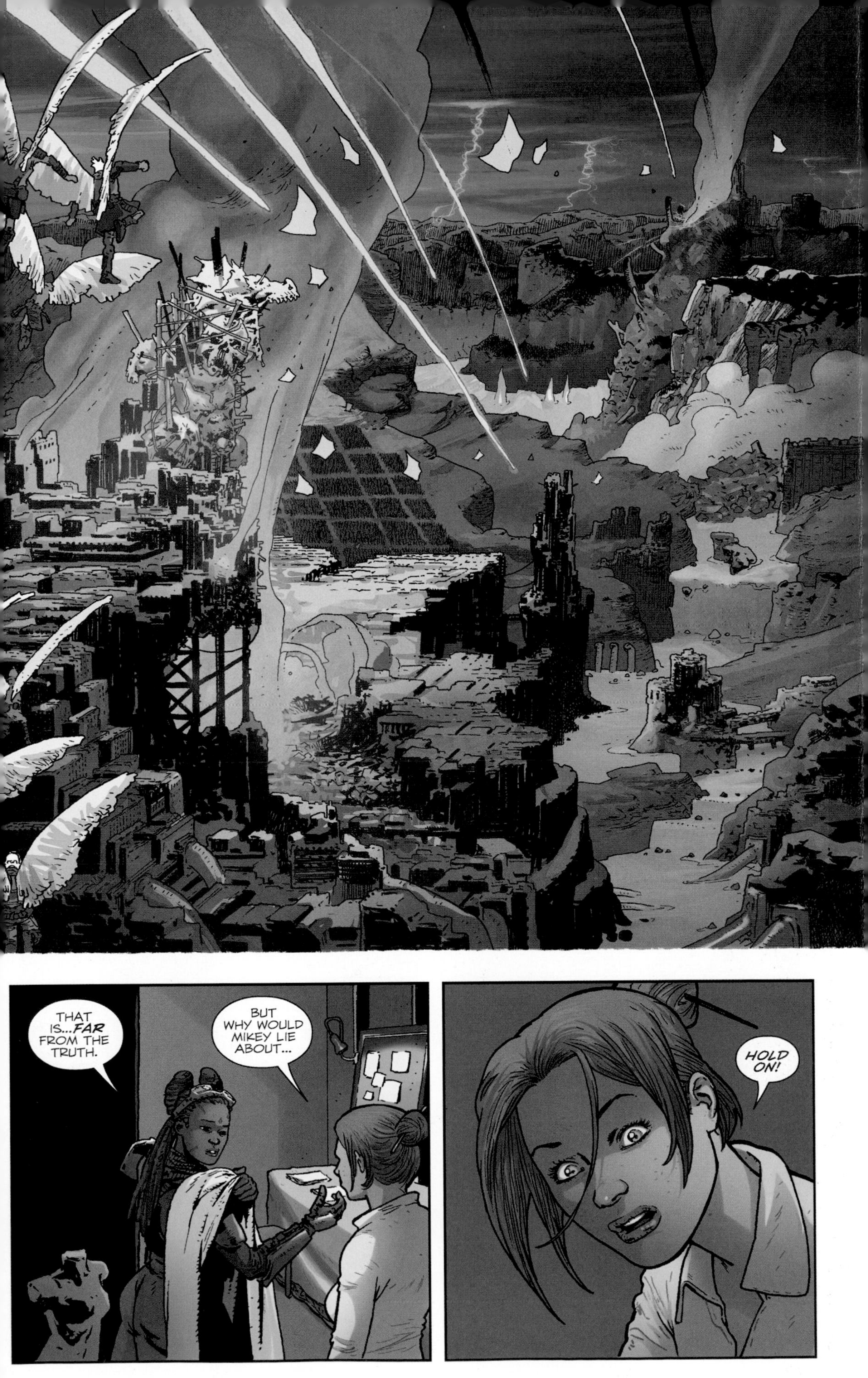
THAT IS...FAR FROM THE TRUTH.
BUT WHY WOULD MIKEY LIE ABOUT...
HOLD ON!

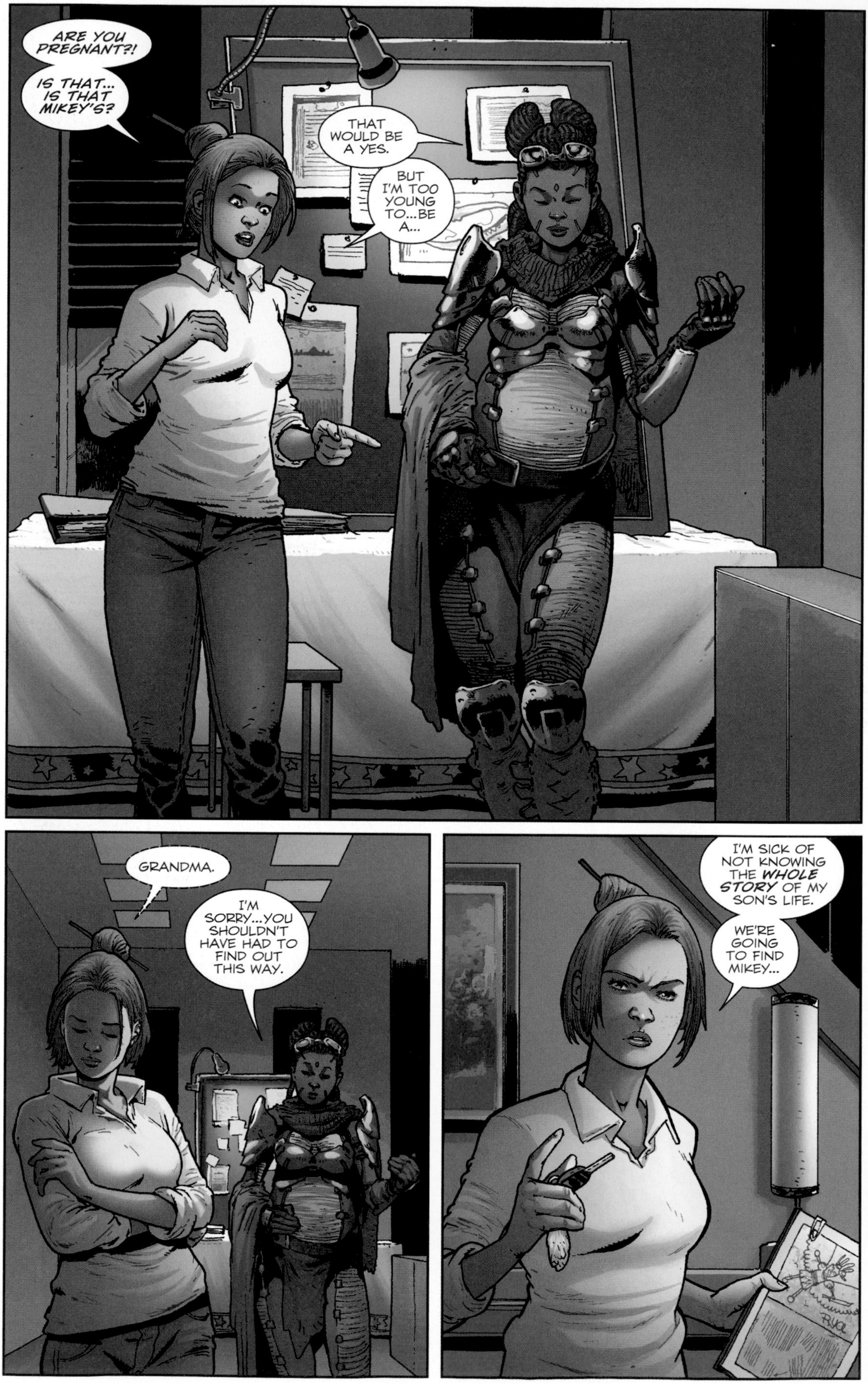
ARE YOU PREGNANT?!
IS THAT... IS THAT MIKEY'S?
THAT WOULD BE A YES.
BUT I'M TOO YOUNG TO...BE A...
GRANDMA.
I'M SORRY...YOU SHOULDN'T HAVE HAD TO FIND OUT THIS WAY.
I'M SICK OF NOT KNOWING THE WHOLE STORY OF MY SON'S LIFE.
WE'RE GOING TO FIND MIKEY...

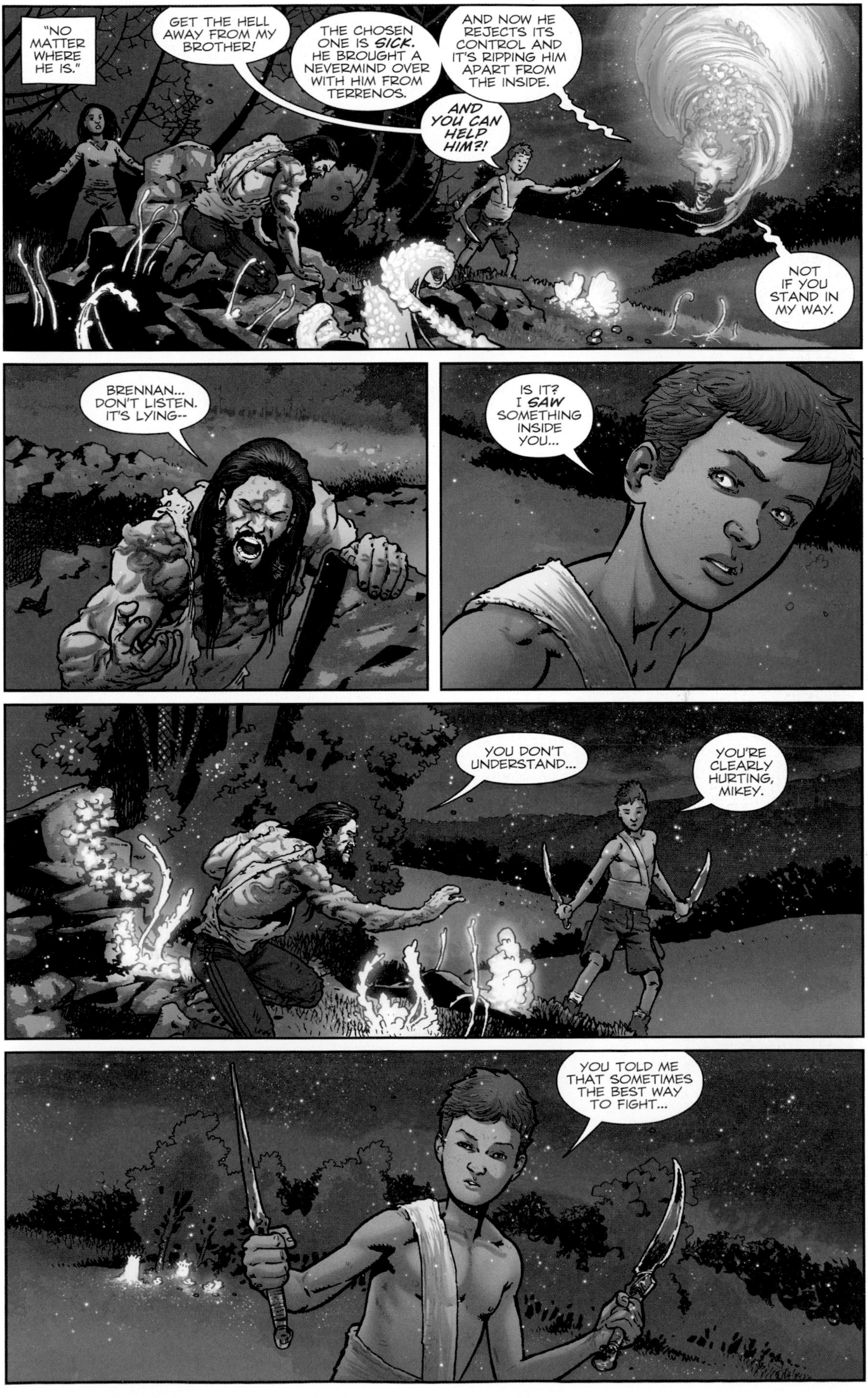
"NO MATTER WHERE HE IS."
GET THE HELL AWAY FROM MY BROTHER!
THE CHOSEN ONE IS SICK. HE BROUGHT A NEVERMIND OVER WITH HIM FROM TERRENOS.
AND NOW HE REJECTS ITS CONTROL AND IT'S RIPPING HIM APART FROM THE INSIDE.
AND YOU CAN HELP HIM?!
NOT IF YOU STAND IN MY WAY.
BRENNAN... DON'T LISTEN. IT'S LYING--
IS IT? I SAW SOMETHING INSIDE YOU...
YOU DON'T UNDERSTAND...
YOU'RE CLEARLY HURTING, MIKEY.
YOU TOLD ME THAT SOMETIMES THE BEST WAY TO FIGHT...

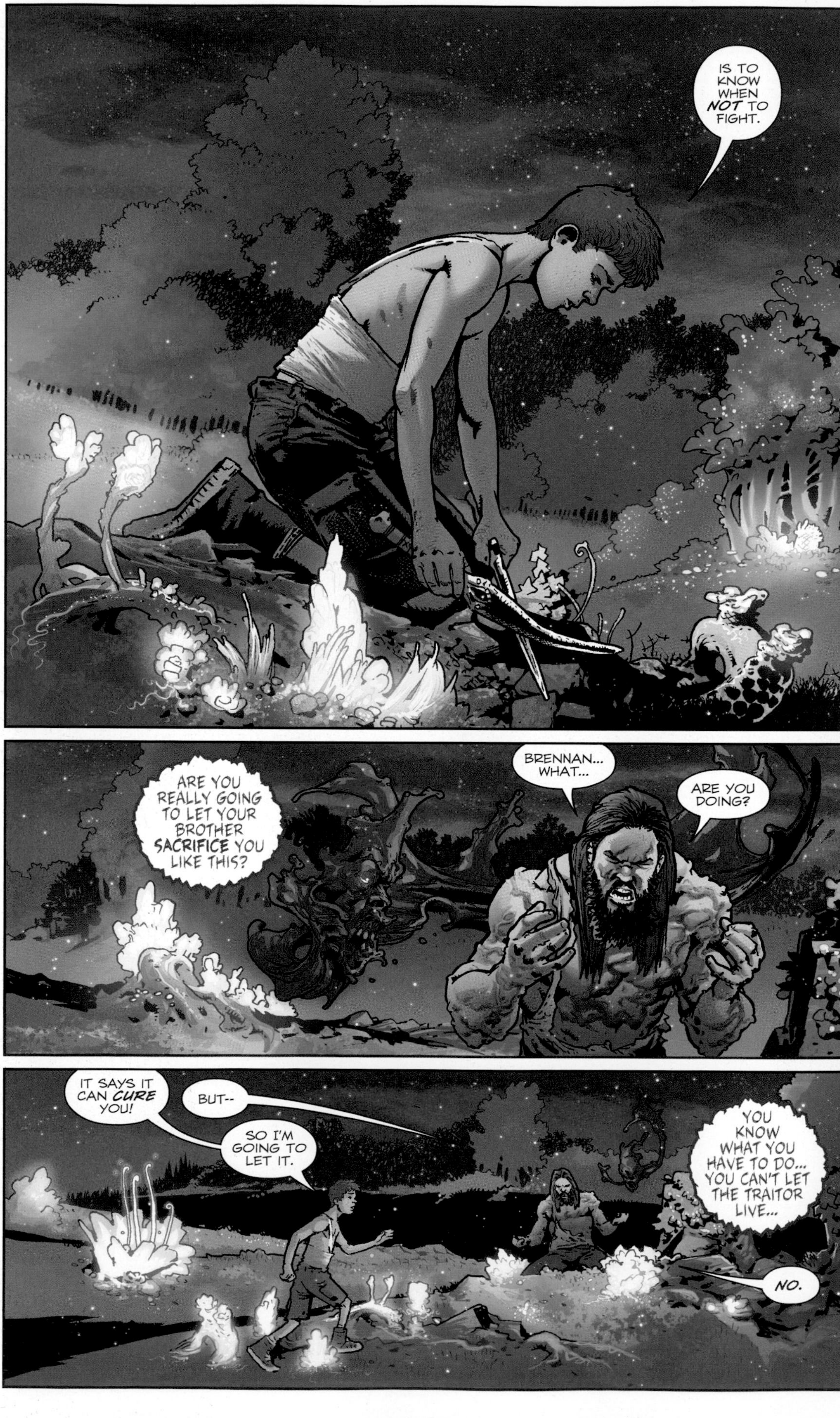
IS TO KNOW WHEN ***NOT*** TO FIGHT.
ARE YOU REALLY GOING TO LET YOUR BROTHER **SACRIFICE** YOU LIKE THIS?
BRENNAN... WHAT...
ARE YOU DOING?
IT SAYS IT CAN ***CURE*** YOU!
BUT--
SO I'M GOING TO LET IT.
YOU KNOW WHAT YOU HAVE TO DO... YOU CAN'T LET THE TRAITOR LIVE...
NO.

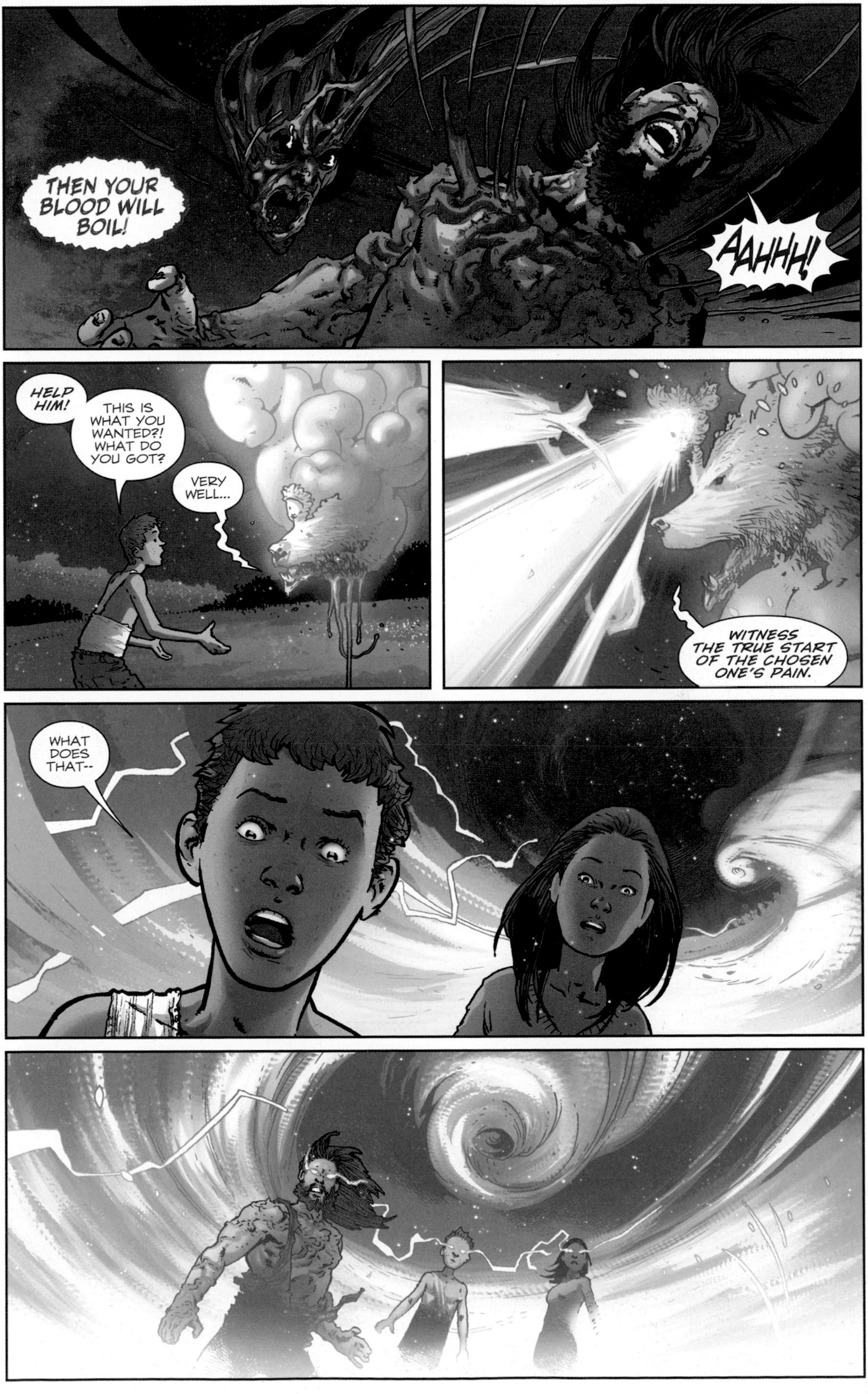
THEN YOUR BLOOD WILL BOIL!
AAHHH!
HELP HIM!
THIS IS WHAT YOU WANTED?! WHAT DO YOU GOT?
VERY WELL...
WITNESS THE TRUE START OF THE CHOSEN ONE'S PAIN.
WHAT DOES THAT--

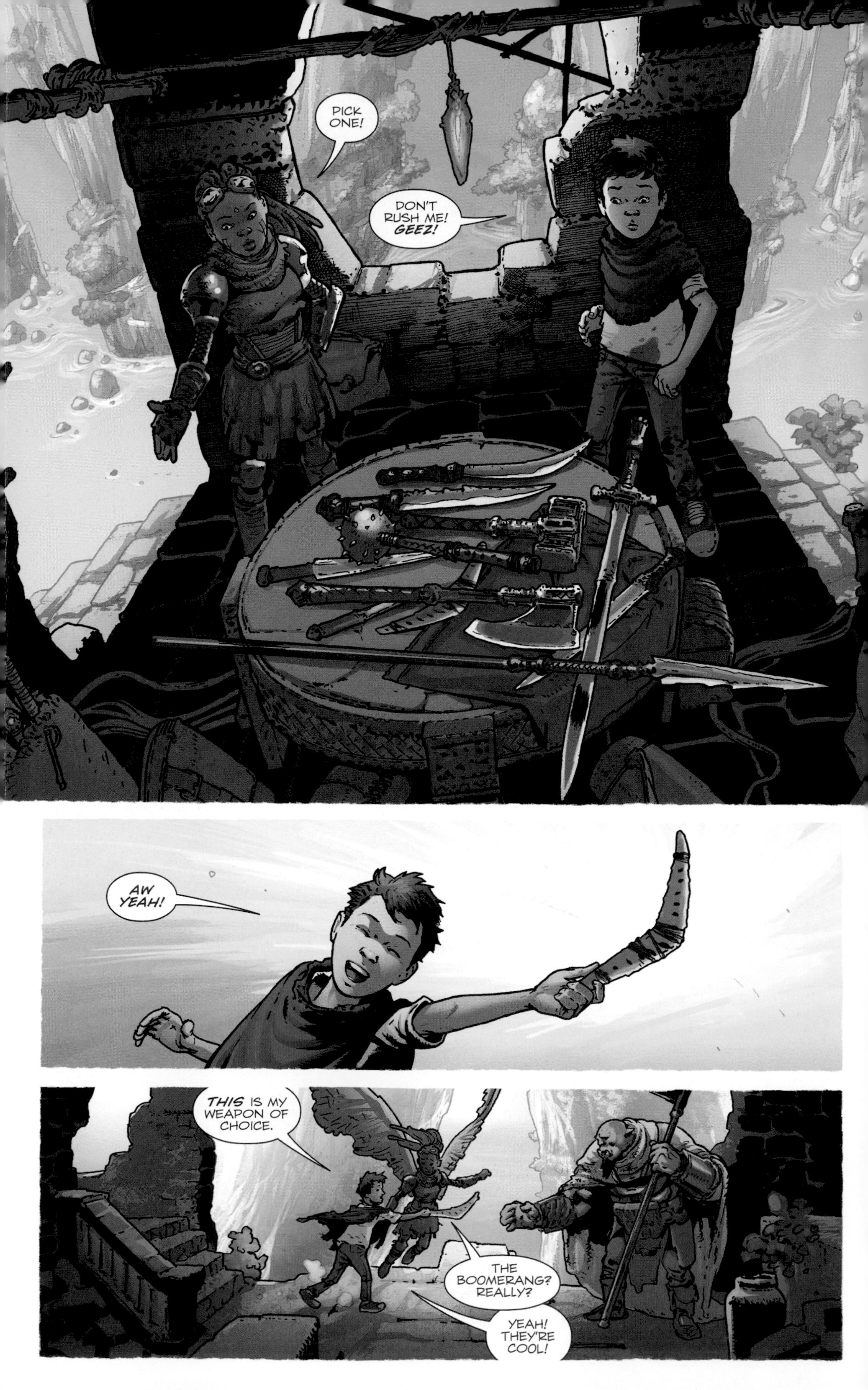
PICK ONE!
DON'T RUSH ME! GEEZ!
AW YEAH!
THIS IS MY WEAPON OF CHOICE.
THE BOOMERANG? REALLY?
YEAH! THEY'RE COOL!

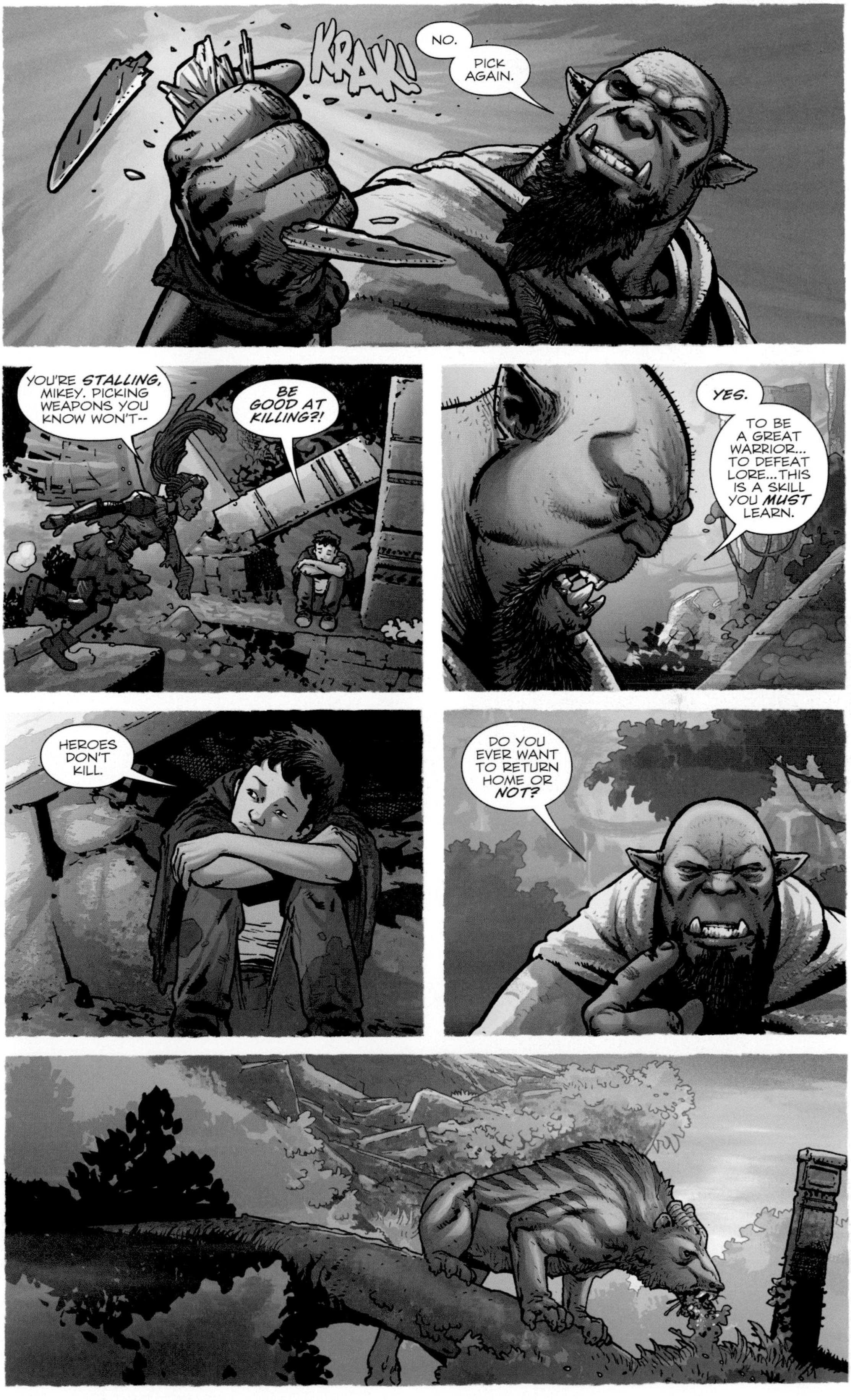
KRAK!
NO.
PICK AGAIN.
YOU'RE STALLING, MIKEY. PICKING WEAPONS YOU KNOW WON'T--
BE GOOD AT KILLING?!
YES.
TO BE A GREAT WARRIOR... TO DEFEAT LORE...THIS IS A SKILL YOU MUST LEARN.
HEROES DON'T KILL.
DO YOU EVER WANT TO RETURN HOME OR NOT?

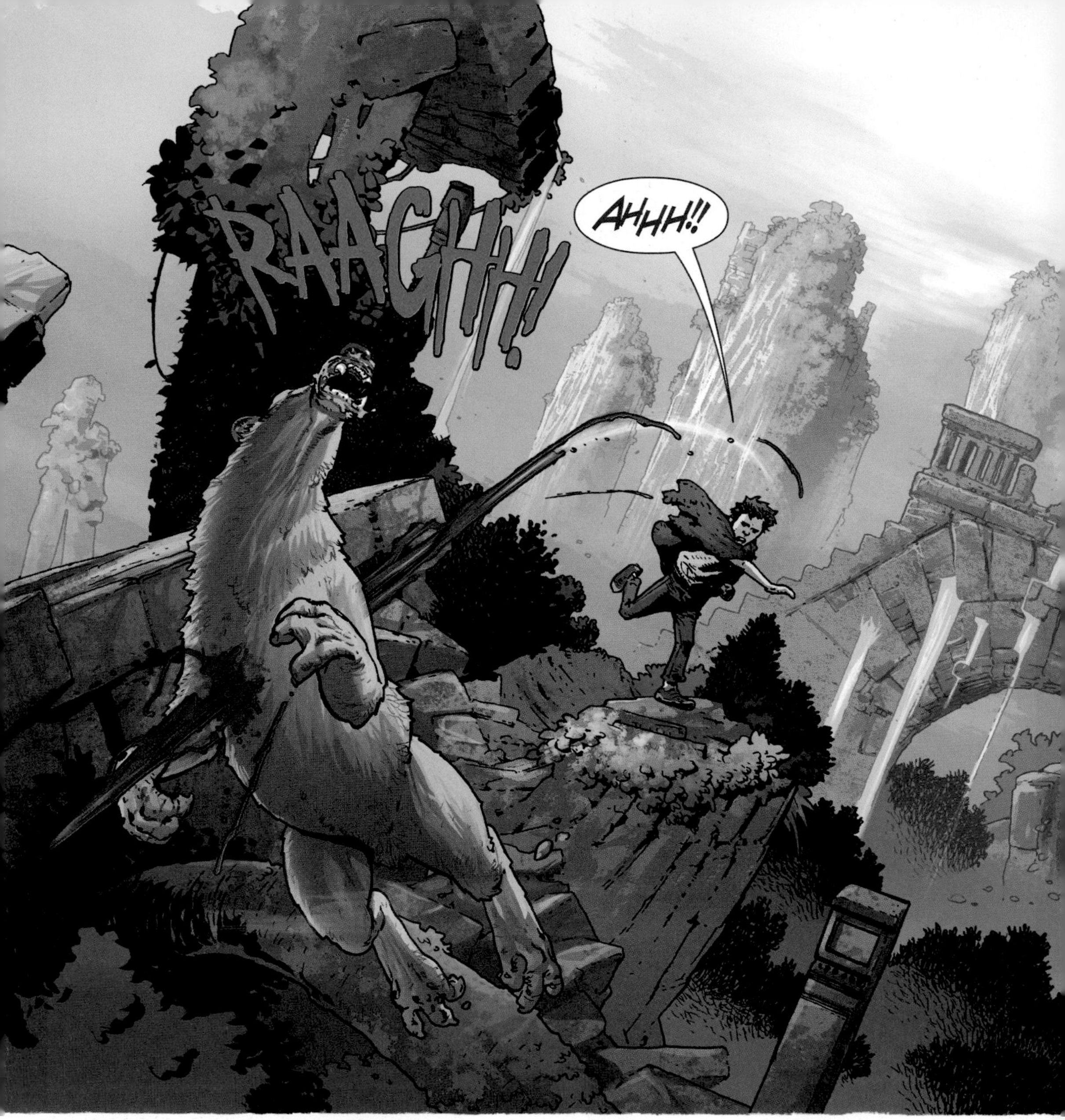
RAAGHH!!
AHHH!!

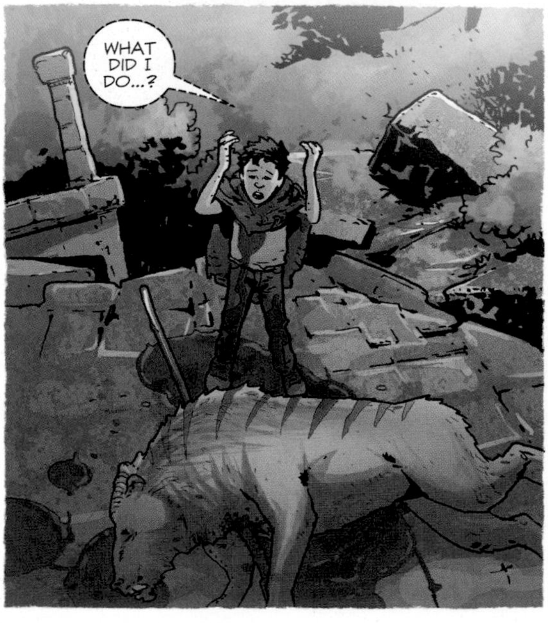
WHAT DID I DO...?

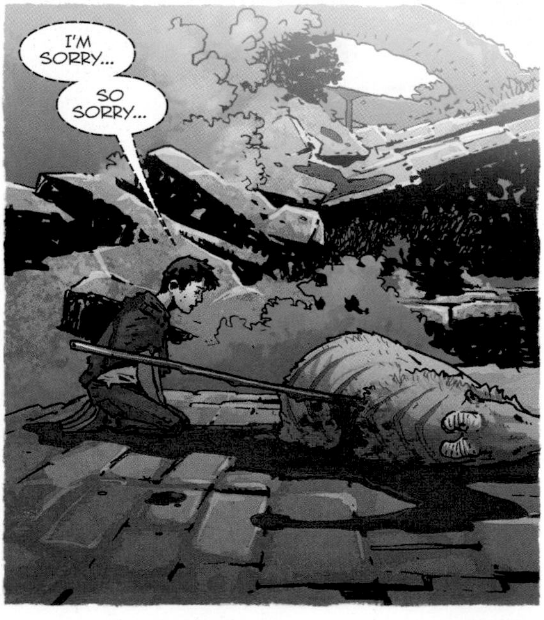
I'M SORRY...
SO SORRY...

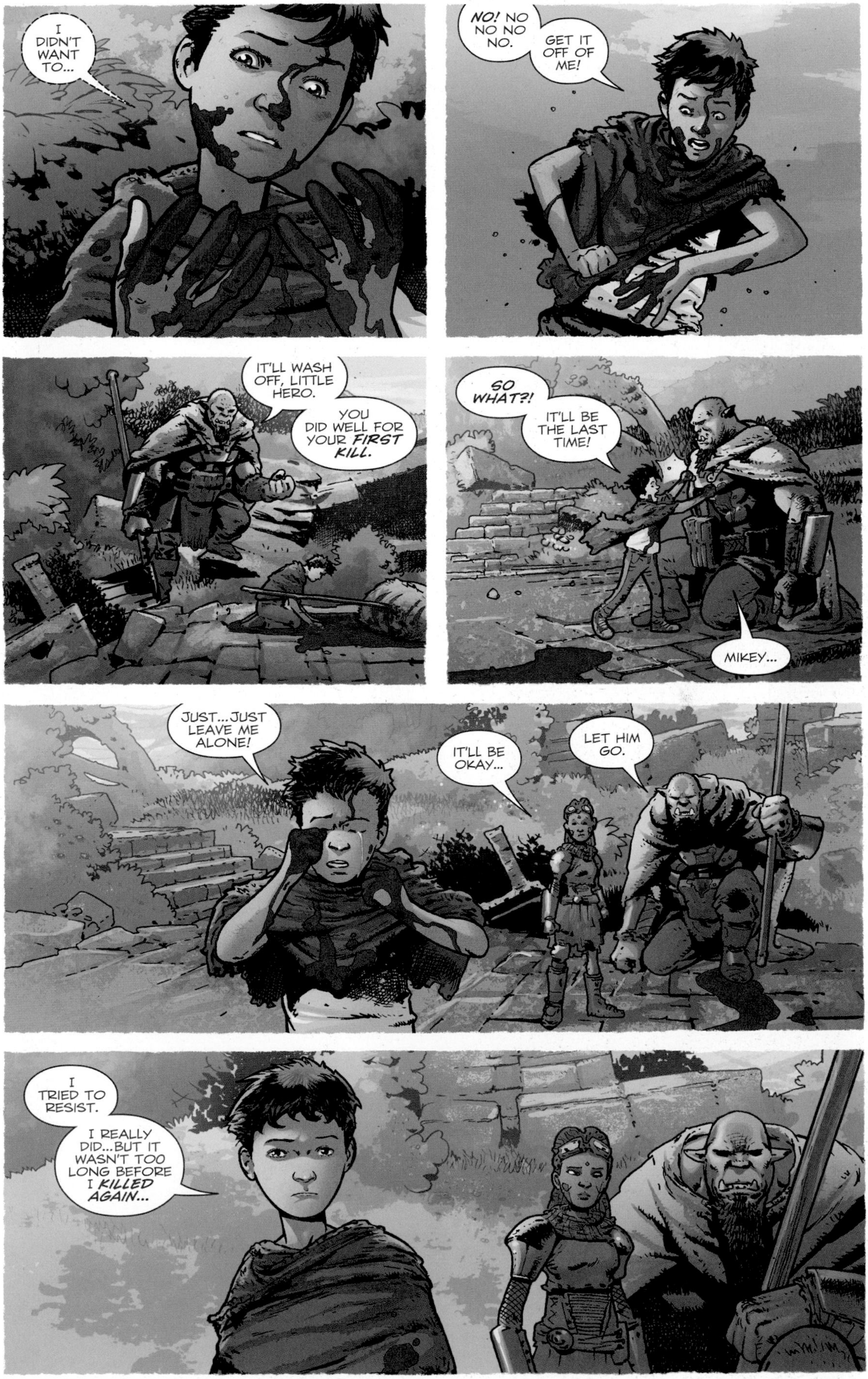

I DIDN'T WANT TO...
NO! NO NO NO NO.
GET IT OFF OF ME!
IT'LL WASH OFF, LITTLE HERO.
YOU DID WELL FOR YOUR FIRST KILL.
SO WHAT?!
IT'LL BE THE LAST TIME!
MIKEY...
JUST...JUST LEAVE ME ALONE!
IT'LL BE OKAY...
LET HIM GO.
I TRIED TO RESIST.
I REALLY DID...BUT IT WASN'T TOO LONG BEFORE I KILLED AGAIN...

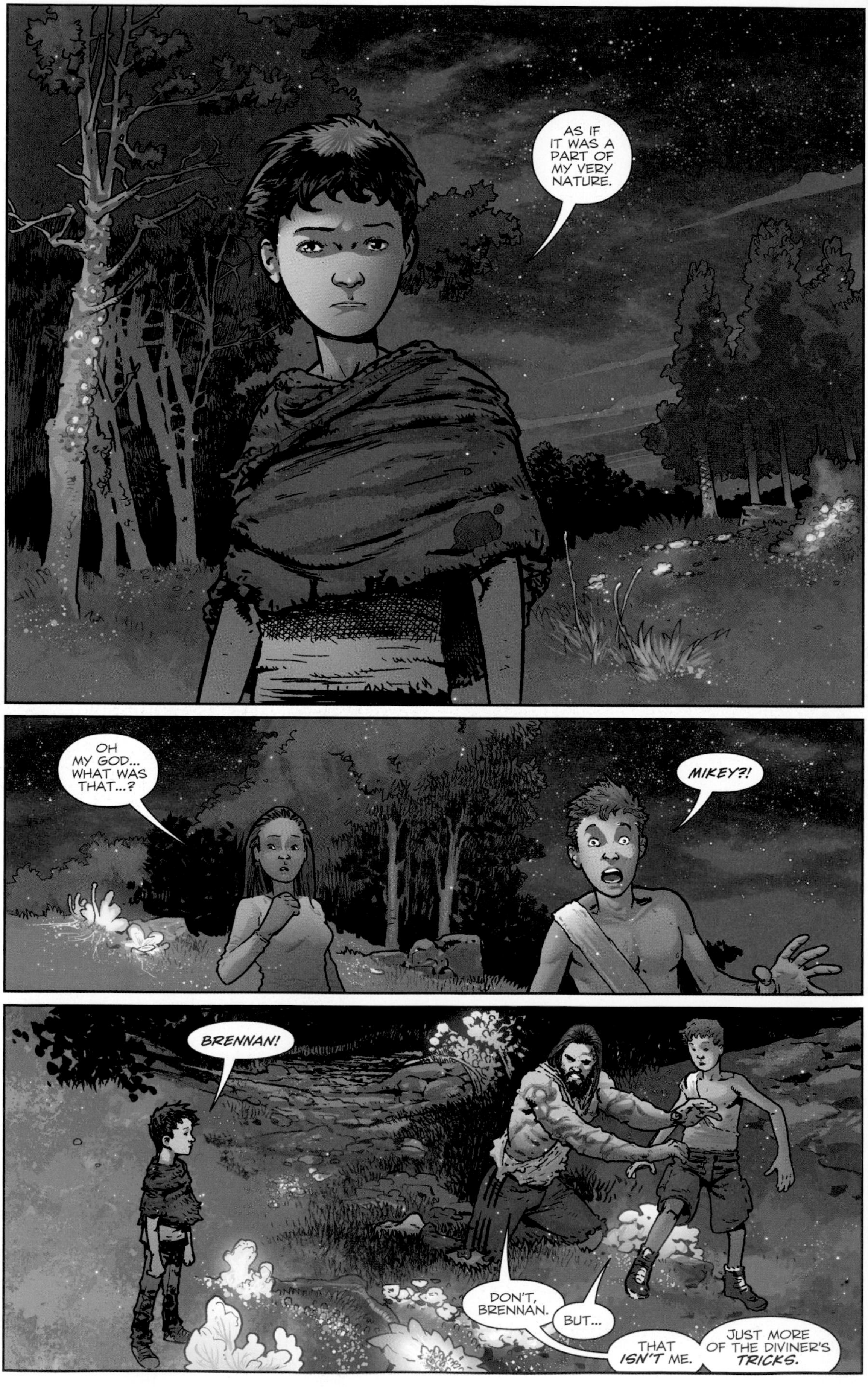
AS IF IT WAS A PART OF MY VERY NATURE.
OH MY GOD... WHAT WAS THAT...?
MIKEY?!
BRENNAN!
DON'T, BRENNAN.
BUT...
THAT ISN'T ME.
JUST MORE OF THE DIVINER'S TRICKS.

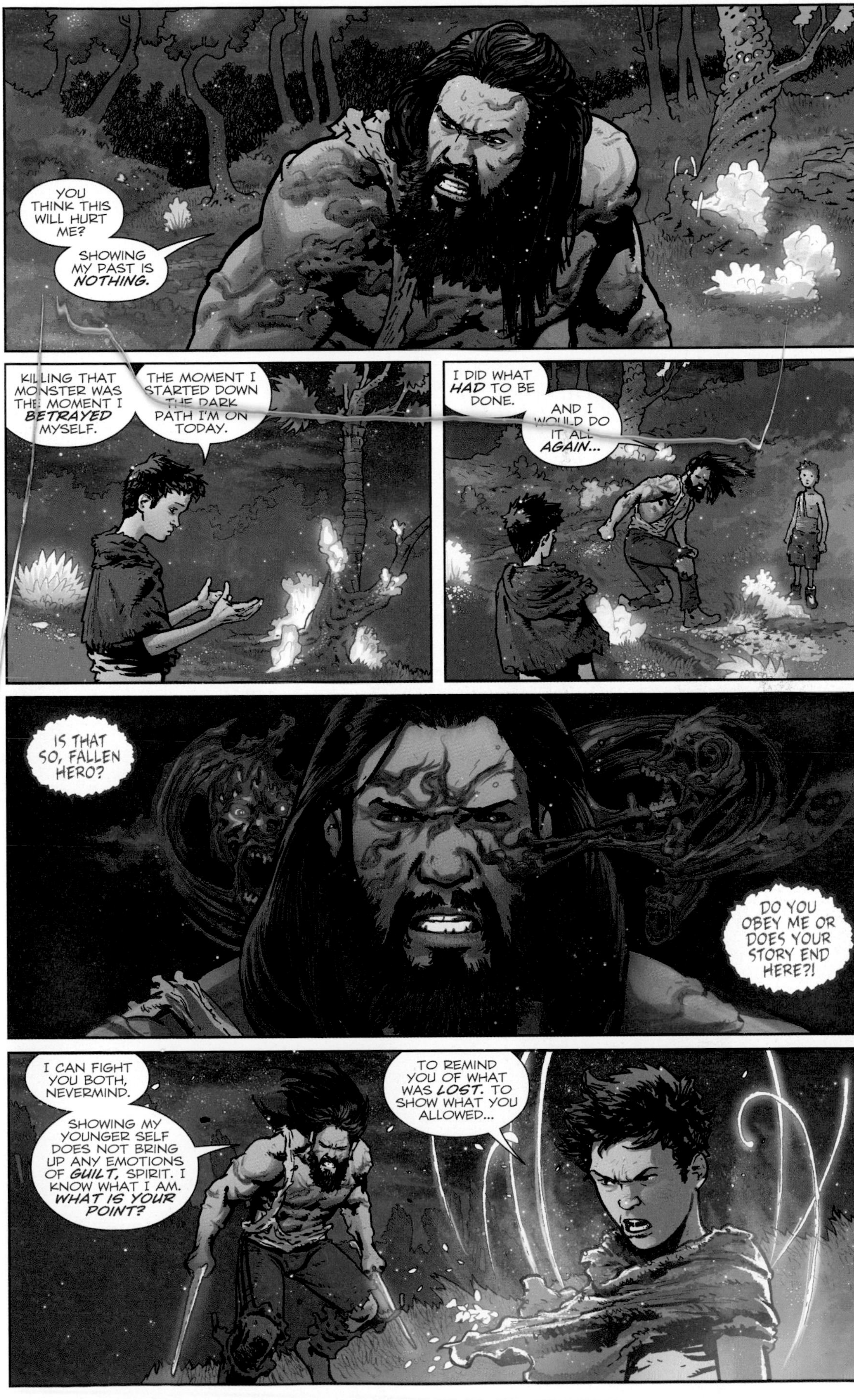
YOU THINK THIS WILL HURT ME?
SHOWING MY PAST IS ***NOTHING.***
KILLING THAT MONSTER WAS THE MOMENT I ***BETRAYED*** MYSELF.
THE MOMENT I STARTED DOWN THE DARK PATH I'M ON TODAY.
I DID WHAT ***HAD*** TO BE DONE.
AND I WOULD DO IT ALL ***AGAIN...***
IS THAT SO, FALLEN HERO?
DO YOU OBEY ME OR DOES YOUR STORY END HERE?!
I CAN FIGHT YOU BOTH, NEVERMIND.
SHOWING MY YOUNGER SELF DOES NOT BRING UP ANY EMOTIONS OF ***GUILT,*** SPIRIT. I KNOW WHAT I AM. ***WHAT IS YOUR POINT?***
TO REMIND YOU OF WHAT WAS ***LOST.*** TO SHOW WHAT YOU ALLOWED...

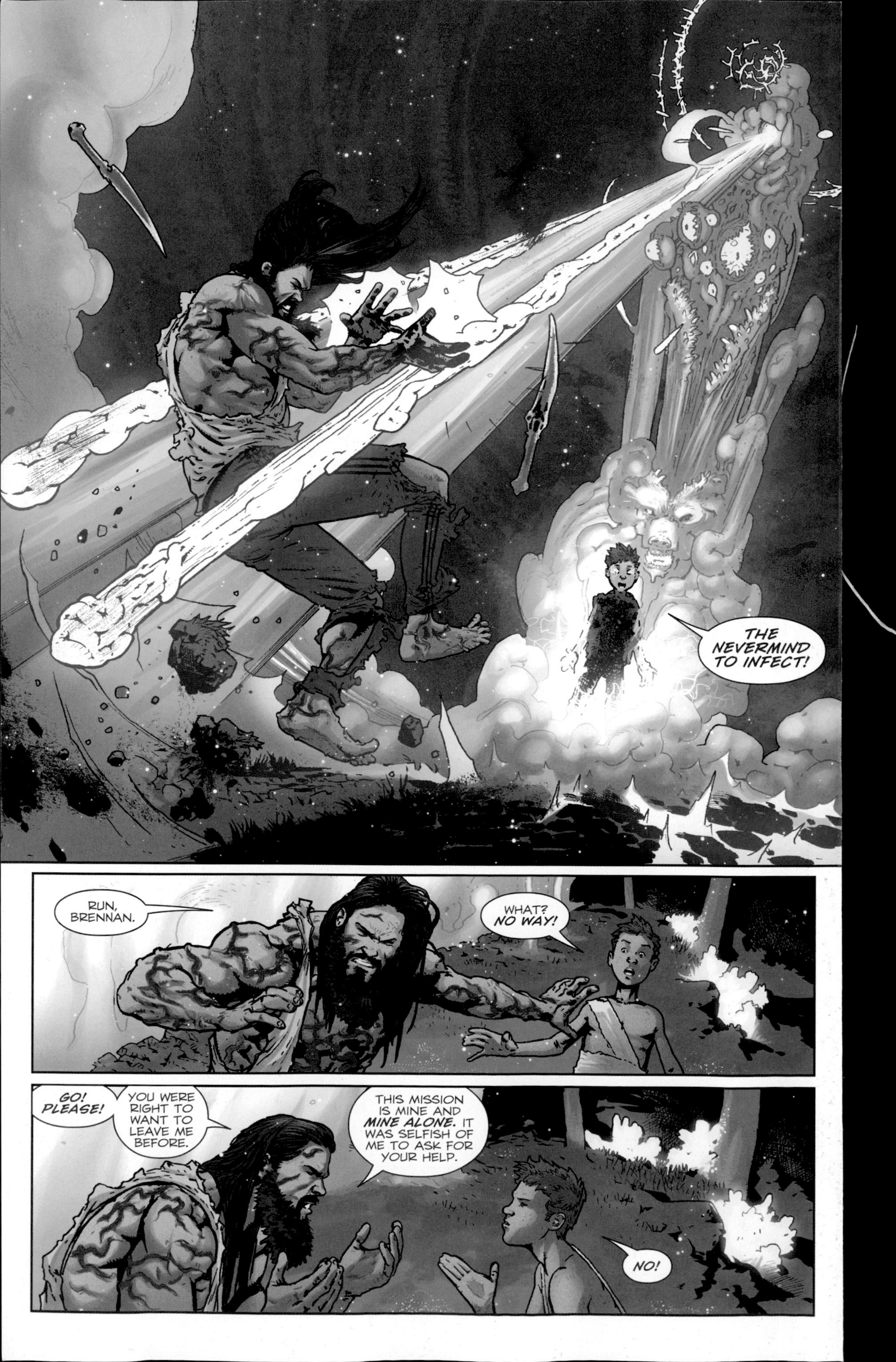
THE NEVERMIND TO INFECT!
RUN, BRENNAN.
WHAT? NO WAY!
GO! PLEASE!
YOU WERE RIGHT TO WANT TO LEAVE ME BEFORE.
THIS MISSION IS MINE AND MINE ALONE. IT WAS SELFISH OF ME TO ASK FOR YOUR HELP.
NO!

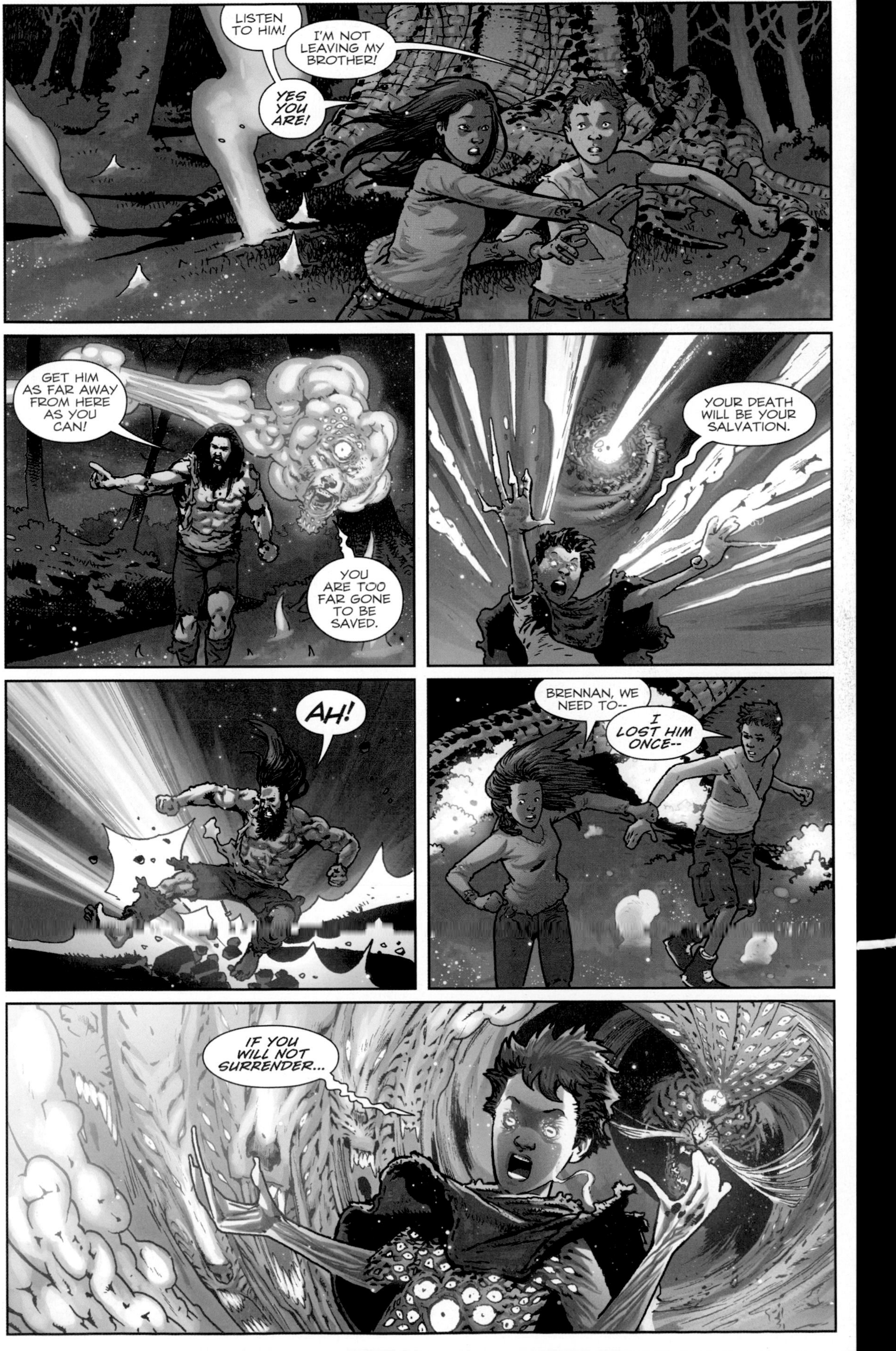
LISTEN TO HIM!
I'M NOT LEAVING MY BROTHER!
YES YOU ARE!
GET HIM AS FAR AWAY FROM HERE AS YOU CAN!
YOU ARE TOO FAR GONE TO BE SAVED.
YOUR DEATH WILL BE YOUR SALVATION.
AH!
BRENNAN, WE NEED TO--
I LOST HIM ONCE--
IF YOU WILL NOT SURRENDER...

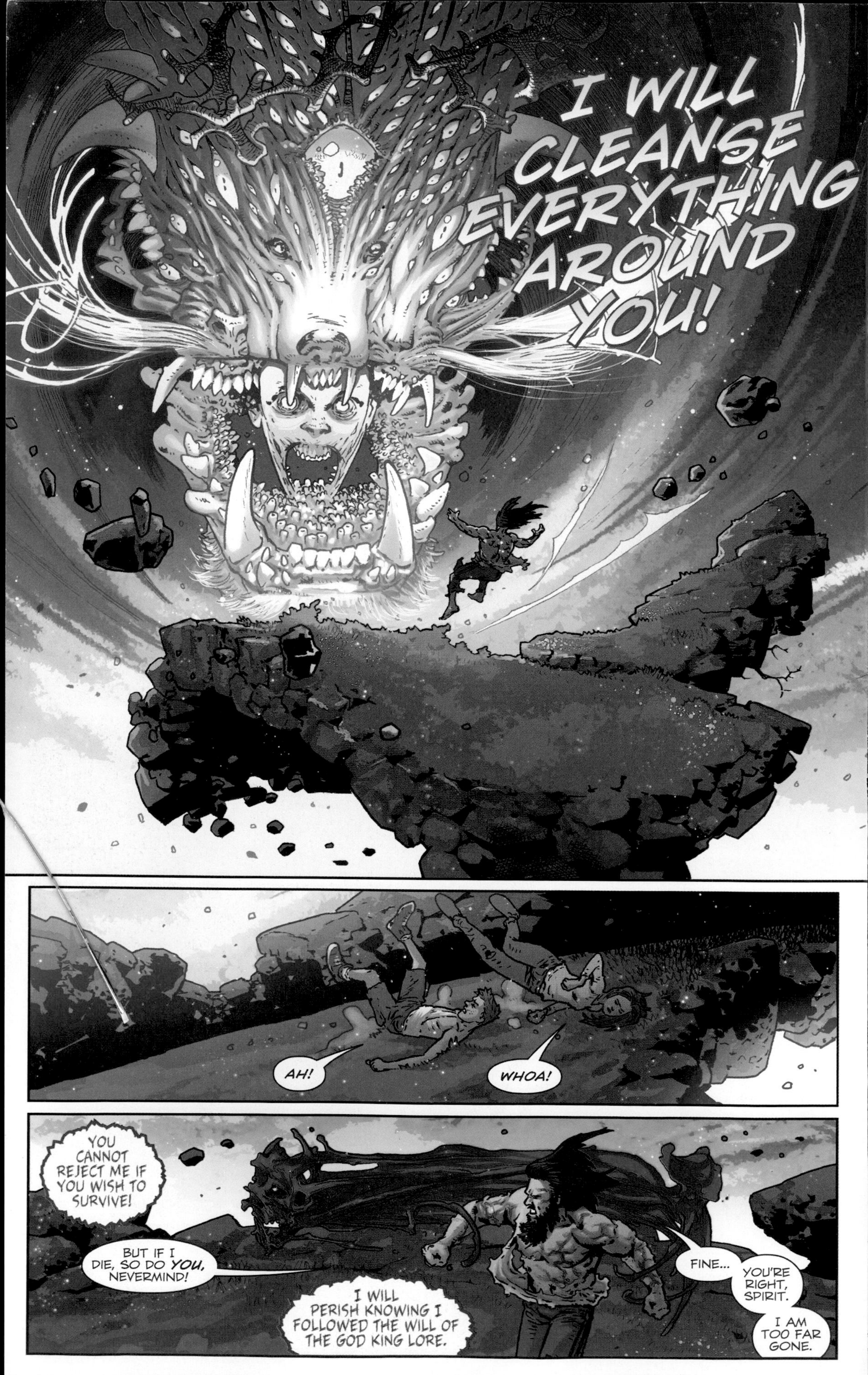
I WILL CLEANSE EVERYTHING AROUND YOU!
AH!
WHOA!
YOU CANNOT REJECT ME IF YOU WISH TO SURVIVE!
BUT IF I DIE, SO DO *YOU*, NEVERMIND!
I WILL PERISH KNOWING I FOLLOWED THE WILL OF THE GOD KING LORE.
FINE...
YOU'RE RIGHT, SPIRIT.
I AM TOO FAR GONE.

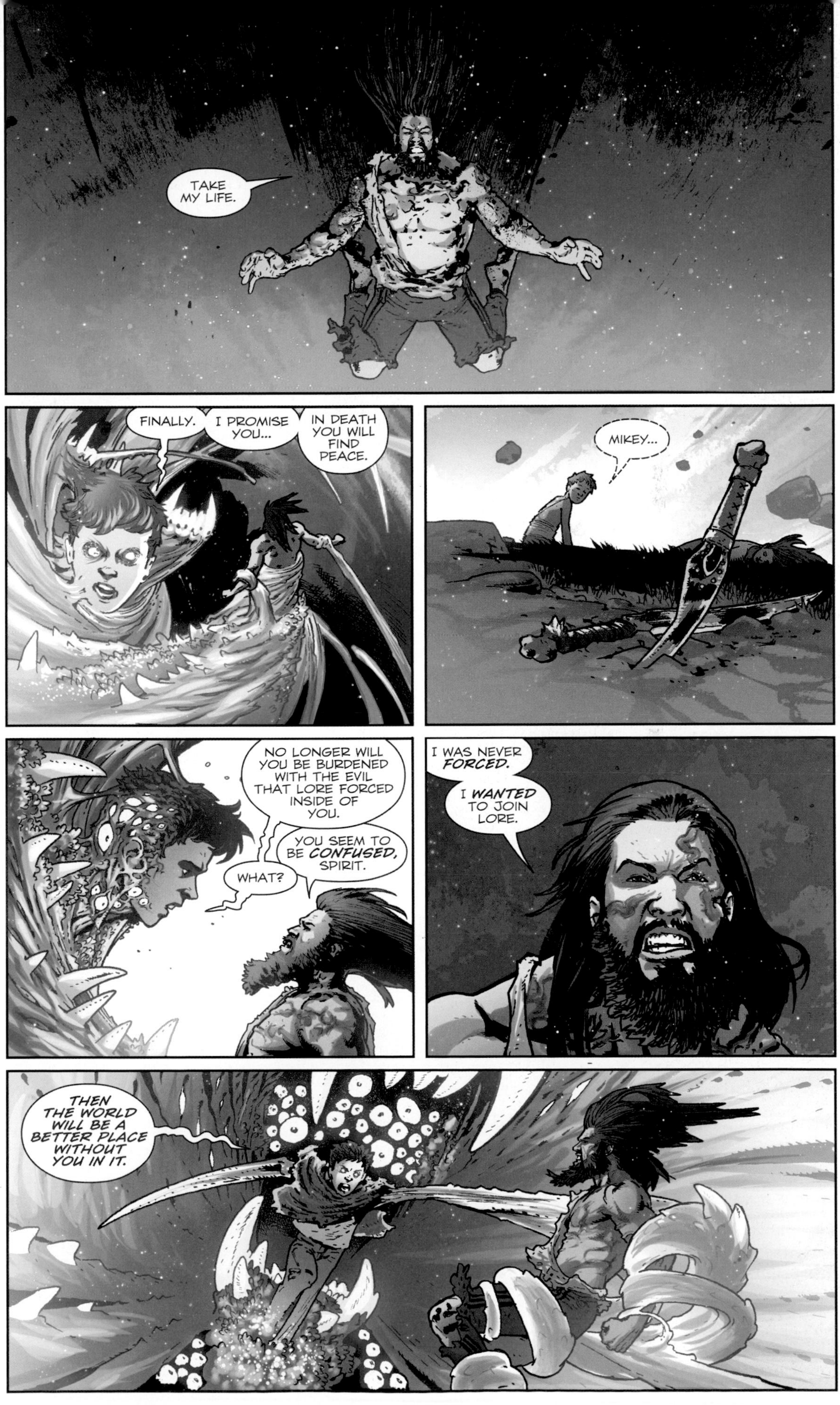
TAKE MY LIFE.
FINALLY.
I PROMISE YOU...
IN DEATH YOU WILL FIND PEACE.
MIKEY...
NO LONGER WILL YOU BE BURDENED WITH THE EVIL THAT LORE FORCED INSIDE OF YOU.
WHAT?
YOU SEEM TO BE CONFUSED, SPIRIT.
I WAS NEVER FORCED.
I WANTED TO JOIN LORE.
THEN THE WORLD WILL BE A BETTER PLACE WITHOUT YOU IN IT.

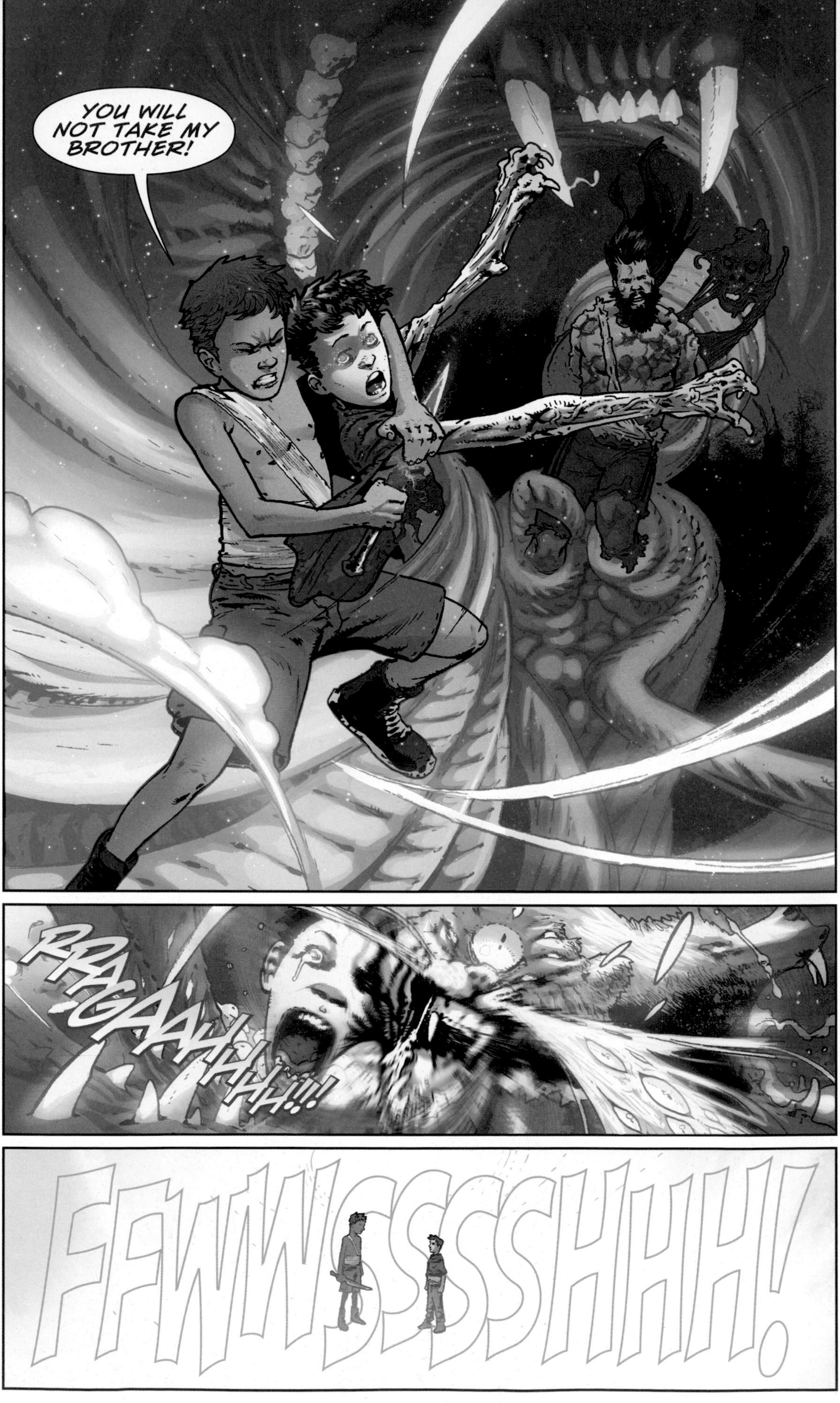
YOU WILL NOT TAKE MY BROTHER!
RRAGAAHHHH!!!
FFWWSSSSHHH!

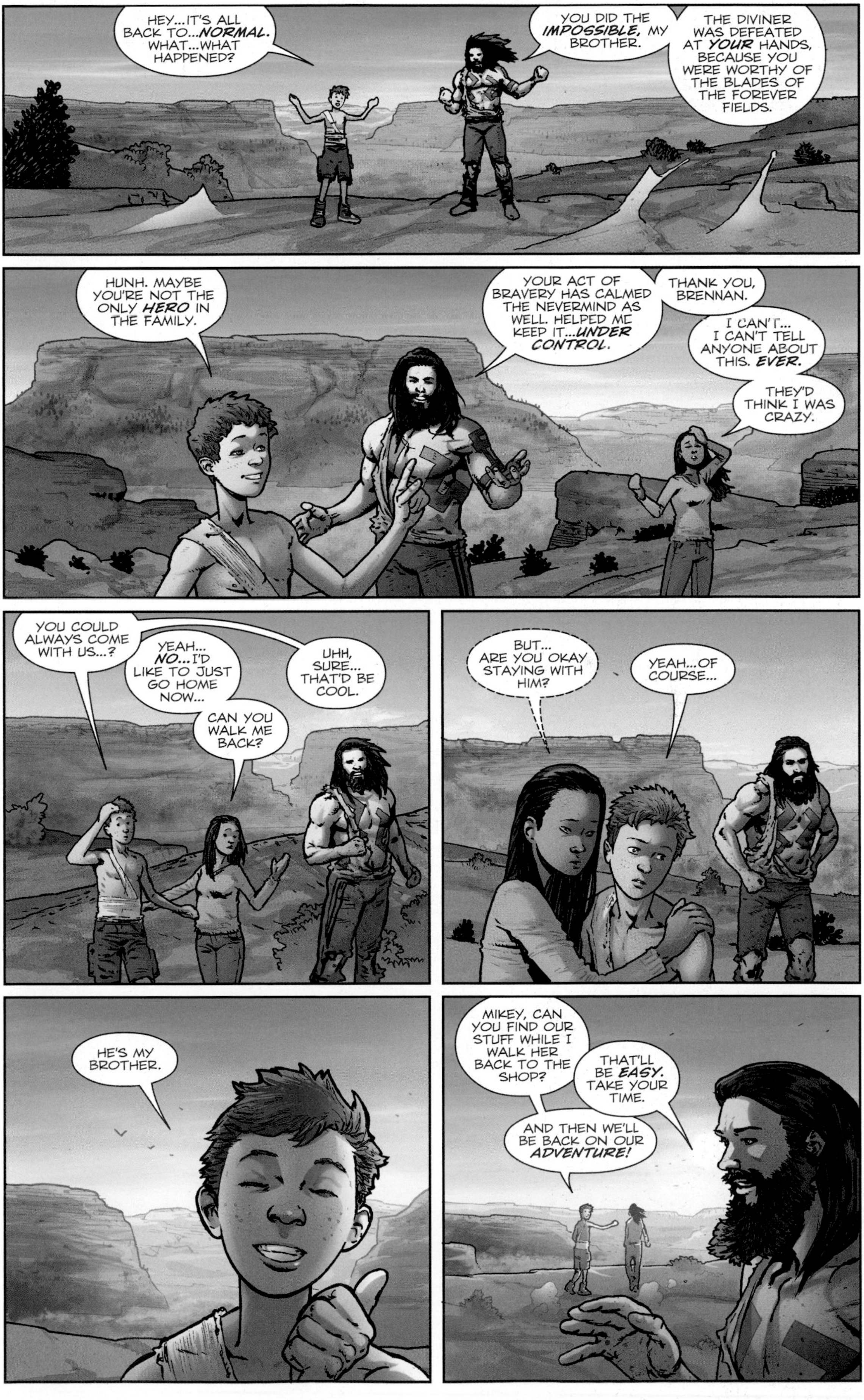
HEY...IT'S ALL BACK TO...NORMAL. WHAT...WHAT HAPPENED?
YOU DID THE IMPOSSIBLE, MY BROTHER.
THE DIVINER WAS DEFEATED AT YOUR HANDS, BECAUSE YOU WERE WORTHY OF THE BLADES OF THE FOREVER FIELDS.
HUNH. MAYBE YOU'RE NOT THE ONLY HERO IN THE FAMILY.
YOUR ACT OF BRAVERY HAS CALMED THE NEVERMIND AS WELL. HELPED ME KEEP IT...UNDER CONTROL.
THANK YOU, BRENNAN.
I CAN'T... I CAN'T TELL ANYONE ABOUT THIS. EVER.
THEY'D THINK I WAS CRAZY.
YOU COULD ALWAYS COME WITH US...?
YEAH... NO...I'D LIKE TO JUST GO HOME NOW...
UHH, SURE... THAT'D BE COOL.
CAN YOU WALK ME BACK?
BUT... ARE YOU OKAY STAYING WITH HIM?
YEAH...OF COURSE...
HE'S MY BROTHER.
MIKEY, CAN YOU FIND OUR STUFF WHILE I WALK HER BACK TO THE SHOP?
THAT'LL BE EASY. TAKE YOUR TIME.
AND THEN WE'LL BE BACK ON OUR ADVENTURE!

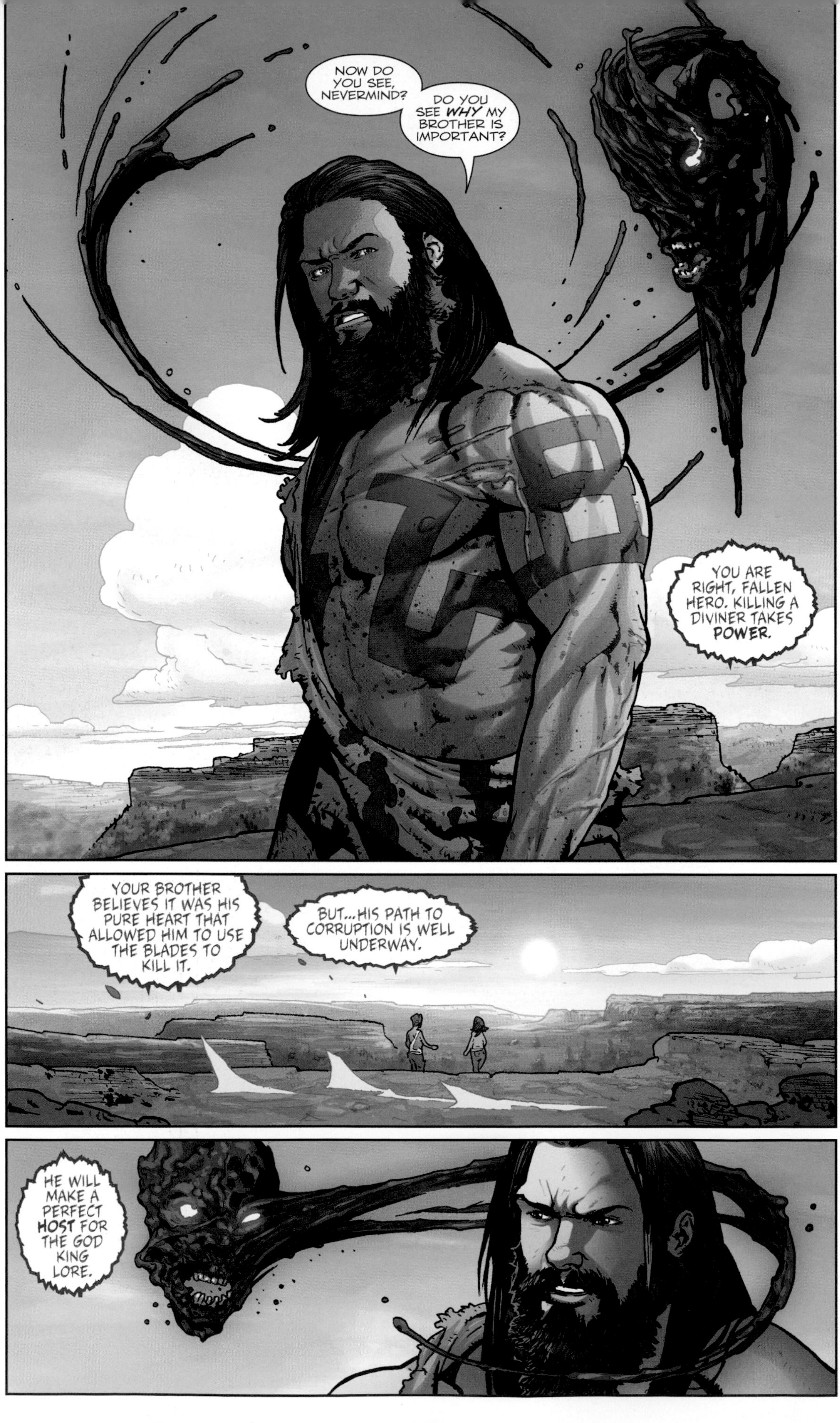
NOW DO YOU SEE, NEVERMIND?
DO YOU SEE WHY MY BROTHER IS IMPORTANT?
YOU ARE RIGHT, FALLEN HERO. KILLING A DIVINER TAKES POWER.
YOUR BROTHER BELIEVES IT WAS HIS PURE HEART THAT ALLOWED HIM TO USE THE BLADES TO KILL IT.
BUT...HIS PATH TO CORRUPTION IS WELL UNDERWAY.
HE WILL MAKE A PERFECT HOST FOR THE GOD KING LORE.

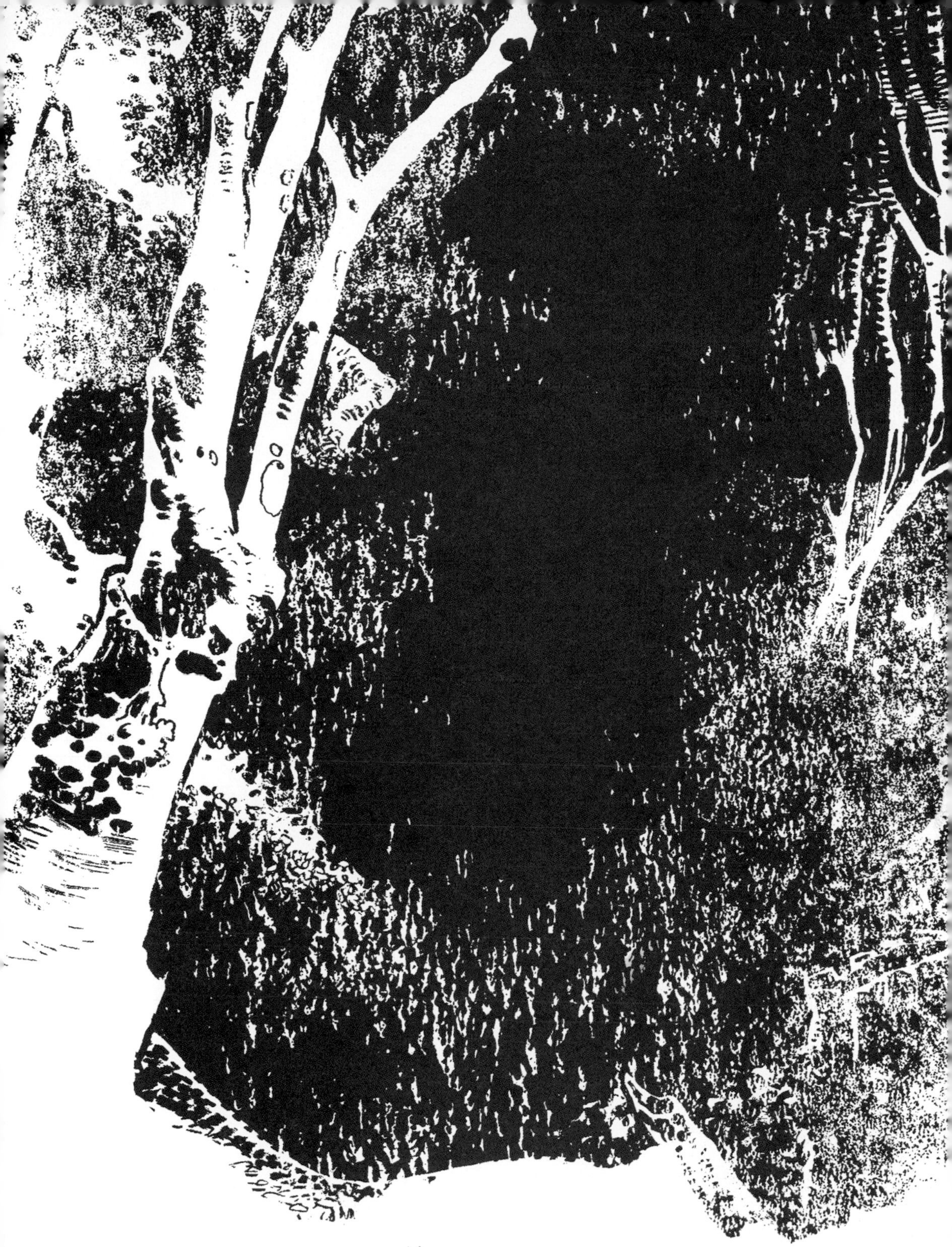

To be continued...

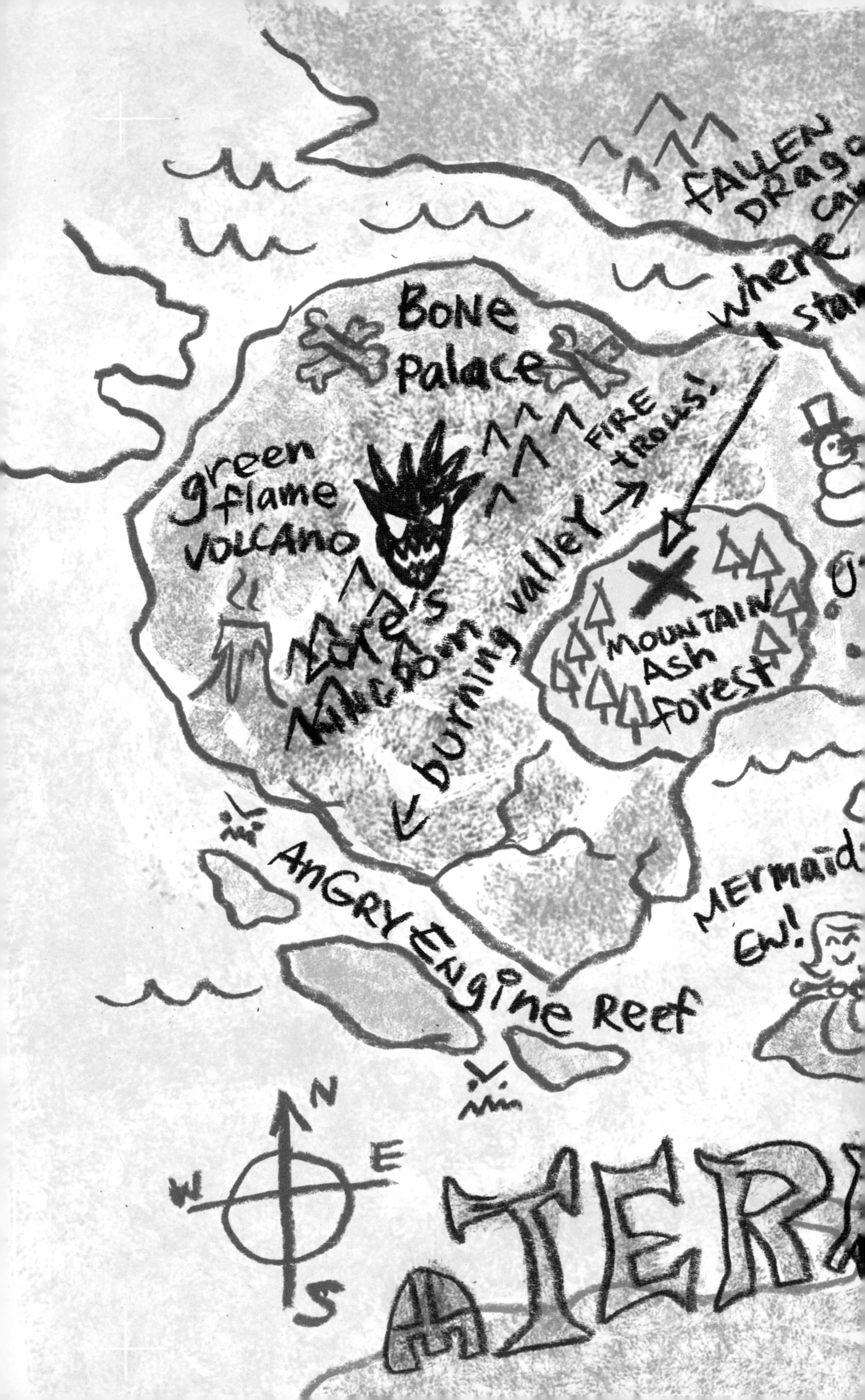

FALLEN
where
BONE Palace
FIRE trolls!
green flame VOLCANO
Kingdom
burning valley
MOUNTAIN Ash forest
ANGRY Engine Reef
Mermaid
Ew!
N
E
W
S

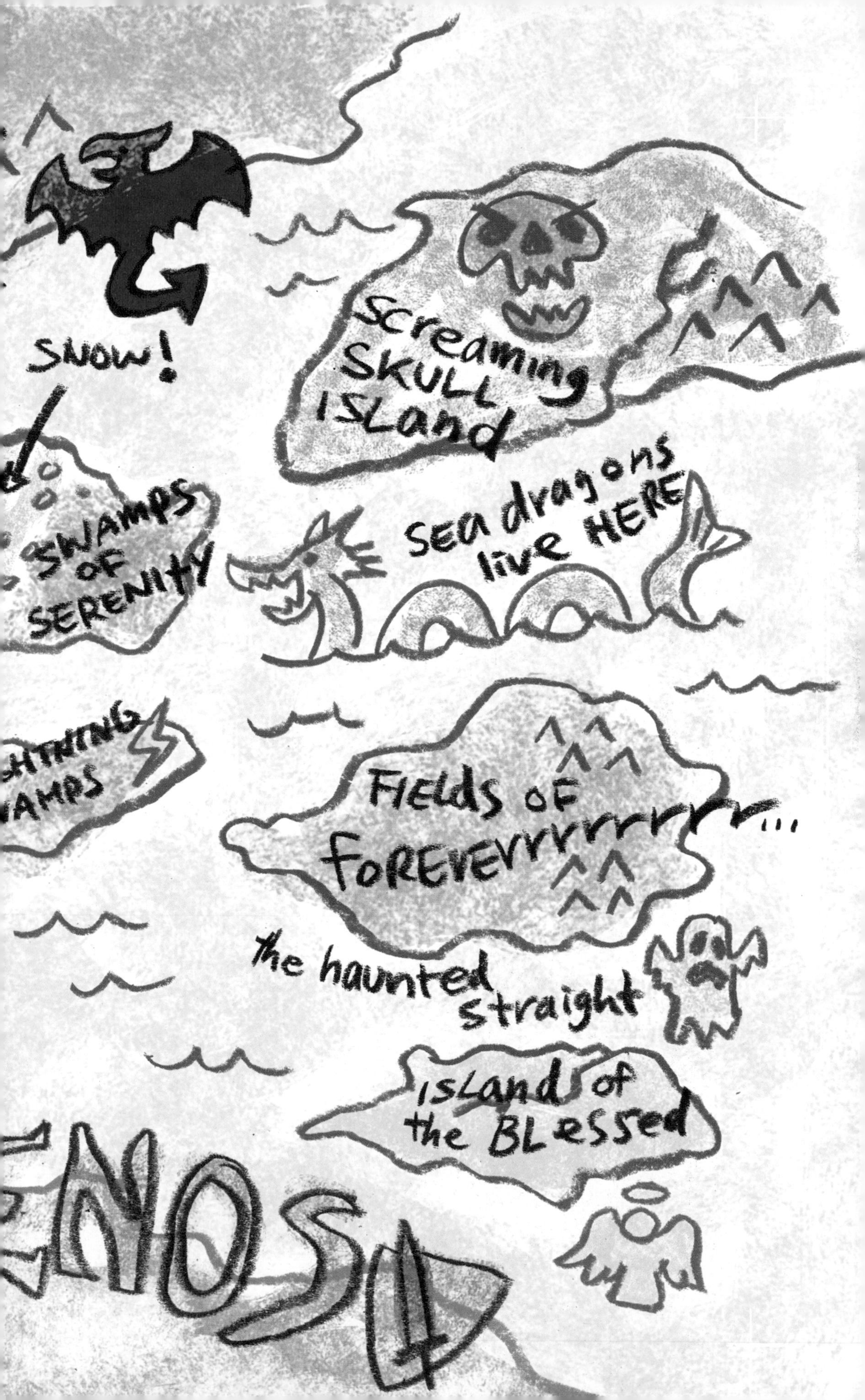
SNOW!
Screaming SKULL ISLand
SWAMPS OF SERENITY
Sea dragons live HERE
...HTNING ...AMPS
FIELds OF foREverrrrrrrr...
the haunted straight
ISLand of the BLessed
...NOS...

“You do what you must to survive.”

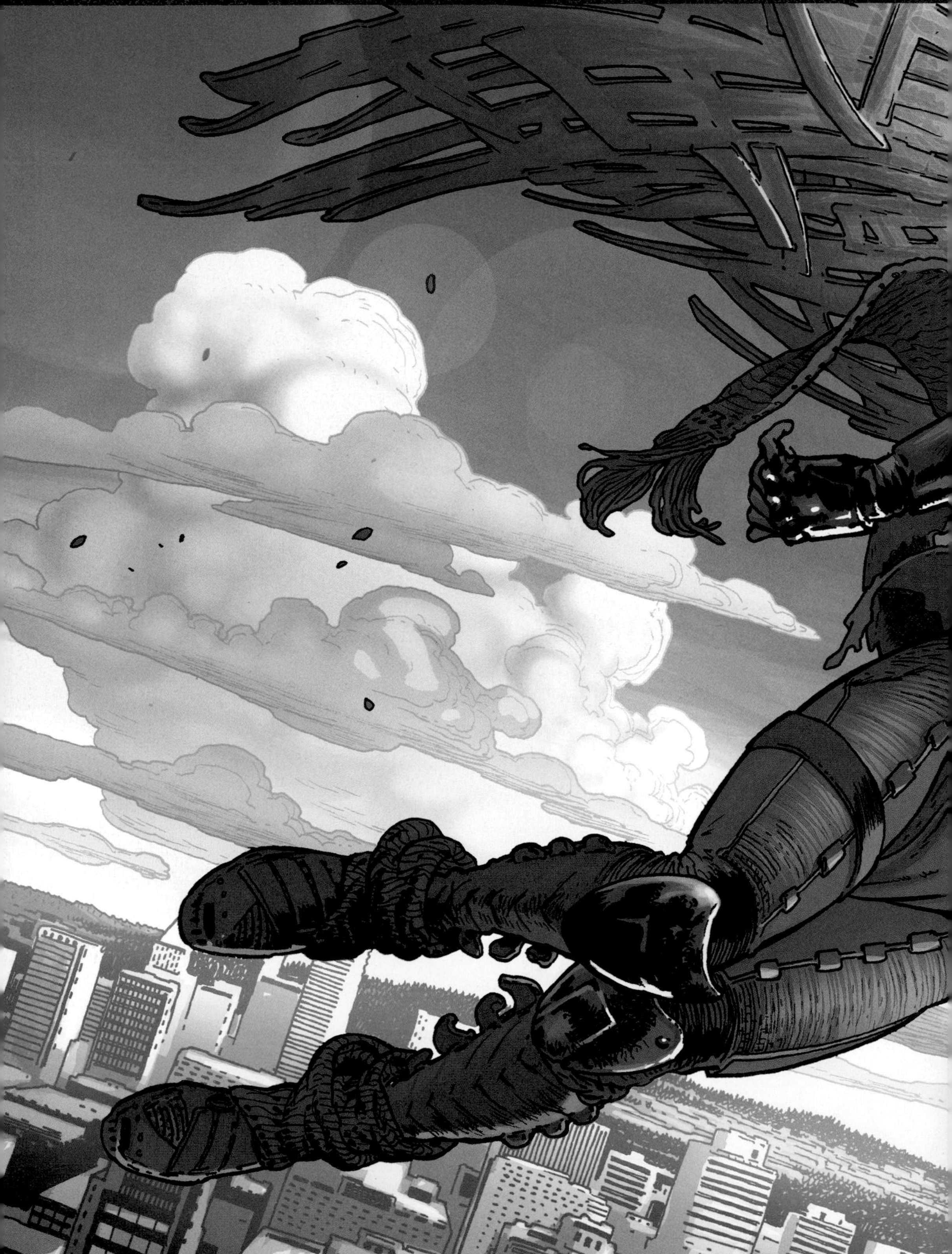

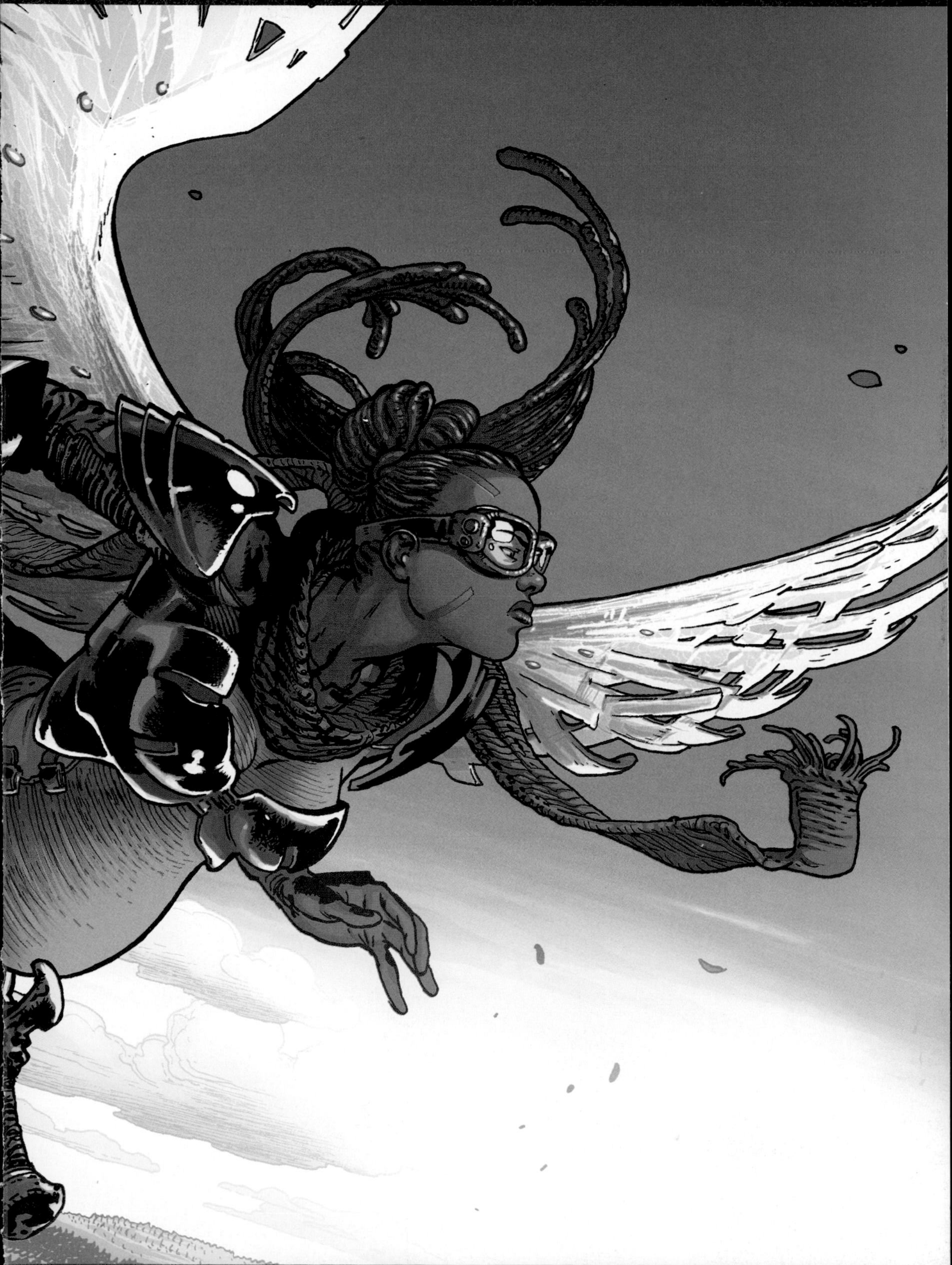

FOR MORE OF THE WALKING DEAD

TRADEPAPERBACKS

ROBERT KIRKMAN TONY MOORE
THE WALKING DEAD
VOLUME 1
DAYS GONE BYE

VOL. 1: DAYS GONE BYE TP
ISBN: 978-1-58240-672-5
$14.99
VOL. 2: MILES BEHIND US TP
ISBN: 978-1-58240-775-3
$14.99
VOL. 3: SAFETY BEHIND BARS TP
ISBN: 978-1-58240-805-7
$14.99
VOL. 4: THE HEART'S DESIRE TP
ISBN: 978-1-58240-530-8
$14.99
VOL. 5: THE BEST DEFENSE TP
ISBN: 978-1-58240-612-1
$14.99
VOL. 6: THIS SORROWFUL LIFE TP
ISBN: 978-1-58240-684-8
$14.99
VOL. 7: THE CALM BEFORE TP
ISBN: 978-1-58240-828-6
$14.99
VOL. 8: MADE TO SUFFER TP
ISBN: 978-1-58240-883-5
$14.99
VOL. 9: HERE WE REMAIN TP
ISBN: 978-1-60706-022-2
$14.99
VOL. 10: WHAT WE BECOME TP
ISBN: 978-1-60706-075-8
$14.99
VOL. 11: FEAR THE HUNTERS TP
ISBN: 978-1-60706-181-6
$14.99
VOL. 12: LIFE AMONG THEM TP
ISBN: 978-1-60706-254-7
$14.99
VOL. 13: TOO FAR GONE TP
ISBN: 978-1-60706-329-2
$14.99
VOL. 14: NO WAY OUT TP
ISBN: 978-1-60706-392-6
$14.99
VOL. 15: WE FIND OURSELVES TP
ISBN: 978-1-60706-440-4
$14.99
VOL. 16: A LARGER WORLD TP
ISBN: 978-1-60706-559-3
$14.99
VOL. 17: SOMETHING TO FEAR TP
ISBN: 978-1-60706-615-6
$14.99
VOL. 18: WHAT COMES AFTER TP
ISBN: 978-1-60706-687-3
$14.99
VOL. 19: MARCH TO WAR TP
ISBN: 978-1-60706-818-1
$14.99
VOL. 20: ALL OUT WAR PART ONE TP
ISBN: 978-1-60706-882-2
$14.99
VOL. 21: ALL OUT WAR PART TWO TP
ISBN: 978-1-63215-030-1
$14.99
VOL. 22: A NEW BEGINNING TP
ISBN: 978-1-63215-041-7
$14.99
VOL. 23: WHISPERS INTO SCREAMS
ISBN: 978-1-63215-258-9
$14.99
VOL. 24: LIFE AND DEATH TP
ISBN: 978-1-63215-402-6
$14.99
VOL. 1: SPANISH EDITION TP
ISBN: 978-1-60706-797-9
$14.99
VOL. 2: SPANISH EDITION TP
ISBN: 978-1-60706-845-7
$14.99
VOL. 3: SPANISH EDITION TP
ISBN: 978-1-60706-883-9
$14.99
VOL. 4: SPANISH EDITION TP
ISBN: 978-1-63215-035-6
$14.99

HARDCOVERS

THE WALKING DEAD
BOOK ONE
a continuing story of survival horror.

BOOK ONE HC
ISBN: 978-1-58240-619-0
$34.99
BOOK TWO HC
ISBN: 978-1-58240-698-5
$34.99
BOOK THREE HC
ISBN: 978-1-58240-825-5
$34.99
BOOK FOUR HC
ISBN: 978-1-60706-000-0
$34.99
BOOK FIVE HC
ISBN: 978-1-60706-171-7
$34.99
BOOK SIX HC
ISBN: 978-1-60706-327-8
$34.99
BOOK SEVEN HC
ISBN: 978-1-60706-439-8
$34.99
BOOK EIGHT HC
ISBN: 978-1-60706-593-7
$34.99
BOOK NINE HC
ISBN: 978-1-60706-798-6
$34.99
BOOK TEN HC
ISBN: 978-1-63215-034-9
$34.99
BOOK ELEVEN HC
ISBN: 978-1-63215-271-8
$34.99

COMPENDIUMS

The ultimate edition of The New York Times bestseller!
THE WALKING DEAD
COMPENDIUM ONE
Robert Kirkman • Charlie Adlard • Tony Moore • Cliff Rathburn

COMPENDIUM TP, VOL. 1
ISBN: 978-1-60706-076-5
$59.99
COMPENDIUM TP, VOL. 2
ISBN: 978-1-60706-596-8
$59.99

SPECIALTY BOOKS

THE WALKING DEAD
THE COVERS

THE WALKING DEAD: THE COVERS, VOL. 1 HC
ISBN: 978-1-60706-002-4
$24.99
THE WALKING DEAD SURVIVORS' GUIDE
ISBN: 978-1-60706-458-9
$12.99
THE WALKING DEAD: ALL OUT WAR HC
ISBN: 978-1-63215-038-7
$34.99

OMNIBUS

THE WALKING DEAD

OMNIBUS, VOL. 1
ISBN: 978-1-60706-503-6
$100.00
OMNIBUS, VOL. 2
ISBN: 978-1-60706-515-9
$100.00
OMNIBUS, VOL. 3
ISBN: 978-1-60706-330-8
$100.00
OMNIBUS, VOL. 4
ISBN: 978-1-60706-616-3
$100.00
OMNIBUS, VOL. 5
ISBN: 978-1-63215-042-4
$100.00

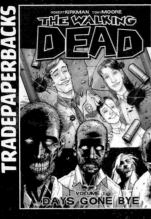

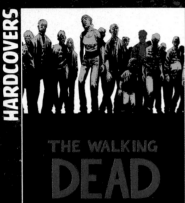

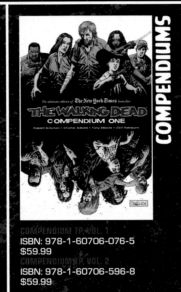

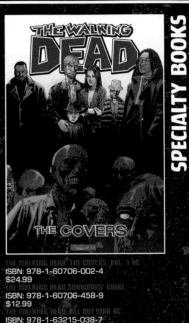

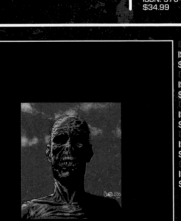

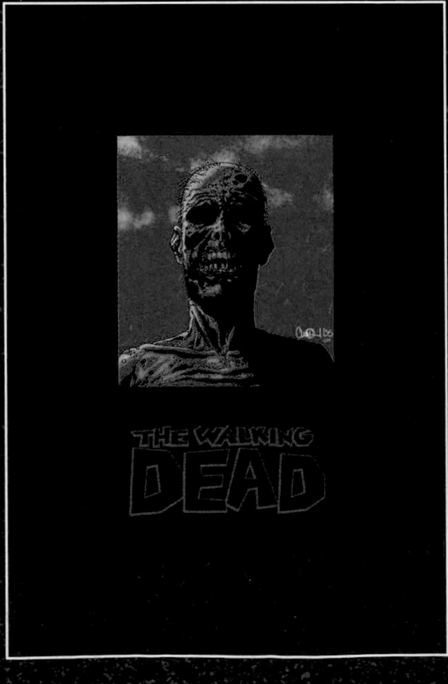

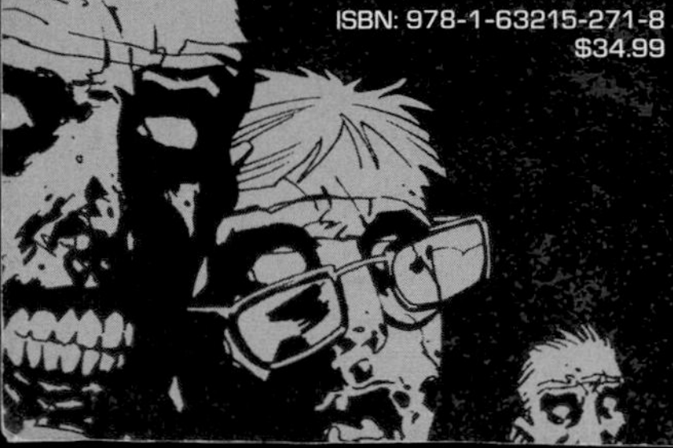

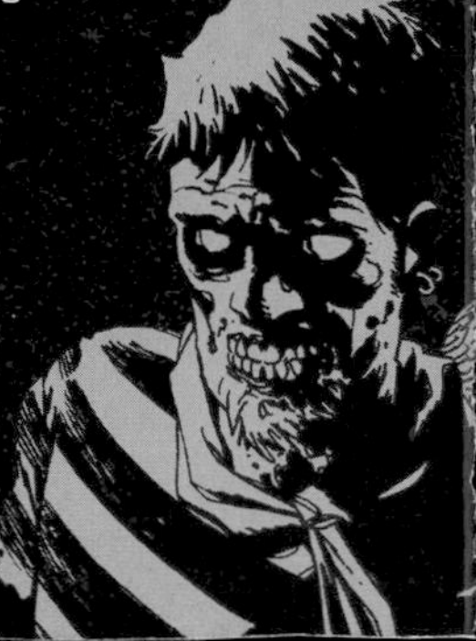

OTHER COLLECTIONS BY JOSHUA WILLIAMSON

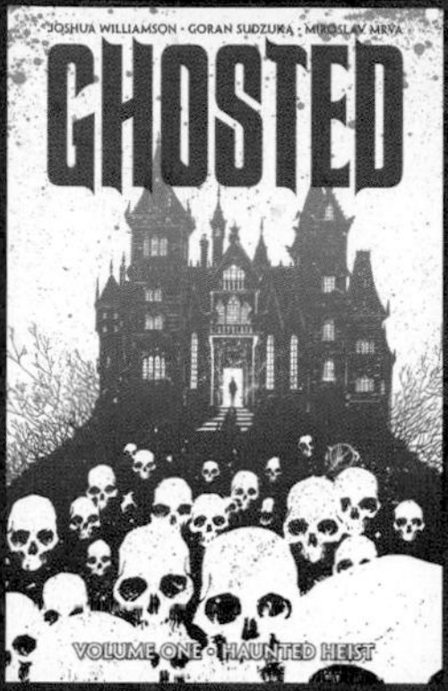
JOSHUA WILLIAMSON · GORAN SUDZUKA · MIROSLAV MRVA
GHOSTED
VOLUME ONE · HAUNTED HEIST

GHOSTED VOL. 1
978-1-60706-836-5
$9.99

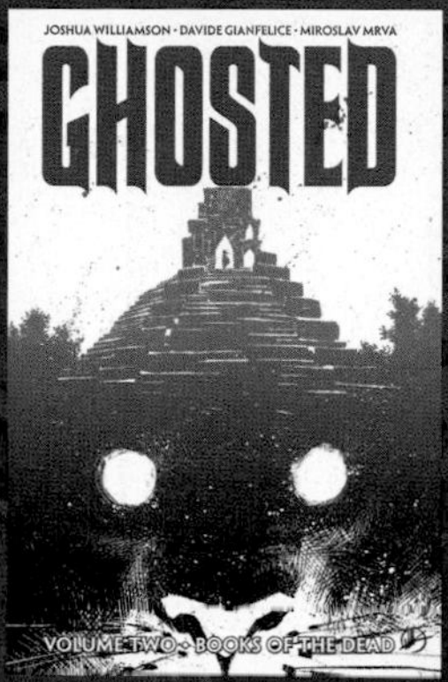
JOSHUA WILLIAMSON · DAVIDE GIANFELICE · MIROSLAV MRVA
GHOSTED
VOLUME TWO · BOOKS OF THE DEAD

GHOSTED VOL. 2
978-1-63215-046-2
$12.99

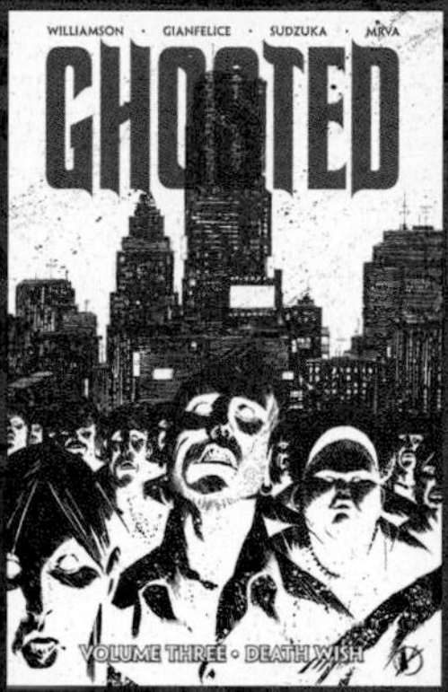
WILLIAMSON · GIANFELICE · SUDZUKA · MRVA
GHOSTED
VOLUME THREE · DEATH WISH

GHOSTED VOL. 3
978-1-60706-051-6
$12.99

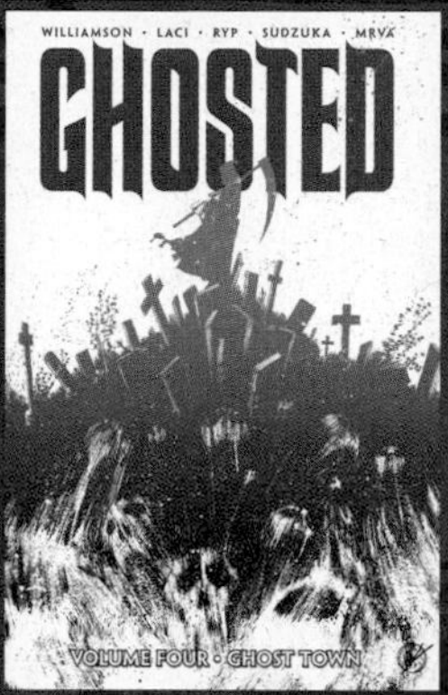
WILLIAMSON · LACI · RYP · SUDZUKA · MRVA
GHOSTED
VOLUME FOUR · GHOST TOWN

GHOSTED VOL. 4
978-1-63215-317-3
$12.99

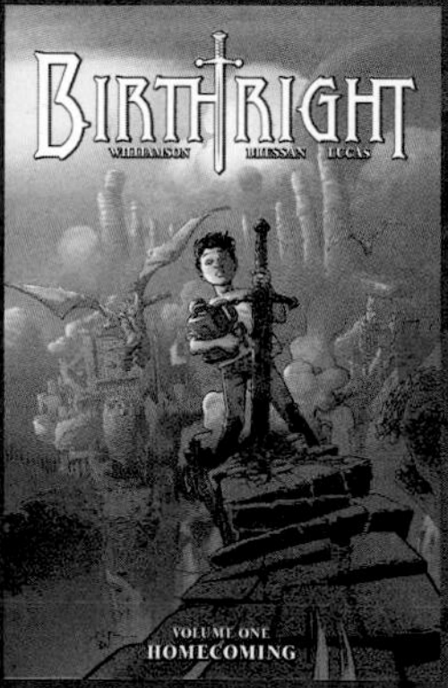
BIRTHRIGHT
WILLIAMSON BRESSAN LUCAS
VOLUME ONE
HOMECOMING

BIRTHRIGHT VOL. 1
978-1-63215-231-2
$9.99

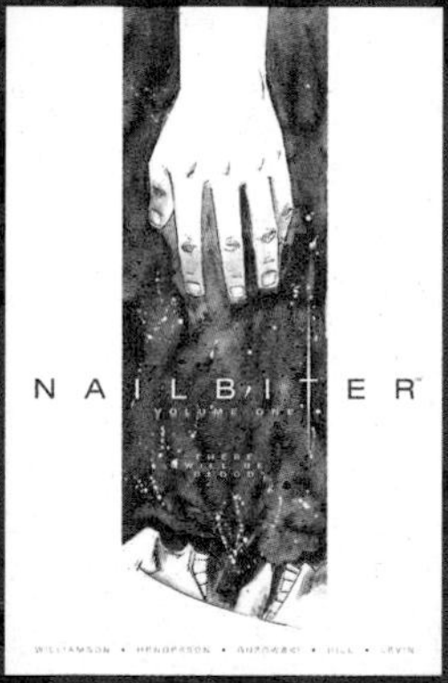
NAILBITER

NAILBITER VOL. 1
978-1-63215-112-4
$9.99

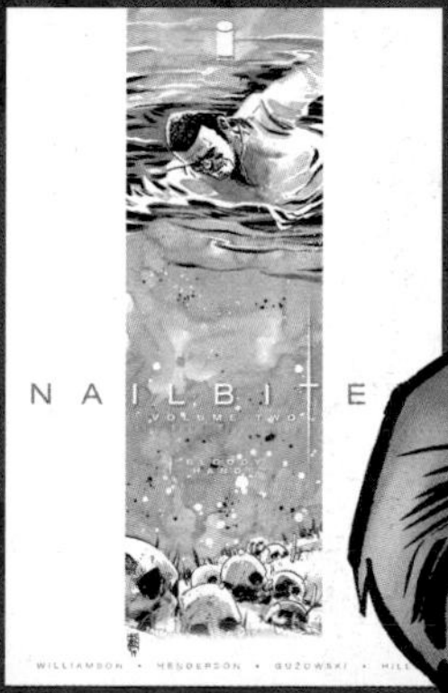
NAILBITER

NAILBITER VOL. 2
978 1 63215-232-9
$14.99

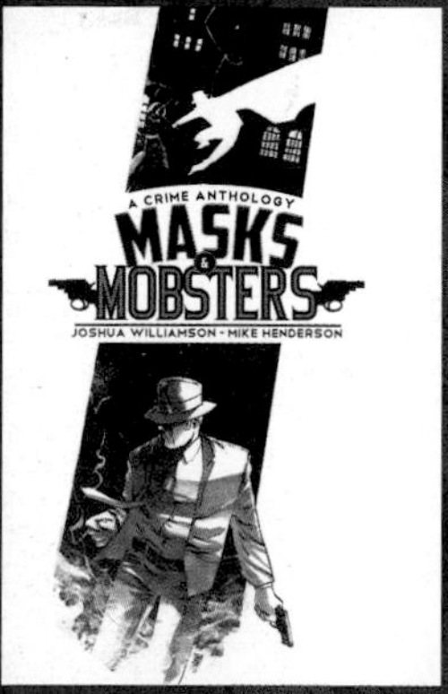
A CRIME ANTHOLOGY
MASKS & MOBSTERS
JOSHUA WILLIAMSON · MIKE HENDERSON

MASKS & MOBSTERS VOL. 1 HC
978-1-60706-765-8
$19.99

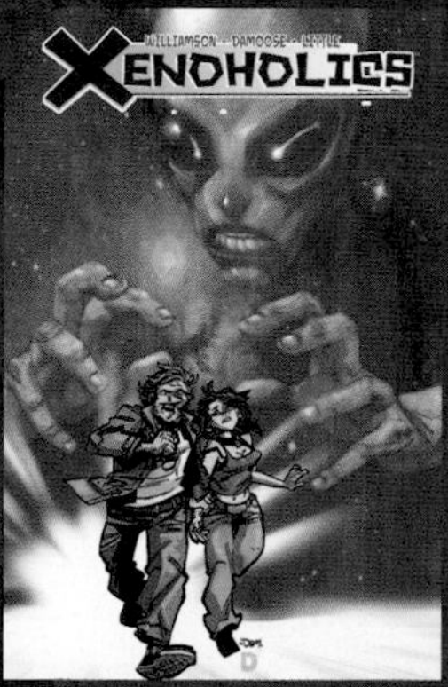
WILLIAMSON DAMOOSE
XENOHOLICS

XENOHOLICS
978-1-60706-557-9
$14.99

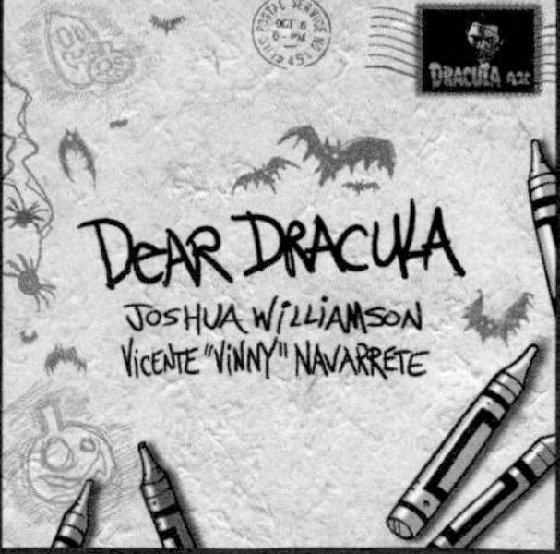
DEAR DRACULA
JOSHUA WILLIAMSON
VICENTE "VINNY" NAVARRETE

DEAR DRACULA
978-1-58240-970-2
$7.99

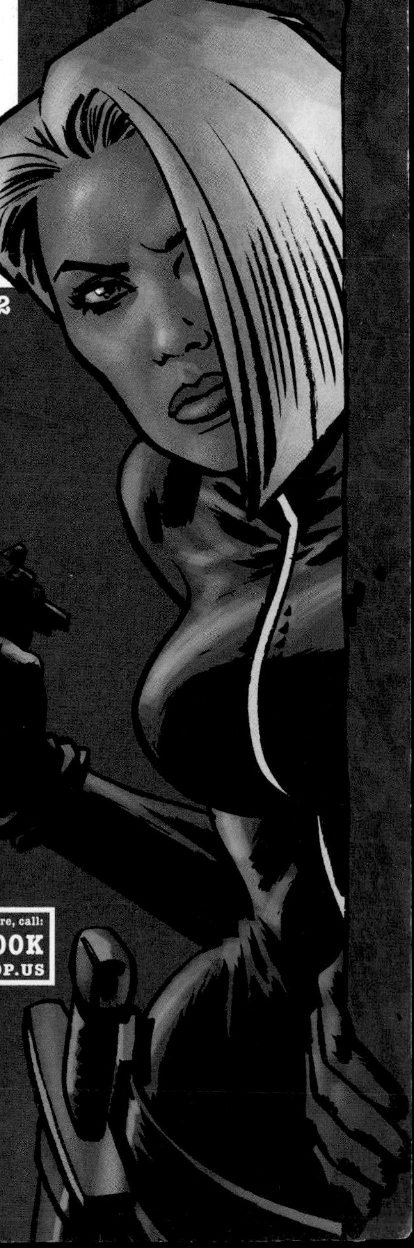

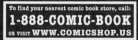

For more tales from ROBERT KIRKMAN and SKYBOUND

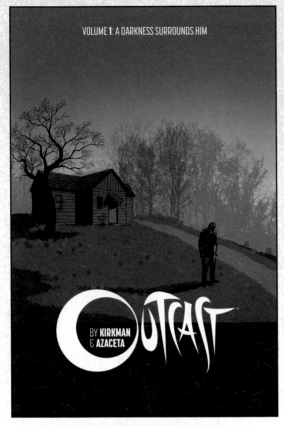

VOL. 1: A DARKNESS SURROUNDS HIM TP
ISBN: 978-1-63215-053-0
$9.99

VOL. 1: FLORA & FAUNA TP
ISBN: 978-1-60706-982-9
$9.99

VOL. 2: AMPHIBIA & INSECTA TP
ISBN: 978-1-63215-052-3
$14.99

VOL. 1: FIRST GENERATION TP
ISBN: 978-1-60706-683-5
$12.99

VOL. 2: SECOND GENERATION TP
ISBN: 978-1-60706-830-3
$12.99

VOL. 3: THIRD GENERATION TP
ISBN: 978-1-60706-939-3
$12.99

VOL. 4: FOURTH GENERATION TP
ISBN: 978-1-63215-036-3
$12.99

VOL. 1: HAUNTED HEIST TP
ISBN: 978-1-60706-836-5
$9.99

VOL. 2: BOOKS OF THE DEAD TP
ISBN: 978-1-63215-046-2
$12.99

VOL. 3: DEATH WISH TP
ISBN: 978-1-63215-051-6
$12.99

VOL. 4: GHOST TOWN TP
ISBN: 978-1-63215-317-3
$12.99

VOL. 1: UNDER THE KNIFE TP
ISBN: 978-1-60706-441-1
$12.99

VOL. 2: MAL PRACTICE TP
ISBN: 978-1-60706-693-4
$14.99

VOL. 1: "I QUIT."
ISBN: 978-1-60706-592-0
$14.99

VOL. 2: "HELP ME."
ISBN: 978-1-60706-676-7
$14.99

VOL. 3: "VENICE."
ISBN: 978-1-60706-844-0
$14.99

VOL. 4: "THE HIT LIST."
ISBN: 978-1-63215-037-0
$14.99